HOW BOSTON PLAYED

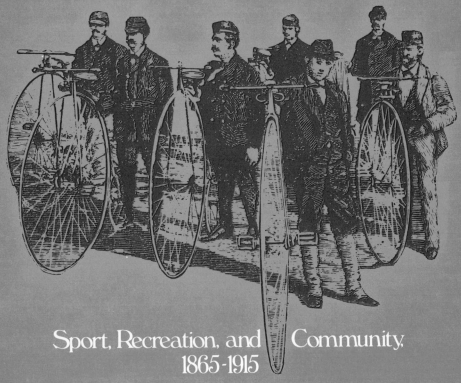

Sport, Recreation, and Community, 1865-1915

Stephen Hardy

NORTHEASTERN UNIVERSITY PRESS

HOW BOSTON PLAYED
Sport, Recreation, and Community
1865-1915
by Stephen Hardy

How Boston Played is a double delight.
It chronicles the birth of Boston sports from
early Redstockings games and college rowing regattas to the exploits of the "Boston
Strong Boy," John L. Sullivan. Looking
beyond sporting events, though, this book
seeks to uncover the sources of the mania
for recreation that swept the Hub following
the Civil War. For, as people increasingly
entered the overcrowded, polluted life of
the city, they sought new means of escape
from their sedentary factory routines.

In **How Boston Played**, Stephen Hardy
examines the response—and surrounding
controversies—that met this new demand
for recreation. From the first public parks
and beaches where urbanites could picnic
and play, to the founding of neighborhood
sporting clubs, a hunger for more activities
swept the city. This was the period that
saw the emergence of the bicycle craze,
schoolboy sports teams, and professional
athletes. Sports were the panacea that
would turn recent immigrants into citizens;
neighborhoods into communities.

As Hardy reveals, the rise of sport did not occur without a struggle. Not everyone acknowledged sport and recreation as wholesome pastimes, nor accepted the community's responsibility to provide and promote events. The touted ideal of sport as an equalizer of class often fell short of its mark, and, occasionally, actually exacerbated racial and class strife.

A well-documented and energetic study, **How Boston Played** provides a fascinating look at the rise of recreation through the intertwined relationships of Boston's social, urban, and sports histories.

The Author

Stephen Hardy is chairman of the Department of Sports Management at Robert Morris College and is also a member of the Editorial Review Board of the *Journal of Sport History*.

1982   220 pp.   Illustrations   ISBN 0-930350-27-8 $19.95 cloth

Order Form

Please send me_____copy(ies) of HOW BOSTON PLAYED @ $19.95 each. I have enclosed $_____. (Note: All individual orders must be prepaid.)

Name _____

Address _____

City_____State_____ZIP Code_____

Northeastern University Press·P.O. Box 116·Boston, Massachusetts 02117

Northeastern University Press
P.O. Box 116
Boston, Massachusetts 02117

Northeastern University Publishing Group   1982

How
Boston
Played

How Boston Played

SPORT, RECREATION, AND COMMUNITY
1865–1915

by
Stephen Hardy

NORTHEASTERN UNIVERSITY PRESS
1982

The author thanks the North American Society for Sport History for permission to use his article, "'Parks for the People': Reforming the Boston Park System, 1870–1915," Journal of Sport History, 7 (Winter 1980), as the basis for Chapter Four of this book.

Editors, Robilee Smith, Anne Lunt
Designer, Mike Fender

Northeastern University Press

Library of Congress Cataloging in Publication Data

Hardy, Stephen, 1948–
  How Boston played.

  Bibliography: p.
  Includes index.
  1. Sports—Massachusetts—Boston—History.
2. Boston (Mass.)—Social conditions. I. Title.
GV584.5.B6H37   796'.09744'61   82–6394
ISBN 0-930350-27-8   AACR2

88 87 86 85 84 83 8 7 6 5 4 3 2 1

Printed in the United States of America

To D. L. H.

Preface

IT IS MY HOPE that this book makes a modest contribution to the historical study of sport and recreation. As the notes to each chapter indicate, increasing numbers of scholars have turned their efforts in this direction during the past decade. All to the good, in my opinion, as these studies tell us much about the meaning of life, both past and present. Our individual and group interests in sporting pastimes—from the jogging addicts to the Little League parents to the millions (this author included) who passively absorbed the action of Superbowl XVI—are the products of long processes of historical development. Moreover, as the best studies make clear, sport and recreation have intertwined closely with broader elements of social, cultural, economic, and political change.

I have attempted to illustrate this relationship as it unfolded during a fifty-year period of Boston's history. My focus on a specific place and time deserves some explanation. A variety of constraints, combined with my desire to investigate the role of sporting activities in the process of community formation, led me to limit my research to one city. Why Boston? It was a logical choice for one who grew up in the Hub's suburbs and has avidly followed the fortunes of Boston's teams and athletic heroes. But there were less sentimental reasons. Bostonians have long been at the forefront of America's sports history. The city has supported teams in most national sports leagues; it provided leaders and pioneers for many of the associations and movements that advanced the rise of American sport and recreation during the nineteenth and early twentieth centuries. Despite this rich tradition, however, I was unaware of any general historical monographs on Boston's sport history. While a number of helpful studies of specific sports, organizations, or individuals existed, the only attempt at a broader treatment was seventy years old, and that was largely reminiscence.

My desire to set Boston's sporting past within the context of her larger social development was aided immeasurably by the earlier work of scholars like Oscar Handlin, Walter Muir Whitehill, Sam Bass Warner, Stephan Thernstrom, Geoffrey Blodgett, Stanley Schultz, and Elizabeth Pleck, to name but a few. Their books and articles made my work far more manageable and accurate. Of course, I am responsible for any errors.

Manageability was a consideration in limiting the study to the fifty years following the Civil War; but the cutoff points made sense to me. While there was much interest and organization in sport and recreation before the Civil War, the real surge came after Appomattox. Likewise, while important events occurred after World War I, they were largely additions to, not major changes in, the structures that had grown between 1865 and 1915. History is ultimately a continuous process, of course, and to that extent any boundaries are artificial.

A word on my use of the terms *play, sport,* and *recreation,* all of which appear in the title. A number of scholars have recently analyzed the differences between these concepts. I am concerned more with areas of overlap. My chapters on parks and playgrounds, for instance, lead me into the areas of unorganized play and noncompetitive recreation. But the highly structured professional baseball games at the South End grounds or at Fenway Park depended on an interest nurtured in youthful games like "one o' cat," played on back alleys, parks, or playgrounds. Likewise, the structures and strategies of the professionals could often filter down to the playground level.

Although I define *sport* and *recreation* broadly, a final caution is in order. My coverage of sports is limited. Avid sports trivia experts will doubtless be disappointed that I do not account for every baseball pennant race, or every marathon, or every Yale or Holy Cross game. I have captured what I hope are the most revealing glimpses of Boston's sporting past; I have not attempted to write an encyclopedia. Perhaps my modest effort will encourage someone to attempt such a monumental task. I wish him—or her—luck!

Any study depends on help and encouragement from others; I have felt especially blessed in this regard. The book had its beginning while I was a graduate student in sport studies and American history at the University of Massachusetts/Amherst. Many faculty helped me along the way. Guy Lewis especially has advised me and has nurtured my appreciation of sport history. Paul Boyer and Mario DePillis were always receptive to my work. All have continually offered thoughtful criticism and suggestions for improvement. John Loy, Harold VanderZwaag, Ron Story, Jack Thompson, Betty Spears, and Jack Tager also gave help along the way.

Many others provided aid at critical stages of my research. Councilor James Michael Connolly opened the doors at Boston City Hall, which allowed easy access to the Parks Department and the city archives, where John Ruck and Bob Hannon patiently answered my numerous questions. Elmer O. Cappers offered helpful information on The Country Club, and gave me a delightful tour of the premises. He also sponsored my stack privileges at the Athenaeum. Francis X. Moloney, assistant director of the Boston Public Library, made numerous suggestions about source material. His tragic death was a blow to all lovers of Bostoniana. His *Tradition of Boston Sports* collection remains an important source for sport historians.

Joe McKenney arranged my access to the Boston public school archives at English High School. The librarians there were most accommodating, as were those at the Boston Public Library, the Athenaeum, the Massachusetts Historical Society, the Schlesinger Library at Radcliffe, University of Massachusetts, Harvard, Brandeis, Boston College, and Boston University. Bill Cleary and Joe Bertagna generously helped me obtain material at Harvard. Bill Flynn and Ernie Roberts also offered assistance at Boston College and the *Boston Globe.* Jack Grinold at Northeastern helped considerably with some of the photographs. Scotty Whitelaw, commissioner of the Eastern College Athletic Conference, fully supported my research and writing during the three years of my rewarding employment with the conference. Chip Dewar, Steve Riess, and Mel Adelman gave timely encouragement.

The book was largely rewritten at the University of Washington, where my chairman, Bob Hutton, provided a working situation that was extremely conducive to research and writing. There also, Jack Berryman was uncommonly generous with his splendid collection of books and articles. Another colleague, Alan Ingham, continually offered criticism and advice during my brief forays into social theory. My intellectual debt to him is great, even if we disagree on many of my ideas.

It has been a pleasure to work with Robilee Smith and her staff at the Northeastern University Press. They helped gather many of the photographs and generally made publishing the book a joy. Anne Lunt's scrupulous editing saved me from a number of embarrassing errors. Lee Wilder of Seattle drew the maps. Pat Rotondi, Earl Raymond, Pat Sheehy, Kari Seeger, and Sandy Houser skillfully typed various drafts of the manuscript.

My biggest debt, however, is to my family, both Hardys and Harrises, who have supported the work in every way imaginable. Above all, I thank my wife, Donna, to whom I dedicate this book. She has patiently endured periodic fits of excitement and despondence with a steady resolve to see the project through. She shares equally any satisfaction of achievement.

Seattle, January 1982   SH

Contents

Illustrations

Part One

SETTING THE SCENE

1/*Introduction: The City & the Rise of Sport*

IN 1906, AN "OLD BOSTON BOY" recalled the sporting scenes around the "Hub" of his youth. He remembered especially the lack of organized play:

> Probably any boy of the present day and generation, if told that fifty years ago there was neither baseball nor football (as we know them today), that tennis, polo, golf, lacrosse, and basketball were unknown, besides many other athletic sports now so common, would at once ask, with surprise, not unmingled with pity, what the boys of that day did, anyway, for sport and recreation.[1]

The athletic germ that infected the country after the Civil War found its most fertile ground in cities like Boston, and there it spawned sporting activities, organizations, and institutions for players and spectators of all ages. Between the Civil War and the Great War, the growth of sport in Boston, as elsewhere, was unprecedented.

Of course there was a long historical background to all of this, for even the town of John Winthrop, yea, even Puritan Boston passed on a legacy of sports and recreations. We find evidence of this in the periodic laws that banned some of these activities, both for their interference with Sabbath observance and for their some-time association with gambling and "misspence of time." As early as 1657 the General Court passed an ordinance to protect the town's inhabitants, "for as much as sundry complaints are made that several persons have received hurt by boys and young men playing at football in the streets." But colonial newspapers and diaries indicate that ball games, horse racing, bowling, skating, and swimming took root. Bowling greens were established on Fort Hill and Cambridge Street by the 1740s; cricket appeared later in the century. Bostonians raced their mounts on the "Neck," as well as in suburbs such as Lynnfield, Medford, and Quincy. On a lower plane, blood sports like cockfighting and bearbaiting recurred periodically. Even boxing enjoyed some popularity by the end of the eighteenth century, as noted pugilists like James Sanford, "the American Phenomenon" from New Jersey, and G. L. Barrett went into business teaching the "manly art."[2]

This was all a modest beginning, compared with what would follow as the nineteenth century unfolded. Boston was at the center of America's sporting scene, along with such old rivals as New York or Philadelphia and emerging cities like Chicago. The self-styled "Athens of America," Boston nurtured a rich tradition in more than arts and literature. She was also a leader in sports and recreation, as even a glimpse at the record book demonstrates.

We can begin with yachting and rowing, since Boston's position as a major port logically ensured her prominence in these activities. This was certainly the case, dating back to the *Jefferson*, an early yacht launched in 1801 by Salem's George Crowninshield, Jr., and named after the new president. Others followed, including the regal *Cleopatra's Barge*, Crowninshield's fifty-thousand-dollar pleasure craft, and the *Sylph*, built in 1834 for John Perkins Cushing. *Sylph*'s designer, Robert Bennet Forbes, was, like Cushing, newly rich from the China trade. Joined by some fellow merchants, Forbes purchased the New York schooner *Dream* the following year, and the races between *Dream* and *Sylph* may arguably be called America's first yacht races.

Of all the illustrious successors to *Dream* and *Sylph*, none brought Boston greater jubilation than the trio designed by Ned Burgess. For three years running, 1885 through 1887, *Puritan*, then *Mayflower*, and finally *Volunteer* each kept the America's Cup in America. These boats were, of course, owned by wealthy Brahmins, but the enthusiasm for races under sail extended to a much wider range of Bostonians. In 1881 the *South Boston Inquirer* reprinted an article on the "poor man's yacht," reminding its readers of the virtues of newer, smaller sailboats then being produced. Even nonsailors could feel the lure of the Atlantic. As the *Boston Herald* argued on the eve of *Mayflower*'s cup defense, "The ocean is the noblest of playgrounds, and it is, of all things, the true playground of the English race."[3]

Yachting did have spectator appeal, but it never rivaled rowing's popularity. For one thing, small-boat ownership was possible for a much wider range of individuals and groups. And whereas yachting matched rich against rich, the rowing race often pitted Irish longshoremen against Yankee bluebloods. Organized regattas began in Boston as early as the 1840s, some off the shores of Chelsea and East Boston. The sport had drama and speed; the distances from two to six miles could be rowed in minutes, not hours. The *Post* described the boats in one early regatta as "skimming like flying fish along the surface of the water."[4]

Rowing enthusiasm continued to grow, and in 1854 the Boston aldermen sponsored a July Fourth regatta on the Charles. The inaugural affair drew an estimated forty thousand viewers, who found perches along the Mill Dam bridge, on adjacent wharves and dwellings, and on boats. With prizes ranging from twenty-five dollars to one hundred dollars, the races proved so successful that the *Herald* expressed hope that "a boat race in the harbor may hereafter be considered as indispensable for the afternoon of the Fourth of July as oration in the forenoon or the fireworks in the evening." Continue they did, into the twentieth century, as a major date on Boston's sporting calendar. The annual regatta has recently been resurrected as a fall classic in Boston, the Head of the Charles Regatta.[5]

Harvard students had an interest in these early races. In 1844, members of the class of 1846 purchased a thirty-seven-foot boat, christened her *Oneida*, and so began the college's history of organized competition. That same year, the class of 1847 organized their own club. The 1846 race of its boat, *Huron*, against a Boston boat, *Wave*, marked the first contest between Harvard athletes and an outside group. These early club crews, however, were mainly social affairs. As Charles W. Eliot, '53, recalled, the strong lapstreak boats of the day "could be used, and were used, both spring and fall as means of bringing home members of the crew who did not propose to return sober from an evening in Boston."[6]

Things were soon to change, though. In 1852, the *Oneida* accepted a challenge from Yale and won the race on Lake Winnipesaukee, which was America's first intercollegiate sports event. Three years later, Harvard's five individual clubs formed the Harvard University Boat Club, which began entering Harvard boats in the local regattas. The 1858 crew rowed in the first racing shell built in America. Her captain, Benjamin Crowninshield, '58, purchased six red silk handkerchiefs for the crew to use as headbands in a June regatta on the Charles, thus beginning the tradition of college colors in general and Harvard's "crimson" in particular. With Charles W. Eliot also in the six-oared shell, the *Harvard* held out to win the June 19 race, besting among other boats the *Fort Hill Boy*, which was manned by Irish longshoremen. The July 5 affair promised an interesting rematch between these crews. The Young Men's Democratic Club, sponsor of the regatta, doubled the course length to six miles (or twice around the stake boats). According to Eliot, the Democrats had a "large Irish element" in their club and hoped that the college boys would tire over six miles. They held up well, however, finishing in a little over forty minutes and well ahead of the *Fort Hill Boy*. The regatta chairman praised the Harvards for demonstrating that "scholars may cultivate manly and healthful exercises with advantage." He also consoled the runners-up by expressing the hope that the "hardy sons of Erin might always be represented in Boston by a club like that of the *Fort Hill Boy*."[7]

In the decades after the Civil War, while Harvard clubs in crew, baseball, football, track and field, and tennis assumed important roles as leaders in the growth of intercollegiate sports, their affairs met with great interest in Boston. The intercollegiate regattas at Springfield or Lake Saratoga, the Yale games in any sport, and especially the fall football campaigns, all were major news. And by the last two decades of the century, Harvard teams began to share the spotlight with varsities from Boston College, M.I.T., Tufts, and Boston University. The excitement, both on and off campus, which surrounded collegiate sporting spectacles symbolized the extent to which Bostonians had embraced athletic competition. John Boyle O'Reilly, editor of *The Pilot*, clearly stated the change in attitude toward sports:

> A few years ago, in New England, a young man who was fond of rowing or riding, or any other vigorous sport, was considered to be on the high road to ruin. It was not respectable even to whistle. . . . This has changed completely.

In O'Reilly's opinion the collegiate contests were worthy modern counterparts of the great games in ancient Greece![8]

The reference to the ancient games was more appropriate than

THE "HARVARD," WINNER OF THE RACE FOR SIX-OARED BOATS, ON THE CHARLES RIVER, BOSTON, JUNE 19, 1858.

June 19, 1858—The Harvard *Beats the* Fort Hill Boy
Courtesy of Special Collections Division, University of Washington Libraries

O'Reilly realized, for only a few years later the first modern Olympic games were held in Athens, in April of 1896. Boston athletes were the heart of the American team, which dominated the games. James Brendan Connolly of the Suffolk Athletic Club won the first completed event, the hop, step, and jump. This was followed by the victorious performances of Ellery H. Clark, T. E. Burke, T. P. Curtis, and W. W. Hoyt, all of the Boston Athletic Association. Thousands of Bostonians thronged Providence Station to greet the returning athletes, while the *Boston Herald* reminded its readers that the ancient Greek city-states had occasionally torn down the walls for their heroes! A number of testimonials followed, including a reception at Faneuil Hall which Mayor Josiah Quincy called "unprecedented." A *Herald* writer was commissioned to compose a victory ode, to be sung to the tune of "Fair Harvard." Boston's Pindar responded, in part:

> Glad victors in strifes that far eras reveal—
>   Valiant heroes in triumph—All hail!
> In your trophies the pride of fair Greece may we feel,
>   And her glow of grand story unveil.
>   . . . .

7

Athenia of old through your prowess appears
   Her deeds of dead ages in view,
Over barriers of age and wide oceans of years
   To this life of our Athens the new.

. . . .

This doggerel hardly challenged the odes of Bacchylides or Pindar, but it satisfied the Boston boosters, who howled with delight when Ellery Clark told them that the Greeks hadn't been sure if Boston was a city in America or if "America was an outlying suburb of Boston."[9]

A year later the Boston Athletic Association sponsored an event created for the Athens Olympics. The Boston Marathon, now one of the world's premier athletic events, began with little fanfare in 1897. New events take time to catch on, particularly if they offer only the sight of anguish and exhaustion. The BAA was prepared, however, for they announced that two bicyclists would accompany each runner, offer all possible assistance "short of carrying him," and finally "see to it that the runner makes all the distance on foot." The Boston Marathon did not linger in obscurity. By the time the subsequent seven-time winner Clarence DeMar entered his first, in 1910, the April race took front-page headlines.[10]

Residents of Boston and its suburbs have long since supplanted the BAA bicyclists as a volunteer support staff for exhausted and dispirited marathoners. Lining the course from Hopkinton to downtown Boston, they are worthy representatives of the Boston fan, a species known widely for its enthusiastic and knowledgeable patronage of sports. It was baseball, of course, where the breed was first identified. It was carefully studied in a book published in 1888, entitled *The Krank: His Language and What It Means*. The author of this analysis followed fans' activity at the Boston ball park, where they pried information from reporters and ticket takers, vilified the umpire, and argued over strategy, all in their own jargon.[11]

The Boston "krank" was not a model of decorum. In 1886 the *Herald* ran an editorial complaining of "baseball rowdyism." Daily crowds of four thousand or more were increasingly intimidating the umpires with shouts of "Hit him and I will pay your fine!" The rowdies were not just boys or hoodlums, worried the *Herald*, but also "men dressed in good clothing and sitting in the grandstand." On other occasions, overflow crowds spilled onto the playing surface, delaying or hindering play. In fact, the Boston crowd was blamed for their team's loss in the third game of the 1903 World Series.[12]

On the other hand, the Boston fans were often recognized for their "fair spirit" and the "squareness" with which they cheered a good play by either team. As one reporter noted in 1911, "This has long been true of Boston, and all the players say that they feel perfectly at home on the Boston field." The players were unable to explain this even-handed disposition, but the author reasoned that, in the case of the Braves fans, it may have been that repeated disappointment had made them "proof against surprise, excitement, or sudden enthusiasm." How true this rings for today's Red Sox fans![13]

Actually the Hub had enjoyed remarkable success in major league baseball, dating back to 1871 and the first professional league. The Boston Red Stockings won four pennants during the short five-year existence of the National Association of Professional Base Ball Players. The club's dominance stemmed from the superb managing of Harry Wright, often regarded as the father of professional baseball. Harry Wright was supported by the all-around play of his brother George, who later opened Wright & Ditson, a well-known sporting goods store in Boston. Other players of note included Roscoe Barnes and Albert G. Spalding, then at the beginning of his influential career in baseball.[14]

These were the first in a long line of Boston baseball stars. The most famous player in nineteenth-century Boston, and possibly America, was Mike "King" Kelly. Born in 1857 in Troy, New York, Kelly had learned baseball as a youth in Washington, D.C., and Paterson, New Jersey. He had enjoyed almost a decade of brilliant play in Chicago when in February of 1887 Albert Spalding (now the White Stockings owner) traded him to Boston for ten thousand dollars. As the *Herald* reported, the trade was a "sensation in the baseball world." A clever performer, Kelly was best known for his baserunning and sliding, which were celebrated in popular song. In 1885 he scored a remarkable 124 runs off 126 hits. Boston fans were well aware of the liberties he took with the rules. He once defeated their club by running from second base to home without touching third! Such were the drawbacks of having a single umpire. Kelly was readily embraced in Boston, however, and his Irish heritage surely helped. He enjoyed his fans as much as they adored

Mike "King" Kelly

Courtesy of the Boston Public Library, Print Department

him. When he died of pneumonia in 1894, the *Herald* reported, five thousand turned out for the wake of "the most popular man who ever played base ball." Of course others took Kelly's place, as the Beaneaters of the 1890s and Red Sox of the early 1900s won pennants and World Series alike. A partial list includes Frank Selee, Hugh Duffy, Jimmy Collins, Cy Young, Bill Dinneen, Chick Stahl, Bill Carrigan, Smokey Joe Wood, and Tris Speaker.[15]

Baseball players probably had the widest fan following, but they were not the only sport celebrities in Boston. Dr. James Dwight and Richard H. Sears were among the first Americans to play "sphairistike," the game invented by England's Major Walter C. Wingfield. This was lawn tennis, and the two Bostonians dominated its early years. In 1881, five years after he began playing the game at Nahant, Dwight helped to organize the United States National Lawn Tennis Association. Sears won the first open championship that year in Newport, and every year after until 1888. The pair won the doubles championship five times.[16]

A few weeks after Dickie Sears won his first tennis open, his brother's wife gave birth to a little girl who the *New York Times* later called a "pioneer in women's sports." Her name was Eleonora Randolph Sears. Clearly a maverick by the standards of her day, Eleonora Sears was a Gibson Girl in looks and an athlete in heart. Tennis came naturally; she was a four-time national champion in mixed doubles. Squash, seen as a man's game, was more of a challenge. Undaunted, Eleo played at the Harvard Club at a time when a woman was persona non grata. These were but the warm-ups for more active pursuits, such as her attempt to practice with a California men's polo team in 1912, a nationally publicized intrusion into a male domain. Ice hockey, football, baseball, and trapshooting were also among her accomplishments. A remarkable athlete, Eleonora Sears was clearly a model for other women who sought to play active sports. But as one biographer concludes, she never saw herself as a crusader; she only wanted to do the things she enjoyed, and her wealth and amazing ability made that possible.[17]

Eleonora Sears symbolized the leadership that Boston provided American sports, and her exploits also illustrated the interest in active recreation that had surged ahead after the Civil War. And it was not just the elite who participated or benefited. For instance, in 1860 Boston had only one central area, the Common, that could be considered open space for public recreation. Yet by World War I, an "emerald chain" of parks surrounded the city. This was the nation's first public park system. During the summer of 1888, Marine Park in South Boston averaged between five and ten thousand patrons every Sunday. On that year's Labor Day, it accommodated fifteen thousand visitors, and as the park commissioners happily reported, "order reigned all day."[18]

Like parks, public playgrounds were born during these years. As late as 1877, the city provided virtually no public grounds for the active sports and games of children and adults. Keep Off the Grass signs had sprouted on the Common. In 1877, one city councilor reproached his colleagues for this policy, and reminded them that free use of the Boston Common was one of the "grandest ideas" that their grandfathers had passed on to them. He further

*Eleonora Sears—Pioneer
Sportswoman*

Courtesy of the Bettmann
Archive

suggested that his fellow councilors had forgotten that "we were ever boys, that we ever loved to play and run and jump, and that we had a place to do these things in." By 1915, in answer to many similar complaints, the city had established twenty-six public playgrounds, many larger than five acres, designed for the games of young and old alike.[19]

Antebellum Boston had no public baths, beaches, or gymnasiums. Early attempts at privately endowed institutions proved to be fads and conspicuous failures. In 1910, however, more than two million patrons enjoyed fourteen public bathing and beach areas; seven public gymnasiums helped more than 150,000 Bostonians on the road to symmetrical physiques.[20]

As we have already seen, general public recreation was only one aspect of the increased popularity of exercise and outdoor activity. School sports were unorganized into the 1860s. One graduate of Roxbury Latin recalled, "In the way of sports and games, we were on our own. We played football at recess, with a rubber ball, spherical in shape." Or as Henry Adams noted in his autobiography, unlike the emphasis of later schoolboy generations, "sport as a pursuit was unknown." By 1895, however, forty-five hundred people were interested enough to watch English High defeat Boston Latin School for the City Championship in football. What is more, both teams were supported financially by organized student athletic associations.[21]

If Americans, Bostonians included, had always been a "nation of joiners," it is interesting that they established few sporting clubs before the Civil War. Yet by the turn of the century, clubs for all sports, representing all classes, in all sections of the city, operated as private promoters of the athletic craze. In 1888, at the first meeting in the new clubhouse of the Boston Athletic Association, which had received over one thousand applications for membership, one speaker noted the significance of the new building:

> Twenty years, yes, a dozen years ago, it would have been impossible to have raised one half this sum [$300,000] for such a purpose. A hundred years ago a club which was organized for the purpose of improving the physique, and where the wicked games of billiards and bowls could be played, would be looked upon not only as a temple for the wicked waste of time, but as a device for the devil for alluring the youth of puritanical Boston. So great has been the change in sentiment that we believe to-day that this noble building has been erected for a noble purpose—the cultivation of these bodies of ours.[22]

By 1888, then, sport had developed its own temples in Boston. The athletic club, like public parks, playgrounds, high school, college, and professional sports teams, flourished in a city that had come to relate such outdoor (and indoor) activities to a "noble purpose." Actually, noble purposes, in the plural, would be more appropriate, for the attractive aspects of recreation or sport could differ from group to group. For some it might be the chance for a quiet picnic in Franklin Park; for others, the opportunity to

"Americanize" immigrant boys through the mysteries of baseball or football. For the baseball "krank" it might mean the satisfaction of seeing a victory over a New York team; for a King Kelly, the chance to play magnificent ball and make good money doing it.

The association with noble purposes triggered the rapid expansion of facilities, teams, participants, and fans in Boston after the Civil War. It was a transformation that had begun earlier, but it gathered force in an expanding city, as part of a collective response to perceptions of social and cultural disorder. The waves of immigrants, the spread of new housing, the rise of modern factories and market systems, and the ever denser and more diverse collection of humanity seemed to complicate urban life. In contrast, parks and playgrounds appeared as pockets of serenity in the swirl of the city. The organized play of young boys and girls promised discipline, citizenship, and teamwork. Adult games and activities appeared to offer escape from the humdrum of daily living. In short, recreation and sports developed as part of a search for order and community that pervaded many nineteenth-century American cities. Boston serves as a prime example of this process.

OTHER HISTORIANS have recognized the importance of the city as the cradle of modern sport, and have essentially agreed that America's transition from a rural-agricultural to an urban-industrial nation played a pivotal role in the expansion of activities such as we have described for Boston. Not only have these historians viewed the city as the fountainhead for the flood of pastimes that swept the country, they have also suggested that elements of a new urban order *caused* the deluge. In brief, they have argued that recreation and sport were both reactions to negative features of city life and products of the city's technological, economic, and social advantages.

An article written in 1917 attempted to link the rise of sports with the closing of the frontier. As the freelands were filled, the author argued, Americans searched for substitute "safety valves" that might vent the pressures generated in a modern industrial society. Urban congestion "stimulated the need" for outlets such as the pioneer life had once provided. As Foster Rhea Dulles later concluded, sports offered "a new outlet for an inherently restless people" who suffered under "the restrictions of urban living." The simple diversions of rural Americans could not adapt to the urban environment. The countryside was inaccessible to most city dwell-ers. But before succumbing to what John Higham called "the frustrations, the routine, and the sheer dullness of an urban-industrial culture," Americans discovered and nurtured games and pastimes that let off steam and at the same time strengthened their bodies and spirits for another round of city life.[23]

These insights are essentially antiurban; they concentrate on the negative features of urban living, such as congestion or the seden-tary routines of work and free time. By themselves, they do not explain the material forces that enabled new leisure pursuits to develop and thrive. In considering this question, a number of historians have cast the city in a more positive light. In this view, the heightened interest in parks, playgrounds, baseball, and bicy-cles was not merely a reaction to the oppression of the modern city; it was a product of an environment that nurtured industry, innovation, and opportunity.

As the principal architect of this argument notes, the city's con-tributions were multiple. Improved transportation increased the scope of competition and enabled more residents to participate or watch. A higher standard of living, more free time, and more discretionary income improved the recreation opportunities of an ever wider segment of the urban population. Swifter, cheaper modes of communication like the telegraph and the penny press helped to whip up enthusiasm for sports and games. Larger, more concentrated populations alone meant a greater market of con-sumers for sporting equipment, entertainment, and information.[24]

The two interpretations are not mutually exclusive. They can be blended to present a general outline that links the rise of recreation and sports to the modern urban complex. Simplified, it suggests that as cities grew in size, population, and density, their inhabitants felt a longing for the outdoor life and recreational pastimes that were being swallowed up by the stultifying regime of the machine age. Just as things appeared bleakest, however, urban economic, technological, and demographic conditions formed the foundation for an arena of new leisure forms, adapted to the pace and life-style of America's cities.

These themes have carried us some distance in understanding the development of American recreation and sports. At the same time, though, it is clear that the arguments contain some serious limitations. For one, they often suggest that mankind possesses what Lucas and Smith call an "unquenchable play instinct . . . universal and timeless." But as one critic of this notion contends, "labelling a behavior as the product of an instinct is not the same as explaining that behavior." Indeed, the idea that a specific sport like football or baseball grew as a result of some inborn need for play seems somehow overly simplistic.[25] There is an additional problem about the idea that sports fulfilled a natural urge or served as a social safety valve. The middle and upper classes, who dominated these activities throughout the nineteenth century, were the classes with greatest access to the pure outdoor life itself, via country homes or vacations to the shore or the mountains. Why, then, would social elites have experienced a need for modern sports? At the same time, why was it inevitable that improved transportation and communication, or increased leisure time and income, would result in a proliferation of something like athletic clubs or schoolboy sports?[26]

Questions like these have prompted historians to reexamine the relationship between the modern city and its recreational life. The results have been thoughtful and imaginative. For instance, a recent book on the rise of "modern city culture" maintains that baseball helped to fuse the fragmented groups which had divided cities by wealth, occupation, language, and ancestry. First, baseball offered all classes and ethnic groups a sense of common history in the form of team records and statistics; people who were otherwise alienated could communicate through the language of box scores and batting averages. Second, baseball taught all residents the proper use of rules and regulations to get ahead; in business as in baseball one could stretch the rules as long as he didn't break them. It was winning that counted most. Finally, a professional ball game demonstrated the importance of meeting exact performance standards; the properly executed work skill, like the perfectly placed squeeze bunt, was the individual's contribution to group performance.[27]

But did the lessons in baseball reach all the people? Perhaps not. A detailed study of professional baseball during the late nineteenth and early twentieth centuries underscores the fact that baseball was limited in the degree to which it actually integrated the public. Admission prices and Sunday laws kept the ball park beyond the reach of most working-class urbanites. Because of this, baseball remained a middle-class sport. Nonetheless, much of its popularity lay in the belief, however false, that it was democratic and integrative.[28]

Other recent studies suggest other reasons for the increase in urban participants and spectators. Sports clubs were an important source of identity in a dense and diversified population. Similarly, teams and heroes could act as symbolic representatives who acted out the struggle of life on behalf of a particular group or even the city as a whole. James B. Connolly's Olympic victory was thus a victory for all Bostonians, and more so for all Irish Bostonians. Along different lines, new forms of leisure sometimes appeared to offer temporary escape from the noise, congestion, and strain of downtown. (But there were ironies to this. Some sources of escape, like Coney Island, presented their patrons with a more frantic, noisier din than they had left!) Finally, many team sports promised to instill values of self-discipline, character, and sacrifice for the good of the group. Many reformers jumped at the chance to organize the games of immigrant children; they would learn on the playground what they didn't get in the classroom.[29]

Boston, like most large cities in the United States, grew and changed rapidly during the late nineteenth and early twentieth centuries. As a modern city, Boston experienced more than increased population, cramped housing, and attendant "social" problems. It became, in the words of Ralph Turner, "a developing structure of thought and behaviour, that effectively altered and transformed traditional patterns of social life." This dynamic process was manifested in a number of concrete ways, such as "in new social services, in new amusements . . . in new standards of consumption, in new relationships of the sexes and the members of families," and in new circumstances affecting health, disease, and death. A basic question in this book is: How were sport and recreation a part of the particular process of city-building in Boston?[30]

Development and change in a city like Boston can be analyzed from three interrelated "perspectives," which were first outlined by Louis Wirth.[31] First, the city can be viewed as a *physical structure*. One can examine the changing functions and forms of various sections of the city, changes brought on by population flow, shifts in technology and economy, uncontrolled land development, or urban planning. In other words, what caused the evolution of specialized business districts, shopping districts, slums, recreation areas, and suburbs?

Next, the city can be considered as a *social organization.* One can focus on the dynamics of its social groups, social institutions, and social relationships. Of interest are the sharper distinctions between income and status groups, the change from traditional social ties like kinship or neighborhood to modern ties like political parties, and finally the rise of specialized agencies to control education, economic production, and recreation.

Wirth's third perspective treats the city as a *state of mind,* or value system, and examines the emotional adjustments of individuals and groups to city life, or the effects of changing social relationships on the urban personality. Here one might consider the ideologies and attitudes that have developed in response to perceptions of the city—how the city affects man's way of perceiving himself and others. Man, in turn, gives the city a personality, as "Big Apple," "jungle," or both.

The first perspective examines the city's anatomy, the second its physiology, and the third, its soul. The distinctions between the groupings are seldom clear-cut; indeed, they are often interrelated. Oscar Handlin demonstrates, for instance, that Irish immigration before the Civil War radically altered Boston's physical structure. The North End became the Irish ghetto, as older residents fled to other residential districts. At the same time, it affected Boston's social relationships and its citizens' beliefs that their city was totally "Yankee."[32]

Sports too can be analyzed as physical structures, social organizations, or states of mind. As physical structures, they transcend the game to include the facilities and environments upon which their existence depends. As social organizations, they are filled with numerous and changing forms of social groups, social behavior, social relationships, and social order. Some are unique to sport, some are reflections of their parent cultures and societies, some are mixtures. Finally, like the city, sport or recreation may be a state of mind, a reified idea, a concept treated as if it were a material thing. In this perspective, advocates have ballyhooed certain pastimes like baseball as panaceas for society's psychic and physical ills. Opponents have condemned other sports as contributors to social decay.

It is clear that as physical structure, social organization, and state of mind, recreation and sport have been integral parts of the process of urban growth. For instance, within the last decade, new civic centers and arenas—physical structures—have often been a central element both in the revitalization of downtown areas and in the improvement of a city's image, its state of mind. In 1972, Indianapolis Mayor Richard Lugar offered great hope for the remedial effects of the new Market Square project: "It will offer new hope for the heart of the city. Sports, along with the theater and the arts, must be a focal point for the renewal of the city."[33] Similarly, Robert Abrams, borough president of the Bronx, defended Yankee Stadium's costly renovation during the city's economic crisis by emphasizing that "Yankee Stadium is part of the chemistry of life in this town." At the same time, however, critics have questioned whether the benefits of arenas accrue less to the city and its inhabitants than to the owners of the sports teams involved.[34]

If the sport facility can alter a city, the opposite can be equally true, with devastating effect. Racial migrations and their ensuing social tensions have transformed recreation areas like the South Side beaches of Chicago or Carson Beach in Boston into powderkegs of violence that erupt at the slightest spark, as happened in Chicago during the summer of 1919. Thus, urban social processes have the power to convert sporting areas, designed as asylums of leisure and relaxation, into symbols of struggles over "turf" or, worse, into bloody fields of racial strife.

As a social organization, sport can affect the mechanisms of social status in the city. This holds true particularly in the case of elite sporting club membership. As one study concludes, "in cities, people rate their fellow citizens by superficial evidence and by symbols such as residential address, occupational titles and club memberships." Research in Kansas City has shown that the clearest index of that city's upper class is membership in an elite country club like the First Jackson or the Missoukana. In turn, the location of the country club can become the most desirable area for upper-class residence.[35]

Along related lines, one baseball historian has uncovered the close relationships between politicians, trolley companies, real estate speculation, and ball clubs. Local bosses were often either club owners or close associates. They offered the teams preferential treatment on matters like municipal services or taxation; they provided inside information on potential developments in real estate or transportation. In return the politicians "used the franchise as a source of honest graft and patronage, as an inducement to encourage people to travel on the traction routes they operated, and to improve their public image."[36] In other words, baseball helped to cement the structures of urban political power, a fact not overlooked by Boss Tweed in New York or Boss Cox of Cincinnati.

Finally, much of the rationale of organized sport, its state of mind or value system, grew as a reaction to the physical environment of the city and to perceptions of suffering and degradation caused by cramped housing and industrial pollution. At the same time, public parks, which were a product of this reaction, altered the physical development of the city by countering unchecked urban growth, by redirecting transportation lines, and by deflecting the patterns of residential land speculation.

While the "perspectives" of the city or sport as physical structures, social organizations, and value systems can help us to make sense of broad relationships, it is necessary that we consider the precise circumstances, events, and personalities which affected them in Boston. If, through analyzing how Boston played, we can bring to life some fragments of her sporting past, and organize them in a framework of change, perhaps we can also reveal something about the meaning of life in the city.

2/Boston's Search for Community

THE RELATIONSHIPS BETWEEN sport and the city begin to make sense when considered in conjunction with notions of community—change in community, and search for it. Indeed, how the forces of urban growth pressured and altered the many forms of community in a city like Boston; how these developments resulted in a wide variety of responses that may be grouped loosely as a "search for community"; how these responses included not only active campaigns to reform the physical, social, and psychological aspects of city life, but also an acceptance of the new urban reality—these questions form the thesis of this book. As an important instrument in this search for community, recreation and sport both shaped the city and were shaped by it.

Looking at a city like Boston in terms of community change and response presents a useful focus of analysis, since the city is, obviously, an amalgam of numerous community forms. But there are difficulties in defining just what is meant by "community." In one sampling of ninety-four definitions of "community" the only common feature was *people*. Of course it is the nature of people's relationships that defines community. The typical notion of the concept has implied a collection of individuals who share not only common interests but also, and more important, a sense of mutual bonding, personal intimacy, affection, and moral commitment.[1] As a recent study of community in American history cautions, no single form can define the concept. It embraces families, neighborhoods, towns, groups of friends, and social classes.[2]

Some scholars, however, have emphasized the importance of locality to the development of community, or in the words of Ernest Burgess, "the community viewed almost exclusively in terms

21

of location and movement."[3] Herbert Gans, author of a community study of Boston's old West End, described this as community in a "combined social and spatial sense, referring to an aggregate of people who occupy a common and bounded territory within which they establish and participate in common institutions." Community here relates to a geographic area, regardless of size; be it the city as a whole, the ward, or the local neighborhood. In this tradition, Max Weber could consider the "urban community" in terms of the entire system within the city boundaries, while Herbert Gans could concentrate on a self-contained "community" within the West End.[4]

Gans, however, recognized the need to go beyond this notion. He and other scholars have questioned the emphasis on spatial limits in defining community, and instead have emphasized the need to think in terms of "nonspatial, nonspace elements," or communities of interest. They argue that the ties binding people into communities can thrive over great distances; intimacy and shared interests do not depend on continuous, face-to-face proximity.[5]

These unbounded communities exist in many forms, from informal networks to more organized social systems. At the simplest level lie the "sentiments, forms of conduct and ceremonies" that can create and nurture a sense of solidarity and "we-ness" that transcends geographic boundaries. They might stem from a common ethnic heritage or dedication to a common cause. Often, however, the members of these networks decide to form structured associations, clubs, or societies in an attempt to ensure the maintenance or expansion of their particular community form.[6] The world of sport can illustrate the difference between these informal and formal systems. For instance, while many people may feel a shared attachment to the goals, ceremonies, and conduct of a sports team, relatively few join the booster club, whose expressed purpose is to advance the team's cause.

Ultimately, then, the community, like the city, can be viewed in a physical-spatial sense, as a locality; in a social sense, as a system; and in a psychological sense, as a state of mind. If its essence is a "sense of belonging" or personal "involvement," it can vary in scope from the local street to infinity. Its form can reside in formal systems of interest or informal networks of shared values and common ways of thinking. The city, a community in itself, is the framework for many autonomous communities. The city and its communities exist in a close relationship; changes in the one usually result in changes in the other. As the city evolves, new neighborhoods and interest groups form to help shape it, in an endless process of action and reaction. Bostonians have experienced a continuing process of city and community development. Most significant to this book, however, is the relationship of this process with a recreation complex that included parks, playgrounds, schoolboy and professional sports, athletic clubs, and bicycle booms.

MOST OF THE EARLY SCHOLARS who studied the city and whose names have become synonymous with urban theory were concerned with understanding the moral consequences of the city as much as they were with describing its growth and operation.[7] To a large degree, their work focused on changes in community forms. Much of the effort stemmed from the work of nineteenth-century intellectuals on both sides of the Atlantic who were concerned with a general corrosion of life and values that seemed somehow the result of contemporary social, political, and economic forces. In Europe, along with the ideas of Maine, Marx, Ruskin, Durkheim, and others, this critical thought crystalized in Ferdinand Tönnies's influential work, *Gemeinschaft und Gesellschaft*, published in 1887. Tönnies outlined the changes that capitalism and its burgeoning centers of production had worked in modern social relations. There had been a weakening of *Gemeinschaft*, the community relations and emotional ties of family, guild, or village. At the same time, the networks of *Gesellschaft* had grown more numerous, particularly in cities. These were artificial society relations, characterized by the impersonal, rational, contractual ties of the corporation.[8]

Following these general critiques of industrial society, intellectuals swung with ease to the swelling city as a focal point for social criticism. In Europe, this trend reached an early peak in the work of Max Weber, Georg Simmel, and Oswald Spengler. Weber concluded that The City, the ideal type that represented the most fulfilling organization of human settlement, had to be found in the past, not the present. Simmel outlined a deterioration of older community attachments that freed the urban resident in ways that were both progressive and pathological. For Spengler, the loss of the older "folk spirit" of Gemeinschaft, devoured by the stone colossus of the city, represented the death of culture itself.[9]

Not surprisingly, the growth of America's cities in the nineteenth century led to equal soul-searching over the impact of urban growth on American social life. Her cities' populations had increased at a remarkable rate even before the Civil War. In 1840, 8 percent of the country had resided in locales of more than eight thousand inhabitants; by 1860 the percentage was 16. Urban growth after the Civil War was equally rapid and chaotic. Chicago's population tripled between 1880 and 1900; New York's swelled from two to almost three and one-half million people. Cleveland, Detroit, and Milwaukee doubled in size. From 1860 to 1910, the number of cities with populations over one hundred thousand increased from nine to fifty.[10]

But the critics of America's growing cities were concerned less with increase in population than with changes in the types of urban inhabitants, and with the new social life and relationships found within the city's reach. Josiah Strong, in a popular book entitled *Our Country: Its Possible Future and Present Crisis,* catalogued the perils of the emerging urban order that many agreed had disrupted older, more stable, forms of community. While his publication preceded the later waves of "new" immigrants from southeastern Europe, he was appalled that the ten largest cities, which contained but 9 percent of the nation's population, held 23 percent of the foreign born. Further, he linked the foreign element to the specter of Romanism. Intemperance was another symptom of cancerous change, Strong declared. In 1880 there was an overall ratio of one saloon to every 438 people east of the Mississippi; but in Boston saloons numbered one for every 329 souls, and in New York, one for every 171.[11]

The cities also became the focal points for the changes in social relations that accompanied a rising capitalist economy. The spread of trolley and streetcar networks encouraged the relocation of industry and the expansion of speculative home building in patterns that sorted the populace by income, occupation, race, and nationality. Many old neighborhoods languished; some dissolved. New neighborhoods sprang from once vacant lots or rural pastures. Many felt a hardening of antagonisms between classes now identified by their relationship to the means of production. Include the large migration of people into and out of the cities, and it is no wonder that some intellectuals feared a weakening of the attachments that had once bound residents to their community. In 1899, Adna Weber, whose study of urbanization still merits consideration, noted the difficulties that this "large floating population" presented to effective city government, since the "thousands of new residents are strangers to the city's history and traditions, have no local attachments and do not readily acquire any civic pride."[12]

Pessimists might paint a bleaker picture. What if ineffective government and lethargy of civic spirit allowed class differences to mushroom into volatile class conflicts? Might not the situation destroy the city itself? Some felt so. Julian West, the hero of Edward Bellamy's immensely popular Utopian novel, *Looking Backward,* offered this view to his twenty-first-century host. When questioned about the social unrest of his day, Mr. West replied, "All I can say is, that the prospect was such when I went into that long sleep that I should not have been surprised had I looked down from your housetop today on a heap of charred and moss-grown ruins instead of this glorious city."[13]

Throughout America, men and women recognized and were bewildered by what Robert Wiebe has labeled a "crisis in the communities."[14] Much of the crisis seemed related to the growth of the cities, which loomed as the most conspicuous sources of change in industrial America. The analysis reached its apogee in the works of Robert Park and Louis Wirth, who believed that, for better and worse, the city had disrupted and weakened the control that older forms of community had exerted:

> But with the growth of large cities, with the vast division of labor which has come in with the machine industry, and with the movement and change that have come about with the multiplication of the means of transportation and communication, the old forms of social control represented by the family, the neighborhood and the local community have been undermined and their influence greatly diminished.[15]

The city seemed to house the greatest community crisis, because the problems of crime, housing, health, immigration, and political corruption were more visible there than in America's towns.

The bleakest descriptions suggested that modern urban life had lost all sense of community. Family, neighborhood, and church were now empty forms. In their place, society had erected artificial and shallow arrangements to bind and control individuals: schools, political parties, professional organizations, and unions. Recent research, however, indicates that traditional community sentiments and structures persisted in the metropolis; indeed, they are alive and well today. What the city nurtured, in fact, was a fragmentation or, as one historian put it, a "bifurcation" of social relations into competing systems of Gemeinschaft and Gesellschaft. The city had been midwife to the birth of new types of social and psychological association. The secret to survival was finding the right mix between old and new.[16]

If it is clear that traditional communities continued in the modern city, it is equally true that many residents perceived the changes around them as serious threats. To certain Bostonians of the late nineteenth century, the changes were obvious and alarming; in reaction they searched for mechanisms to ensure what they hoped would be a true sense of city-wide community. Other Bostonians simply sought to get by, working out their networks of mutual interests and attachments however they could. The actions and struggles that grew out of these perceptions and adjustments to change shaped the social organizations and ideological images of organized sport and recreation.

A PERSON'S SENSE of community solidarity, or its lack, is always a relative notion. In the industrial age, with its swift and highly visible changes, inhabitants of towns and cities have often felt that each succeeding generation has experienced a less cohesive community than its predecessors. In this regard, the past has been viewed with fondness and the future with trepidation. It has mattered little that the past might have been, in fact, less serene than the present would have it; what motivates a search for community are perceptions or recollections of a better, more stable past.

During the nineteenth century this sense of change and loss in community solidarity had a recurring pattern in Boston. Foreign immigrants, new factories, labor disputes, and sprawling tenements had surged over the city in successive and concurrent waves. Thus, the past community often loomed ever better than the present.

At the turn of the twentieth century, one old resident recalled the town of his boyhood and noted that "her glance fell upon a homogeneous population, for no influx of foreigners had then entered her gates, bringing with them their griefs and prejudices."[17] Poverty existed before the Irish masses arrived in the 1840s, but there also existed a belief that the problem of poverty could be solved. As one charity worker reminisced, "The poor were personally subjects of knowledge and cognizance to the more favored classes . . . every man was known by his neighbor . . . none were overlooked, nor could escape in the crowd."[18] Struck by the apparent beneficence of Boston's fortunate classes, Harriet Martineau remarked, "I know no large city where there is so much mutual helpfulness, so little neglect and ignorance of the concerns of other classes."[19]

In general, older Bostonians recalled the Hub that existed before the Irish invasion as a community blessed by God and man. Oscar Handlin paints such a picture in *Boston's Immigrants*. Though subject to periodic financial panic and underdeveloped industry, Boston was a healthy and comfortable city: "With the utmost confidence in himself, the Bostonian could look out upon the world with an unjaundiced and optimistic eye." Surely, as Edward Everett Hale recalled, Boston was a good place in which to be born and a good place in which to grow to manhood.[20]

Perhaps, though, this community was not quite so serene. A recent interpretation of the town's incorporation into a city in 1822 concludes that the transition reflected a real break from the communal, homogeneous population and values that might have existed before. Boston's first mayor, Josiah Quincy, was faced with the prospect of governing a growing population beset by splintering factions in which conflict, not consensus, held political sway.[21] Workers' strikes and labor agitation loomed on the horizon for a city in which 10 percent held over half the wealth. Periodic outbursts of rioting against and among minority groups or neighborhoods, although largely spontaneous and always widely condemned, nonetheless reflected the tensions inherent in a social and cultural environment that was increasingly heterogeneous. The flames that in 1834 consumed the Ursuline convent in Charlestown clearly were fanned by religious intolerance, which saw Protestant pastors like Lyman Beecher preaching of Papist plots and Catholic subversion of American principles.[22]

If the first three decades of the nineteenth century were not as halcyon as later memories made them out to be, perhaps the reason for the distortion is more easily understood when one realizes how much worse the next two decades were. Certainly the 1840s and fifties were years of turmoil and rapid change, largely induced by the great influx of Irish. These developments set in motion many of the mechanisms that later worked to shape the development of sport. Among them were a concern for physical changes in the community, such as land and housing; a discernible flight by residents to outlying suburbs, interpreted by contemporaries as an attempt to escape the problems of the city; and a search for common bonds among various social groups. When organized sport finally burst into full bloom thirty years later, these responses to community change were again in full swing.

From 1810 to 1840, the population of the city and its immediate suburbs (most were later incorporated) increased from approximately 50,000 to about 125,000. In the next decade alone, the population increased to over 200,000—a growth of 68.5 percent. These ten years witnessed the largest percentage growth of the period, but the population continued to swell, approaching 290,000 souls on the eve of the Civil War. Moreover, these figures represented the population at a given instant. Actual turnover of population was much greater, perhaps to the level of half the population every one or two years.[23]

The sheer increase and turnover in population would bring change and problems, to be sure; but of even greater concern to Bostonians was the character of the increased population. While the early immigration had been dominated by rural New England stock, much of the later influx bore a Hibernian tongue and carried a Catholic missal. In 1820, foreigners composed only 12 percent of the city's total population; by 1845, the number of foreign born and their children had risen to about 33 percent. Ten years later, this group, mostly Irish, represented 53 percent of the total. The "natives" were now in a minority.[24]

The alarmed reaction was predictable, a portent of later responses to East European immigrants. In 1851, an article on immigration, published in an educational journal, summarized the fears of many Bostonians. The author anxiously wondered about the "ultimate effect of this vast and unexampled immigration." Could Boston preserve herself from "demoralization," or better yet, improve and purify the foreigners? Or would the hordes "spread ignorance and vice, crime and disease, through our native population?" The answer was not clear.[25] But cultural differences, heightened by mutual religious hostility, contributed to the short-lived success of the Know-Nothing party in the early 1850s, and heightened the sense of group conflict that lingered to occasionally envenom Boston's social and political life until the twentieth century.[26] Reverend Edward Everett Hale felt compelled to urge his flock at the South Congregational Church to work through benevolence to ensure that the city, now more than half foreign, would remain true "to the glories of its early name." A year later, in 1857, he lamented the feeling of "less public spirit . . . less pride in the good name of Boston."[27]

Immigration meant cramped housing in the city's oldest districts. Citizens were sympathetic to the physical plight faced by the poor in slums and at the same time alarmed at the increasing amounts of public funds used to support them. While one committee recognized that the abominable conditions in the North End clearly fostered "sullen indifference and despair," Boston's mayors complained about the twofold increase in poor relief from 1850 to 1860.[28]

If the foreign immigrants were forced by poverty to suffer in the slums of Boston's oldest sections, the more fortunate classes developed their own residential enclaves within the city limits or struck out for the immediate suburbs and, in the words of one City Council committee, began "increasing the taxable property in those from the profits of business transacted within our limits." This pattern of residential segregation and suburban flight would become even more pronounced after the Civil War.[29]

In the midst of this first great flow of different people with conflicting values and beliefs, Boston's ethnic and social clusters began to develop and nurture a sense of their own consciousness as distinct peoples. While gradually emerging as Bostonians, the Irish still felt the need for their Shamrock Society and Charitable Irish Society, Scots for their Caledonian Club, Germans for their Turnverein. At the same time, frustrated by the failure to assimilate these newer groups, the old stock began to solidify its own distinct identity, until by the 1850s it had developed its own ideal type, the Boston Brahmin.[30]

The upsetting of community identity and cohesion, the anxieties over rapid growth, and the fears of change brought about by the heavy Irish immigration during the 1840s and 1850s were ameliorated to some degree by the common focus and effort of the Civil War. Anglophobia united old Bostonians and new Irish immigrants. The need for efficient military units assured the Irish a new sense of equality and worth. Both in the field and at home in the factory, Irish contributions to the war effort were well recognized; in turn, Boston showed a new tolerance of its immigrants.[31]

This period of relative "community" spirit is an important break; for although it is clear that the decades before the war had been tense and troubled, the problems that occurred after Appomattox were of greater dimension. While urbanization became more intense, immigration took a new twist, with the arrival of groups yet more alien than the Irish. As the city expanded in size, housing became more segregated by ethnicity and income. The old political order gave way to a new regime, heavily influenced by bosses, machines, and sons of Erin. There is little wonder, then, that a younger generation viewed its predecessors with a sense of yearning for "those simpler days." What is significant is the fact that these perceptions of troubled times occurred during a period when parks, playgrounds, and organized sports mushroomed.

FROM 1835 TO 1900, the population of Massachusetts increased from 660,940 to 2,805,346. Further, the distribution of this population had gone from 81 percent rural to 76 percent urban ("urban" being areas of 8000 or more inhabitants). The Bay State was experiencing urbanization, and nowhere was this felt more than in her capital. State and federal census figures between 1860 and 1900 show a greater than threefold increase in Boston's population, from 177,840 to 560,892. Each decade the percentage increases topped 20 percent; from 1870 to 1880 alone, the increase was 44.8 percent.[32]

But sheer population increase doesn't tell nearly the whole story. Census figures put the increase from 1880 to 1890 at 85,638. By careful analysis of listings in city directories, Stephan Thernstrom has been able to estimate that the actual immigration between 1880 and 1890 was as high as 790,000, and that the exodus of people was equally staggering. Thus, by comparison, the net population change for this decade was modest; but only because "two very powerful migratory currents flowing through the community nearly cancelled each other out, leaving only the small rivulet registered by the new figures." It also appears likely that total migratory levels were similar right up to World War I.[33]

If the size of population growth posed a threat to community solidarity, new waves of immigrants further destroyed any sense of homogeneity. We have seen that the natives were already in the minority by the Civil War. Their relative size continued to shrink; by 1880, 64 percent of Boston's inhabitants had been born of foreign or mixed (one foreign) parentage. By 1910 that figure had increased to 74 percent. Where once a "Yankee" breed had dominated the Hub, by the turn of the century, her inner streets were a patchwork of racial and ethnic enclaves that could be clearly distinguished, catalogued, and analyzed by social statisticians.[34]

Boston expanded and reshaped her physical dimensions drastically after the Civil War. In the six years from 1867 to 1873, Roxbury, West Roxbury, Dorchester, Charlestown, and Brighton entered her fold by annexation, thereby increasing the city's territory by 441 percent. This new territory, plus the continued reclamation of land, as in the Back Bay area, created new havens for housing development, speculation, and migration by the middle and upper classes.

Thus, the city was further segregated in its residential patterns, from the opulent architecture of the Back Bay, to the middle-class "cottages" of West Roxbury, to the tenements of the North End. These artifacts themselves proclaimed the dispersal of community identity. As the narrator of *Looking Backward* reminded his audience of the year 2000, housing was the benchmark of social status:

> For it must be understood that the comparative desirability of different parts of Boston for residence depended then, not on natural features, but on the character of the neighboring population. Each class or nation lived by itself, in quarters of its own. A rich man living among the poor, an educated man among the uneducated was like the one living in isolation among a jealous and alien race.

By 1900, Boston was "very much a city divided."[35]

The inner city contained the business district; the North, West, and South Ends, three impoverished neighborhoods; and the Back Bay, the reclaimed area housing the well-to-do. The North End, where Paul Revere's house still stands as a colonial landmark, was the city's oldest neighborhood. By the middle of the nineteenth century, however, it had become a foreign land, as successive waves of immigrants drove out older stock. First the Irish, then Italians and Russian Jews; by 1920 it was 90 percent Italian clusters of Campanians, Sicilians, and Abruzzesi. Nearing 30,000 in population at the turn of the century, the North End was one of Boston's most congested areas. The West End was similar; in 1910 it housed 189.6 persons per acre, in a city that averaged 27.2 per acre. Its population in 1900 stood at 34,500, with Jews and Irish predominating, but with sizable pockets of British, blacks, some Italians, and scattered "natives." The South End was in constant flux. At mid-century it had grown as a haven for the upper middle class who were leaving the older neighborhoods. The 1870s saw its swift decline, as the wealthier moved to the new Back Bay, and workers moved in from the North and West Ends to be nearer the piano and furniture factories in the area. Row houses quickly converted to apartments and lodging houses. By 1895, the South End's 40,000 inhabitants were mainly Irish who were striking out toward Roxbury or South Boston. It also housed growing segments of Jews and blacks, a floating third of native-born lodgers, and blocks of Italians, Greeks, Syrians, Chinese, Armenians, Germans, British, and Scots. With the notable exceptions of the Back Bay and Beacon Hill, the inner wards were the poorest, the densest, and the most disease ridden.[36]

By 1900, these core areas were surrounded by a "zone of emergence," which included East Boston, Charlestown, parts of Cambridge, the nearer ends of Roxbury and Dorchester, and South Boston. The "zone of emergence," coined by contemporary reformers, was an appropriate name. Its residents were mostly established immigrant groups, largely Irish, who followed factories and jobs toward cheaper land. They were lower middle class and upper working class, striving for a piece of America's promise. Although usually mortgaged and converted to multiple family use, 65 percent of the zone's residences were owned by occupants.[37]

To the south and west lay the "streetcar suburbs" of the middle and upper classes. Separate villages and towns until they were annexed, these outlying areas offered breathing room and country houses, if not ownership, to white-collar workers seeking an escape from tenements and concrete alleys. By the twentieth century, however, many of these districts were also feeling the squeeze of uncontrolled development.[38]

While some neighborhoods prospered, others languished. Those

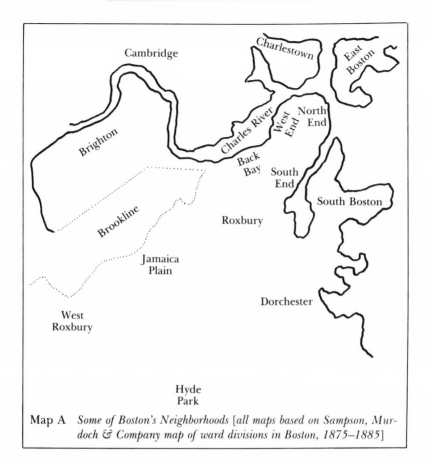

Map A   *Some of Boston's Neighborhoods [all maps based on Sampson, Murdoch & Company map of ward divisions in Boston, 1875–1885]*

who could not or would not remember earlier slum studies were shocked to see accounts of the housing and living conditions in the North and West Ends. Benjamin O. Flower, reformer, social activist, and publisher of *Arena* magazine, referred to the slums as "Civilization's Inferno" or the "Social Cellar," and warned of the uprising, rebellion, and plague fostered in such conditions. The city's director of physical training, Edward Mussey Hartwell, pointed with alarm to the high death and disease rates brought about by crowded conditions and inactivity; he stressed that Boston's death rate was higher than that of London or Berlin.[39]

Local government was strained by the demands for remedies to social problems and by the need for increased services to the old city and its new suburban areas. The municipal debt had increased almost fourfold in the fifteen years after the Civil War, unleashing a fiscal conservatism that had a braking effect on projects like public parks.[40] Moreover, voters overlooked the traditions of genteel political control and began electing politicians who offered, and appeared to provide, the best services for their particular needs. Through this process the Irish began to enjoy serious political success. Benjamin Butler, seen as a demagogue by Boston's first families, successfully rallied Irish support in his victorious gubernatorial campaign of 1882. Irish-born Hugh O'Brien became, in 1884, the first of his stock to enter the mayor's office, but his fellow immigrants had been gaining strength in the Common Council for years.[41]

Boston's political life during this period was by no means a simple matter of Yankee Republicans against Irish Democrats. Those were the main battle lines, to be sure; and issues like control of parochial schools or enforcement of liquor laws could pit natives against immigrants. On the other hand, for over a decade Patrick Maguire, the Irish boss of local Democrats, worked closely and successfully with Yankee mayors like Frederick O. Prince, Nathan Matthews, and Josiah Quincy, who were also Democrats. Only when Maguire died in 1896 did party control loosen, creating opportunities for local ward bosses like John F. ("Honey Fitz") Fitzgerald in the North End, Martin Lomasney in the West End, James Donovan in the South End, and James Michael Curley in Roxbury's zone of emergence. The political boss might be vilified by the Back Bay banker as a corrupt and prodigal obstruction to good government, but his constituents knew him as a man who could help pay the rent, secure legal assistance, find a bed at the hospital, or gain work on a construction gang.[42]

Strains appeared in other areas. Statisticians offered cause for alarm to those concerned with organized labor. Carroll Davidson Wright's study of strikes in Massachusetts outlined a deterioration of labor relations. Fully 27.6 percent of the strikes from 1830 to 1880 had occurred in the six years following the financial failure of 1873. Wright additionally suggested a link between the growing foreign-born population and the increased number and severity of workers' strikes. In the mid-eighties the state witnessed 555 strikes, almost four times the total that Wright had found in fifty years. John Boyle O'Reilly's poem "The City Streets" issued a warning to capitalist plutocrats:

> Not gold, but souls, should be first in an age
>   That bows its head at the sacred word:
> Yet our laws are blind to a starving wage,
>   While guarding the owners sweat-wrung hoard.
>   . . .
> Take heed, for your Juggernaut pushes hard;
>   God holds the doom that its day completes;
> It will dawn like a fire when the track is barred
>   By a barricade in the city streets.

This tension continued into the twentieth century; Fitzgerald and Curley both used it to great effect in their campaigns.[43]

Clearly, Boston experienced changes and tensions in her physical, social, and political structures in the decades between the Civil War and World War I. It was, however, the contemporary perceptions of these changes that laid the basis for individual and group responses to the city and its problems. Edward Everett Hale put it mildly when he noted the effects of immigration on the city:

> Upon this simple village life, if you please, an ocean of foreign emigration was about to fall; and the Boston of today, more than half European by birth, does not recognize the homogeneous population of the Boston of 1840.

Even though Hale did not believe that the country was inherently more salutary than the city, he came to fear the "strange loneliness" that the growing city imposed: "the loneliness which is so terrible because there are thousands all around." Other perceptions of urban change and disorder were more alarmist than Hale's.[44]

Change was most shocking to the Brahmin class. They considered many of the era's popular leaders—Ben Butler in politics, Henry Ward Beecher in religion, P. T. Barnum in entertainment—to be, as Van Wyck Brooks has put it, "singularly coarse."[45] Elites from other cities sympathized with the plight of their Bostonian brethren. When Frederick Law Olmsted wrote to Horace Cleveland of Chicago expressing fears that Hugh O'Brien's election to the mayoralty might hinder park development, Cleveland bitterly responded: "It is enough to make the old Bostonians of past generations turn in their graves to think of the city being given over to Irish domination and I cannot but fear that you will suffer discontent from this last throw of time's whirligig."[46]

As early as 1878, Francis Parkman, writing in the *North American Review*, warned of the "inevitable strain" that arose in crowded cities, where the poor and ignorant outnumbered the wealthy and virtuous, where "bloated wealth and envious poverty" were forced to coexist, creating "a tinseled civilization above and a discontented proletariat beneath." Universal suffrage, he declared, might succeed in the small village, but not in the metropolis.[47] Fourteen years later, Senator Henry Cabot Lodge described the afflictions that threatened Freedom's Birthplace. Immigration had filled Boston with poor illiterates who were "unfamiliar with American habits and ways of thought." The closeness of wealth to poverty gave rise to "professional politicians," elected by the poor, who were indifferent to fiscal responsibilities that fell "only on those who are taxpayers." Such conditions offered temptations and produced evils "which in many American cities have reached an alarming height." Lodge had more faith than many of his kinsmen, however, and he maintained that Boston could overcome this latest peril if her citizens were but true to the traditions of their Puritan forebears.[48]

Others of the Brahmin stock, however, were not so sanguine. Many began to withdraw from the active and very public role they had once played in Boston's life, working either behind the scenes or not at all. Charles Eliot Norton removed himself to Ashfield, where he wrote to James Russell Lowell that there was "but one Irish family . . . in the township." Charles Francis Adams, Jr., retired to Lincoln, where the farmers seemed more steeped in the ways of his own ancestors. No longer trusting the abilities of Boston Latin School to educate their children, the upper class invested their sons, their money, and their prestige into St. Paul's, Andover, Groton, Exeter, and a limited number of other boarding schools. This was by no means a wholesale class desertion of civic responsibility, for many remained active in reform politics, in cultural affairs, in philanthropy. But the "aristoi" of America's Athens were clearly now on the defensive.[49]

The same sense of hopelessness and fear, fed by the lurid accounts of urban depravity that enlivened the popular press, added fuel to the middle-class drive to the outlying suburban areas of Boston. These perceptions of urban chaos undoubtedly slowed down the annexation of further towns into Boston's fold and minimized the willingness of the suburbs to enter into metropolitan schemes of cooperation.[50]

Reformers like Robert A. Woods were similarly convinced that the forces of industrialization, immigration, population growth, and unplanned housing had dispelled older, more penetrating forms of community cohesion. Woods, who came in 1892 to the Andover House settlement in Boston's South End, and who spent the remainder of his life directing settlement and reform work in the Hub, organized numerous studies of the urban environment. What he and his colleagues perceived was a destruction of the neighborhood, the one urban link to the stability and cohesion of the traditional village:

> Neighborhoods come to be made up of people who have no local attachments and are separated from one another by distinctions of race and religion. There is no concerted action for a better social life, no watchfulness over common interests.[51]

Much of the problem could be seen in the migration by so many of the upper working class and lower middle class to zones of emergence, way stations on the road to the suburbs. Here, Woods and his workers noted, "people no longer live among neighbors and friends, and children lose all sense of that common unity of feeling which under ordinary circumstances would be outraged over the violation of primary ties."[52]

But to Woods and many others of the middle and upper classes, the threat of community chaos sounded alarms not for retreat but for action. As Paul Boyer has recently argued, urban reformers redoubled their efforts with great urgency as they perceived that "the very survival of the social order was riding on what happened in the great industrial cities." Social workers like Woods led the charge into the heart of the city, supported by numerous philanthropists who financed the work of organizations like the settlement house, the church mission, the YMCU, and the YMCA.[53]

If the wealthy Brahmin and his middle-class clerk recognized the disruptions around them, what can be said about the mass of workers and their families, struggling to survive in the North End or grasping at a dream of home ownership in Roxbury Crossing? Did they experience a sense of crisis and anomie? How did they react?

Their strikes and their votes indicated that workers recognized the same inequities—the results of rapacious capitalism—that Boston's George McNeill outlined. A prominent figure in the Eight Hour League and the Knights of Labor, McNeill contended that, "whereas [the worker] is the most important factor, he is treated as the least. . . . When at work, he belongs to the lower orders, and is continually under surveillance; when out of work, he is an outlaw, a tramp—he is a man without the rights of manhood,—the pariah of society, homeless, in the deep significance of the term."[54]

Yet the working class was often divided, especially by ethnic antagonisms. Witness this attack on North End immigrants:

> These people are the very scourings of the slums of Italy. They are imbued with socialist ideas, taught under the Crispi method of civilization to despise religion and to be indifferent as to their political and social mores. They are a dangerous as well as an undesirable element.

The source was not the Brahmins' *Evening Transcript*, but Patrick Maguire's *Republic*, lashing out at the Italians who were threatening the stability of Irish political and religious organizations.[55]

Workers could be alienated from their work; as ethnic groups, they could be alienated from each other; as families, they could be unsettled and mobile; they could intelligently grasp the significance of the changes around them. But at the same time, these "other Bostonians" could experience a real sense of community. The chaos and crisis of the urban slum districts was never as great as many reformers claimed. Perceptive analysts discovered that community did exist in civilization's inferno, although it was a form of association that most outsiders could not appreciate. Street identity, ethnic identity, and gang identity did exist among the masses, and the cleverest reformers worked with these forms, not against them. Nonetheless, those who articulated their life in the inner wards sometimes wondered what had ever saved them "from the seemingly inevitable consequences of such an environment," and one senses that the anonymous inhabitants groped for more

organized forms of association and identity in response to a perceived need for them.[56]

THROUGHOUT THE NINETEENTH CENTURY, then, Boston experienced tremendous changes both as a city and as a
community of communities. Her physical and social structure and
her state of mind were altered by her relationship to a burgeoning
economy of capitalist free enterprise. While some groups had more
options in responding, no segment of Boston's society was immune
from the effects of change. An unregulated approach to production and consumption had encouraged a dislocation of residential
communities, like the North End, where once a mixture of social
classes had lived and worked in proximity. What developed instead
were divisions of space, with separate areas for production, services, shopping, and housing. Beyond this, housing itself became
segmented by class and status. The rings or zones of housing in
Boston illustrate this tendency. Both new immigrants and old natives had to adjust to this process of change. They did so by
continually redeveloping their communities.[57]

Robert A. Nisbet calls this a "quest for community," which, he
claims, "springs from some of the powerful needs of human nature—needs for a clear sense of cultural purpose, membership,
status and continuity." In a similar vein, Gunther Barth argues
that nineteenth-century city people "sought new ways of life to
strengthen their commitments to a common humanity." Bostonians embarked on this quest between 1865 and 1915, as they had
before and as they have since. Clearly, it affected their behavior,
as they sought a more stable, more meaningful existence for themselves and their city.[58]

Bostonians restructured their communities in various ways and
at various levels. Some campaigned for active "reform" causes
which they hoped would refashion the city and its social life in
such a way as to recapture what they believed had once been a
city-wide community. Herein lay crusades to save souls and raze
slums, to close saloons and open settlement houses, to control the
environment with parks and playgrounds, to develop loyal children through adult-directed games. Their efforts, however, often
clashed with the interests of local neighborhood groups who themselves were actively seeking to shape and control the space and life

on their street or in their ward. The conflicts and compromises between these broad and narrow visions of community played themselves out within the context of a political structure that was itself changing and adapting. As we shall see in Part Two, this could lead to some interesting skirmishes in City Hall.

The reformation of community was not always so active and conscious an assault. At the same time, many residents chose not to fight the city, but rather to exploit its opportunities and avoid its hazards by adapting to the new forms of community that its social and economic institutions had created. In this vein existed a more "receptive" establishment of community, in which Bostonians adopted new styles of association that were in many ways the products of the same rapid growth and change that activists felt threatened community life. Gunther Barth has recently examined the apartment house, the metropolitan press, the department store, the ball park, and the vaudeville house in this light, arguing that in different ways these institutions helped to forge a common "city culture."[59] I shall include in this category organized sports clubs, the collective interest in the bicycle, and shared attachments to heroes and teams. At their core these were new forms of identity and patterns of consumption that were clearly shaped by the realities of urban life. While at times these associations could bond together the city's divergent classes and ethnic groups, they could just as easily highlight differences and foster conflict. The added paradox, of course, was that a given individual more than likely participated simultaneously in both the active and receptive reformations of community.

Organized recreation and sport were vehicles with which to engineer or control the city and the life within it; they were in turn shaped by the urban reality. The remainder of this book focuses on this complex interaction, as Bostonians played it out around a century past.

3/ *Vicious Amusements & Wholesome Recreations*

THE CHANGES IN URBAN LIFE and conditions, growing ever more visible during the nineteenth century, elicited responses that affected the course of recreation and sport when they bloomed in full after the Civil War. By the same token, sporting activities played a significant role in community search and formation during this period. In order to appreciate this relationship, it is necessary to examine the ideological background against which it developed. Arguments about the relative vice or virtue of sports and pastimes are of a long lineage—many ancients, including Cicero and St. Augustine, questioned the effects of athletics, chariot races, and gladiatorial combats. The modern city, however, gave the problem a new sense of urgency. Ultimately, certain interested groups—principally clergy, journalists, and social reformers—fashioned a popular philosophy that championed the use of certain sports as remedies for urban vice and immorality. In short, they defended "sport" as a form of innocent "recreation." We are so likely to confound the two concepts today that it is worth examining their fusion a century ago.

In large measure, the problem of sport has historically been a part of the larger problem of leisure. If, as Daniel Rodgers outlines, the work ethic has been an integral part of America's moral life, and if the concept of work has been glorified in the nation's culture, then Americans have been equally concerned with what their people do in their "nonwork" time.[1] If work has served to enhance the community, then nonwork activity has been carefully scrutinized to ensure that it has not destroyed progress made on the job. Sport has been and remains basically a leisure activity; that is, one consumed by participants and spectators in their hours away from work. Thus, it is not surprising that thoughtful people have questioned whether sport has served to cultivate or debilitate the body and spirit of the individual and the community.

Rodgers has outlined the dominance of the work ethic in America as it awoke to an industrial age. The work ethic elevated work over leisure in "an ethos that permeated life and manners." It surfaced "in countless warnings against the wiles of idleness and the protean disguises of the idler." But even when work was exalted over nonwork, it was necessary for moral guardians like the clergy to organize leisure activities into a ladder of legitimacy, rising above such noxious pursuits as the brothel or the saloon to exercises in social and individual salvation, like Bible study. Within the overall scheme of the work ethic, sports have occupied various positions on the ladder of nonwork affairs. For instance, because of their obvious connections with organized gambling, such sports as cockfighting, boxing, and horse racing have typically been held in lower regard than rowing or sailing.[2] What is significant to our study, however, is the fact that by the end of the nineteenth century, most sports had assumed a level of high legitimacy. Indeed, they became for many almost a panacea for social and individual ills, and nowhere was this more evident than in cities like Boston.

If, like Michael Marrus, we define leisure as "free activity, determined by individuals who make a choice independent of direct obligations of work, family, or society," then it is clear that the rise of the modern city and its related modes of production created an "emergence" of leisure, and with it, an aggravated problem of nonwork pursuits. The swirl of life in the growing city eroded many of the old customs and traditions that had controlled nonwork time. More important, the precise coordination of efforts demanded in a capitalist economy created clearer divisions between work time and nonwork time. The regimentation of time evolved slowly, and it was met with some resistance by workers who maintained traditional, self-paced patterns of work and leisure, filled with self-imposed holidays like "Blue Monday." Also, the erratic cycle of booms and busts meant that workers had frequent stretches of slack time. Ultimately, though, as E. P. Thompson points out, the factory clock, the division and supervision of labor, and the money incentives of the wage system all served to punctuate a new rhythm of work and leisure.[3]

Assured a larger and steadier audience, the market forces of the city nurtured the creation of a booming enterprise in commercialized amusement, as witnessed not only by the tremendous growth of the theater, the music hall, the dance hall, the museum, and, ultimately, organized sport, but also by the stunning popularity of amusement apostles such as P. T. Barnum. Thus the new problem of leisure. If urban man was faced with more clearly defined, if not larger, segments of free time, what could he do with it? What activities could he pursue that would not destroy himself or his community? By the end of the century, many had found the answer in organized sport.

In Boston, the concern for work and idleness was as old as the Bay Colony itself, for the fear and loathing of the idle man or mind were firmly entrenched in the Puritanism of Governor Winthrop and his followers. From the beginning, nonwork activity was scrutinized to ensure that it served the community's calling to God. One minister summarized this philosophy while the "chosen ones" yet remained in England, reminding his flock that they must constantly "performe service to God," in all activities, no matter how trivial, "yea even in our eating and drinking, lawful sports and recreations, when as we do them in faith."[4] It is always dangerous to impose present-day meanings on words taken from the past; and such a course would be quite precarious in dealing with Puritan attitudes toward sport. While our society tends to consider sport, recreation, and amusement as largely interchangeable terms, our forefathers treated them as separate entities, with distinct relationships to the problem of work versus idleness.

The Puritan held that sport, as a physical exercise and diversion, might be legitimate as long as it was taken as recreation; that is to say, as long as its purpose was to restore the body and spirit to a more efficient state of proper usefulness. William Burkitt, an English Puritan whose works were popular in New England, carefully outlined the possibility in a seventeenth-century "self-help" guide. God never intended man to endure constant toil, Burkitt argued, so He "adjudged some Diversion or Recreation (the better to fit both Body and Mind for the service of their maker) to be both needful and expedient." The rub, of course, lay in letting "Religion" choose the activities which were "healthful, short, recreative, and proper." Burkitt's instructions contained sentiments that echoed repeatedly in colonial Boston.[5] The town's intellectual leaders, including John Winthrop, John Cotton, Increase Mather, and Cotton Mather, countenanced diversions that were "recreative" in nature, provided they were not taken to excess, were followed in the proper spirit, and were not disruptive of community welfare. At the same time, however, these guardians of virtue lashed out against idle amusements, like dancing or gambling, with arrows "drawn from the quiver of the Scriptures." Contrary, then, to many existing interpretations, it is clear that there was no monolithic "Puritan" attitude toward sport. Lawful or unlawful sports were part of a larger, subtly distinguished continuum that spanned work, recreation, amusement, and idleness. As Cotton Mather insisted, he and his intellectual colleagues never meant to insinuate that "a due pursuit of Religion is inconsistent with all manner of Diversion."[6]

In this light, the well-documented laws of the Colony and Commonwealth that proscribed sport were not a blanket condemnation. Closer inspection reveals that these laws were directed at Sabbath merriment, corruptive gaming and gambling, or disruptive sports such as football and horse racing which made the streets unsafe for the ordinary citizen. (Street sports were a recurring urban problem, and played a crucial role in motivating the early playground movement.) While the Puritans detested idleness and debilitating amusement, they harbored no similar hatred of recreation and lawful sports.[7]

One must also remember that the Mathers and their ilk clearly had greater reservations about idle amusements than did many of their brethren. The numerous, repetitive laws as well as the repeated jeremiads citing wanton amusements as causes of famine or disease are all testimonies to this fact. The growth of the commercial seaport and its dilution of central, Puritan values aggravated the situation in the eyes of clergy like John Danforth, who fretted over the "vile profanations of prosperity" in places like Boston; where good harvests turned to "bad revels," where "streets of people" supported "bad houses of Entertainment," where "Precious Sabbaths" suffered "notorious profanations."[8] As we have seen, however, both lawful and unlawful sports and amusements enjoyed increasing popularity as Boston prospered.

Nonetheless, the early intellectual traditions concerning sport and its relationship to work and idleness are quite important because they were perpetuated by later clergy and, to a degree, worked their way into the attitudes of businessmen and workers alike. Into the early decades of the nineteenth century, the morality of free-time activities was still an issue. Even "innocent" amusements could be found guilty by a conservative theological persuasion which felt that "they counteract the designs of all religious institutions whose restraining and reforming influence is beneficial to men in time, and eternity."[9] At the same time, however, temperance societies and temperance laws like the Fifteen Gallon Law, passed in 1838, found widespread support among merchants and skilled workers alike. They also met with heavy resistance from other members of the same occupations.[10]

The tensions over temperance laws underscored the problem that Puritan intellectuals had grappled with two centuries earlier. Even if the Bostonian's principal calling *was* work, commerce, banking, or industry, it was clear that man could not labor during all his waking hours. Those who tried would find themselves burned out, physically, mentally, and emotionally. But this observation didn't answer the nagging question of what activities would be socially or spiritually profitable while one was off the job. The question was old, and yet there was no consensus in an answer. Moreover, there was no agreement about who could suggest or impose an answer. Boston's emergence as a city gave a new sense of urgency to this problem of leisure. While gambling, drinking, and bawdy houses had appeared as manageable aberrations in colonial Boston, their nineteenth-century counterparts appeared in more threatening guise, which in turn led to a more concentrated search for rational and innocent recreations.[11]

AS THE DECADES TURNED in the nineteenth century, then, the concern over amusements focused increasingly on the city. Many popular novels retold the ancient tale of the rural virgin, of either sex, corrupted by the sins of the city. But even if the author meant to moralize, the metropolis usually emerged as a warehouse of fun and excitement as well as a haven of vice and corruption. Indeed, only a fine line separated the two, and how many worried if the former turned into the latter? Where else to find the splendor of the opera or the art gallery, the roar of the music or the concert hall, the electric atmosphere of the theater, the chance to strike it rich in the gambling den? Were not the saloons, the billiard parlors, and the brothels more fun than the drudgery of farm and village? Many thought so, for much of the urban growth during the first half of the century came from rural American migrants. And the popular books of the day did nothing to dissuade them from striking out for the city.[12] It was not just the country bumpkin, however, who yielded to the baser pleasures. Investigative reporters like George G. Foster provided their readers with lurid descriptions of bordellos and groggeries among the "proletaires" and of gambling houses packed with members of prominent families. The images were as inviting as they were menacing.[13]

It is no wonder that reformers focused on amusements as a critical problem that spread rapidly in the urban environment. In this regard, Boston was like other cities. As early as the 1820s, the North and West Ends were labeled as shelters of vice. The City Missionary Society detailed all the "facilities and fascinations of crime" to be found in Ward 6, including gaming houses "fitted up with imposing splendor," and dancing halls "ablaze with light."[14] Ann Street (now North Street) harbored brothels known as the "Tin Pot" and the "Beehive." Raids by vigilantes and later by Marshal Tukey's police proved to be short-lived solutions. "Nymphs" of the night had other haunts, such as the notorious "third tier" of many popular theaters where, as one historian of Boston's theaters put it, "a portion of the house [was] set apart by custom for the abandoned and profligate of both sexes."[15]

There were numerous theaters in Boston; dozens opened in the decades before the Civil War. Not all offered a third tier, and many endured but short and uncertain existences. Nonetheless, they presented a varied menu of amusement, from serious drama to minstrel shows and musical burlesque. What is more, the admission price was within popular reach—in 1852, the Howard Athenaeum's tickets ranged from 12½ to 75 cents. The traveling circus was also an annual attraction. As an advertisement for "Welch and Delavan's Olympic Circus" announced during the summer of 1843: "They crack the lively whip in Atkinson Street— merry music, gay horses, bold riders."[16]

Those who sought their amusement at the gambling table could easily locate a game of faro, "policy," or "dead props." The more bloodthirsty could seek out a rat pit. A veteran Boston police captain described the operation at one North End rat pit of long standing. The animals' arena was located in the basement of a saloon, so the patrons could pass the time between events mingling with the barmaids who tempted with "vermillion cheeks and low-necked dresses." A trapdoor led down to the rat pit, a tightly secured "board crib," three and one half feet high and eight feet in diameter. Rows of board seats surrounded most of the pit, except for the proprietor's work area. Here stood a wire-covered flour barrel half-filled with live rats, which the proprietor fished out with tongs. When a set number had been placed in the pit, a "ratting" dog was brought out and held by an assistant, while the patrons, who had paid a 25-cent admission, bet with each other on the speed with which the dog could dispatch the rodents. Betting completed, the dog enters the fray, "the growling, and chomping, and squealing, and scratching is soon over," time is called out, the bets decided, "and all hands go up and liquor." The exhibitions would continue, with different dogs, until the barrel of rats was empty. The next night's performance would be ensured by the enterprise of local denizens who scoured the stables at night, bagging rats for a shilling apiece—five dollars for "a pretty good evening's work."[17]

The third tier, the faro hall, and the rat pit saw a social mixture: sailors on leave, young society "swells" (possibly some of Charles W. Eliot's fellow rowers!), professional thieves, downtrodden immigrants. By the 1840s, school authorities were of the opinion that a major purpose of the public school system was to combat the base amusements of the city by inculcating an appreciation for the "higher" over the "lower" pleasures. The idea was that schools could cultivate "a taste for simple and innocent pleasures, rather than a love for vicious excitement." A laudable idea, but perhaps unrealistic amid the temptations of the city. Shortly thereafter, the superintendent of the state reform school observed that truancy from school was the first link in a chain of delinquency that consisted of debasing excitements like "horse racing, the bowling saloon, the theatrical exhibitions, and other similar places of amusement, debauchery and crime." The associations formed in these havens of iniquity became schools of crime that offered as a curriculum profanity, drunkenness, and lust. For many, however, these course offerings were far more attractive than those of the public school.[18]

The problem of amusements in the urban setting had become more acute and wide-ranging. In reaction, one can see during the first half of the nineteenth century a splintering of attitudes and

The Rat Pit

in some cases a blurring of the once-rigid distinction between idle "amusement" and wholesome "recreation." Old-light Protestants, however, tended to retain the sharp contrast. As the *New Englander* of 1851 reminded its readers, the difference between amusements and recreations lay in their respective purposes and motives: "the motive of the latter being to recruit and restore, and thus prepare for greater usefulness; the motive of the former being a love of pleasure, or the desire of personal gratification." Traditional sports like cockfighting or horse racing were included with gambling and tippling as degenerate amusements. Straining the horse beyond its power or setting cocks to the death duel was clearly an abuse of man's dominion over God's creatures. Worse yet, as one minister reasoned, was the infectious patronage of brutal sports by members of the social elite: "With such examples of irreligion, profanity and cool calculating cruelty 'in high places,' is it wonderful that the inferior classes of society become dissipated, careless and indifferent about divine things?"[19] Charles Dickens complained that "the peculiar province of the Pulpit in New England (always excepting the Unitarian ministry) would appear to be the denouncement of all innocent and rational amusements." It seemed to Dickens that the only legitimate sources of excitement were the church, the chapel, and the lecture room.[20]

As Dickens insinuated, the amusement problem was aggravated by the failure of conservative theologians to suggest realistic alternatives. At the same time, he was perceptive in noticing that some Unitarians were reconstructing the question at hand. Realizing that amusements were a fixed part of the urban scene, that they could be neither eradicated nor reduced, these clergy chose to consider how to single out the better forms, which some called "Christian" amusements, and direct the people toward them. Moreover, a number suggested that exercise and athletic sports might serve as a model of proper amusements.[21]

In several of his public lectures and addresses during the 1830s, William Ellery Channing set the framework of this new perspective. Advising on the "ministry for the poor," Channing recognized the threat of "stirring amusements":

> Human nature has a strong thirst for pleasures which excite it above its ordinary tone, which relieve the monotony of life. This drives the prosperous from their pleasant homes to scenes of novelty and stirring amusement. How strongly must it act on those who are weighed down by anxieties and privations! How intensely must the poor desire to forget for a time the wearing realities of life! And what means of escape does society afford or allow them?[22]

Very little, that Channing could see. As a result, many succumbed to intemperance; not just the poor, but "multitudes in all classes." As a solution to alcohol and other degenerate amusements, Channing expressed the hope that "by the progress of intelligence, taste, and morals among all portions of society, a class of public amusements will grow up among us." Some of his possibilities included music, dancing, the theater (at least legitimate drama, without a third tier!), and recitation. But Channing also considered "physical education." He had no specific activity in mind, but he sounded like the author of a modern *Joy of Jogging* manual as he argued that "physical vigor is not only valuable for its own sake, but it favors temperance, by opening the mind to cheerful impressions, and by removing those indescribable feelings of sinking, disquiet, depression."[23]

Channing's suggestions were continued in the next decade. His protégé, the energetic and controversial Theodore Parker, in his *Sermon on the Moral Condition of Boston*, chastised his fellow citizens that "there are no amusements which lie level to the poor in this country . . . save only the vice of drunkenness." Parker saw a ray of hope in the recent work of some local philanthropists who had treated a group of the city's poor children "to a day of sunshine, fresh air, and frolic in the fields." Parker was some fifty years ahead of the movement for organized play; similar answers to the amusement problem were emerging on other fronts. A book entitled *A Plea for Amusements* argued that if wholesome alternatives, such as "athletic institutes" for gymnastic exercises, "would be established in all our towns and cities, for the free use of the people . . . we shall see to it, that we have enough healthy sources of recreation to empty the gambling rooms, the tippling shops, and the brothels." Slowly, these and similar treatises were making the case that amusement could serve the purpose of recreation; the answer was not suppression but reform.[24]

This sentiment gathered momentum. In 1857, Boston's Edward Everett Hale, Unitarian minister, prolific writer, and tireless crusader for urban reform, reviewed for the *Christian Examiner* eight articles on the subject of public amusements and public morality. Rejoicing that the "interest which now seems to be excited in the subject" might foster further discussion among his fellow clergy, Hale argued that the church must not withdraw from the realities of the urban world but must rather jump in with both feet to ensure that amusements remained wholesome. But with insight, Hale added some new dimensions to the question. He agreed that the "haste of the age," with its "increased competition, increased demands, increased and increasing labor and accelerated methods of meeting the demands" necessitated an antidote like amusements. He then discussed the new leisure time of the working class, and noted that "all this complicated labor question, the discussion of ten-hour systems, of the work of women, of the work of children, asks what men, women and children are to do with the hours of rest."[25]

In his own lecture on the subject, Hale further recognized that the problem of amusements existed only in the city:

> So long as we live in the country, the subject does not come up for discussion, for there God provides the best entertainment for everybody. Every boy can find it in the trout streams, and every girl among the buttercups. But when we choose to bring people into crowded towns; to substitute pavement for the meadows, and mains six feet under ground for the trout's brook, we must substitute something for the relaxation and amusement which we have taken away.

Indeed, Hale linked the very growth of the city to the lure of its amusements. There was no use in arguing that the countryside provided better economic opportunities, if all the while the magnet attracting native immigrants was not the fact that "they think they shall grow rich," but rather that "they are tempted by the excitement of crowds, of concerts, of bands, of theatres, of public meetings, of processions, or exhibitions, of parties, of clubs, or in general of society."[26]

Finally, Hale stressed that the solution lay in discovering and nurturing amusement forms that were at once both wholesome and popular. He recalled walking downtown while pondering the whole question, and seeing a sign in bold print that read, **"Rare Sport for Everybody."** Excited that he had fallen on the answer to how the city might amuse all, rich and poor, learned and simple, he hurried to read the fine print, only to discover the promotion of one "celebrated terrier," Mad Jack, who was scheduled to enter the rat pit that day with the assigned task of killing one hundred rats in five minutes. Dismissing that sport as no solution, Hale concluded that private enterprise could not be expected to provide amusements that were attractive to all tastes and at the same time soothing to the harried urban resident. He knew that the commercial alternatives were either degradation or boredom:

> So a sad public returns next morning to its filing of iron, its balancing of accounts, its sewing of seams, or its digging of mud, without one wrinkle smoothed, without one care lightened. The killing of rats has not soothed it; the death-rattle of Camille hath not soothed it; and the lecture certainly has not rested it. The evening has been killed, and that is all.

Hale earnestly hoped that the church and the city government would join hands and actively foster public amusements for all citizens.[27]

Moreover, Hale hinted that "a right understanding of athletic amusements" might reveal the answer to the problem. In his opinion, the clergy spent too much time exposing the evils of gambling and not enough effort promoting the advantages of cricket and football. Throughout his career, Hale would value athletics for building health, courage, and character, qualities essential to survival in the city. In this regard, he must be numbered among the apostles of "Muscular Christianity," a consortium of clergy and intellectuals who advocated physical exercise both as an antidote to the sedentary habits of urban life and as a solution to the problem of free time. Included in this group were Hale, Henry C. Wright, Ralph Waldo Emerson, Oliver Wendell Holmes, and Thomas Wentworth Higginson.[28] At mid-century, these men first suggested sport and exercise as the ideal urban amusement.

Of all the Muscular Christians, Thomas Wentworth Higginson alone rivaled Hale in his devotion and zeal for athleticism. In fact, his reputation as an athletic advocate probably surpassed that of Hale. Born in Cambridge of a successful merchant family, Higginson graduated from Harvard College in 1841 and from the Harvard Divinity School in 1847. A striking figure over six feet tall, Higginson was throughout his life an activist and reformer. He cut a dashing figure as commander of an all-black regiment during the Civil War, a service that was the culmination of his outspoken abolitionism. Also a committed advocate of temperance and women's suffrage, Higginson found time during his ministry at Worcester to pen a series of articles for the young *Atlantic Monthly*, extolling the virtues and necessities of athletic exercise.[29]

In the first article, entitled "Saints and Their Bodies," Higginson stated his desire to crush the impression "in the community . . . that physical vigor and spiritual sanctity are incompatible." With the growth of cities, the dominance of the business mentality, and the loss of the outdoor life, Higginson found that "it has been supposed that a race of shopkeepers and lawyers could live without bodies." He hoped that the "terrible records of dyspepsia and paralysis" would urge a reaction in favor of outdoor activities and exercise. Having laid out his basic thesis in this essay, he continued to build his argument in future articles for the magazine. Along the way, he called for improvement in dietary habits, the adoption of exercise in the school curriculum, and the need for exercise among the nation's female population.[30]

Higginson specifically treated the city in his article entitled "Gymnastics," an outstanding description of the exercise rage sweeping many eastern cities in the early 1860s. Addressing the urban reader—the "average American man, who leaves his place of business at nightfall with his head a mere furnace of red-hot brains and his body a pile of burnt-out cinders, utterly exhausted in the daily effort to put ten dollars more of distance between his posterity and the poorhouse"—Higginson advised him to eschew the Chess Club and "come with me to the Gymnasium." Echoing the thought of many contemporaries, Higginson stressed that neglect of physical health was a vital problem facing all Americans, on the farm or in the town. And the danger was compounded in the city, with its constant "mental excitement." As a solution, the gymnasium offered a program of exercise that could be altered to suit the physical needs of anyone, no matter how fatigued or excited.

Beyond this, Higginson noted, the gymnasium helped to prevent the young men in cities from patronizing vicious amusements, particularly when it divided their evenings "with the concert, the book, or the public meeting." Not only would there be little time left for alternatives, there would be little energy as well. Higginson stressed that "it is the nervous exhaustion of a sedentary, frivolous, or joyless life which madly tries to restore itself by the other nervous exhaustion of debauchery." The "honest fatigue" of exercise called for "honest rest." The argument must have been pleasing to colleagues like Edward Everett Hale.[31]

Higginson and Hale were spokesmen for an increasingly popular opinion that physical exercises in the gymnasium or on the playing field, were important and legitimate sources of urban amusement. These activities were clearly more wholesome and desirable than those found in the commercial temples of dissipation: the billiard parlor, the music hall, the saloon, and the rat pit. Beyond this, they contributed to health, a quality under siege in the city.

The arguments of these clergy, and their replications in the popular press, were significant in a number of ways. They signaled the beginning of a new current of thought that flowed against the older tide condemning activities pursued for their own sake. They linked the amusement problem itself to broader concerns about social life in the city: wasteful indulgences among elites, degenerate escapism among impoverished workers, sedentary and enfeebling work routines among clerks and storekeepers. The ailment, and its solution, involved all classes. The call for public action laid the groundwork for the first major civic response to the problem: the development of a public park system in the 1870s and 1880s. Finally, the gradually favorable climate of opinion helped to explain the development before the Civil War of organized sports clubs in rowing, cricket, and baseball.[32]

SPORTS AND AMUSEMENTS continued to grow in northern cities during the war years, as urban social life quickly recovered from the initial shocks of Fort Sumter and Bull Run.[33] The amusement problem, however, appeared to worsen. The decades after the Civil War were filled with a growing perception that the inhabitants of the industrial cities enjoyed (or were burdened by) increasing amounts of free time. During this period labor unions increased their demands for fewer hours. The movement for a ten-hour day had begun as early as the "Ten-Hour Circular" and strike of 1835 among Boston's skilled workers. Agitation continued during the 1840s. By 1865, a Grand Eight-Hour League had formed in Massachusetts; the tension reached a peak in Boston with the May Day strike of 1886. Relief came slowly. In 1874, Massachusetts passed a Ten-Hour Law for women and children in manufacturing, but it was easily evaded by crafty operators. State and municipal workers got the nine-hour day in 1891. The Massachusetts Bureau of the Statistics of Labor monitored the downward drift of the average workday, including the trend toward a partial holiday on Saturday. During the second half of the century the average work week in nonagricultural industries declined from sixty-six to fifty-six hours.[34] The interests of capital resisted shorter hours for workers, arguing that there would be a corresponding increase in "intemperance, vice and crime." A spokesman for the Eight-Hour League protested this vehemently, and claimed that the short workday had filled the meeting halls and the reading rooms.[35]

Many remained unconvinced about the effects of more free time, but it seemed that the distinction between work and leisure was growing sharper. Sensing this, the Reverend O. B. Frothingham described the conundrum that faced all classes:

> How to employ leisure, is the problem we have to deal with. Everybody has leisure, more or less. Nobody works literally all the time. In every day there are vacant hours, that should be used to balance the occupied ones.

A new generation of investigators approached the problem, and the answers were always the same: things were getting worse.[36]

In 1867, the American Christian Committee examined thirty-five cities in an effort to identify the obstacles that confronted the mission of the church. Among the commonly identified afflictions were "the multiplied temptations of the city in the way of debasing amusements." In Boston, the YMCA urged contributions so that it could press its assault on the lure of the city's sporting establishments, gambling halls, fifty-nine billiard halls, fifteen hundred saloons, and hundreds of houses of prostitution.[37] Boston supported all levels of amusement, for rich and poor. But the last decades of the century saw increasing attention focused on the dissipations in the poorer districts. The popular press headlined the infrequent police raids on streetwalkers; they ran investigative reports on the numerous dens of organized gambling, and young clerks driven to suicide by their losses. Newspapers walked a tightrope, however, since they commonly ran advertisements for the same "low and vulgar" entertainments that they condemned in editorials.[38]

Reformers like the Reverend Henry Morgan were less compromising. Morgan, an independent Methodist minister, ran his own mission in the South End. In 1880, he wrote a fictional "story of real life," entitled *Boston Inside Out! Sins of a Great City!* The novel sold more than five thousand copies in a few weeks, as Bostonians tried to guess who could have been the model for Father Titus, the power-mad priest who has a harem of "nieces"; or Frank Gildersleeve, the despicable Brahmin rake who violates young Minnie Marston's virginity while she is under anesthesia in a dentist's chair! The reader could also follow Morgan's investigations into "Boston's darker side," with its two thousand liquor dens and one thousand bawdy houses: "As I strayed through the streets, the dark curtain of midnight was pierced by myriads of flashing lights. Strains of bacchanalian song, drunken shouts, and ribald laughter greeted my ear."[39]

In the next two decades, Boston's settlement workers, under the direction of Robert A. Woods at the South End House, published nonfictional accounts of life in the city's working-class districts. In their view, degrading amusements, along with poor housing and unstable, transient populations, constituted a most serious threat to neighborhood life. The South End's cheap theaters attracted the masses to its vaudeville and its burlesque. Places like the Dime Museum, the Grand Opera, and the Columbia Theatre, packed the crowds at 10 cents for a gallery seat and 50 cents for a box. The experienced observer could pick out a cross-section of residents: "the corner loafer, the out-of-work, the casual laborer, the mechanic, and the clerk . . . the cheap and flashy aristocracy." The theater, along with the dance hall, the pool room, and the saloon, had little competition, causing one reformer to utter the much-echoed sentiment that "the parents, clergy, teachers and social workers in this region regard the problem of providing healthful amusement for young people as one of the most serious which they have to face."[40] The more alarming realization was that commercial amusements were simply filling a large void created by the inactivity of public agencies. This led to a vicious circle which saw "inferior amusements degrading the people; degraded people enjoying inferior amusements."[41]

The call for action *was* being sounded, however, with an argument that followed the lines of antebellum reformers like Hale and Higginson. The trend that had begun slowly before the Civil War emerged more clearly. Moralists were forced to accept amusements as an integral component of urban life. They could not be suppressed through stern warnings about their idle nature. Rather, the dominant theme emphasized a search for alternatives by which to combat the attraction of commercialized dissipations. After summarizing the opinions of nine sermons on the subject, an article of 1867 in the *New Englander* concluded that all must "recognize the need which human nature has of amusement and recreation." The answer lay less in suppression than in the "Christian duty to bring recreation within the pale of Christian thought, and to make such provision for innocent enjoyments as to protect our youth from sinful indulgences and perilous amusements." A few years later James Freeman Clarke, popular pastor at the Church of the Disciples, stressed the same ideas in a series of public lectures on "self-culture."[42]

Was there an alternative form of amusement that was, at once, healthy, "Christian," uplifting, and attractive to all elements of the urban population? Many found an answer in certain types of physical recreation and sports. Increasingly, from Edward Everett Hale to Robert A. Woods, urban critics and reformers concluded that sports and athletics, whatever their deficiencies, were far more desirable than the billiard parlor or the brothel. In a more positive vein, this group supported outdoor exercise as a vehicle to health, an endangered quality in the urban environment. When properly directed, sports and games could develop morality and character, as playground advocates would continually stress. They were, at the same time, popular with the masses.

The Protestant church felt the effects of this ideological change. By the turn of the century, the church was promoting organized sports both as a wholesome alternative to commercialized entertainments and as a powerful agent for strengthening the moral fibers of humanity, so frayed by urban living. In Boston, the YMCA, the YMCU, the Berkeley Temple, and the North End Union added a new Christian dimension to exercise. Under the direction of Robert J. Roberts, whose motto advised, "If you have time to eat you have time to exercise," the YMCA was a focal point of activity. In 1888, the "Y" began leasing the Union Athletic Grounds on Dartmouth Street; the facilities included a ball field, a running track, a cycle track, and tennis courts. Exercise and sport could bring people to Christ by improving the temples of their souls. Moreover, these forms of amusement could lure the wayward back into the fold, where their spiritual regeneration might begin. As Charles Dickinson of the South End's Berkeley Temple concluded, if manly sports and innocent games could reach young men and keep them "from the streets and the saloons," then every church should have a gymnasium and a ball field.[43]

Along similar lines, Robert A. Woods and his fellow reformers advocated organized forms of sport and exercise as desirable alternatives to the amusements found in the inner wards and in the zones of emergence. Time and again, they heaped praise upon the public parks and playgrounds, the municipal baths and gymnasiums, the private athletic clubs, and gymnastic organizations like the German Turnverein. To Woods, recreation was ultimately a "way to liberation and exaltation of life," and sport was a desirable avenue of recreation. After examining the entire spectrum of popular amusements, one reformer concluded that "amateur athletics are the most wholesome and encouraging phase of the whole general problem; indeed, they are less a phase of the problem than an effective solution."[44]

The problem of urban leisure and the solution of sport came to a head in two related issues. The first was the saloon and the attempts to combat its widespread influence among the working classes. The second was the broader question of the Sabbath laws. At the end of the century, numerous cities grappled with the liquor and saloon questions, Boston among them.[45] The attempts to control liquor licensing could lead to confrontations between

Yankee Republicans and Irish Democrats. In 1885, Republicans struck at Democratic "rum power" by securing state legislation which put Boston's police, and therefore liquor licensing, under the control of a commission appointed by the governor. As one Yankee put it, "the administration of law in Boston is a farce. . . . The liquor interest controls affairs in the city."[46] In 1895, the Committee of Fifty for the Investigation of the Liquor Problem conducted a survey to determine the extent of the saloon's influence in Boston. The committee, which included such influential citizens as Charles W. Eliot and Francis A. Walker, concluded that the saloon succeeded because it offered more than drink; it was "ministering to a much deeper desire than that for alcoholic liquors. . . . Nothing less than the satisfaction of the deeper thirst for fellowship and recreation" could explain its success.[47] The saloon lured the worker into its embrace with its bright lights and its "cheery exterior in the midst of the prevailing gloom." Once inside, the weary worker enjoyed music, baseball scores, fellowship and gossip, racing news, pool, kinetoscopes, and other entertainments along with his beer. More alarming was the awareness of the saloon's central position in the machinery of ward bosses and criminals. But the most startling revelation was the saloon's popularity. A headcount by Boston patrolmen indicated that daily patronage of Boston's six hundred saloons amounted to almost half the city's population.[48]

The Committee of Fifty cited a number of solutions to the saloon problem, including stricter enforcement of licensing codes, wider and sparser distribution of saloons and, more important, the provision of attractive substitutes that might offer companionship and amusement without the evil of liquor. Once again, organized sport and exercise headed the list of ideal substitutes. Raymond Calkins, who examined the substitutes for the saloon, concluded that "possibly the gymnasium is the most effective substitute; it offers a definite aim to its habitués, something to work for, and it satisfies, at the same time, the primary social desire and the purely physical demand." The athletic club, cycling and cycle meets, and even professional baseball games, when properly directed, could prove attractive enough to lure workers out of the saloon. Further, these substitutes would satisfy social and physical cravings in a wholesome manner.[49]

Reformers knew that the "liquor problem" existed seven days a week, so their concerns for temperance sometimes led them to challenge the orthodox Sabbath. The General Court had, in a series of restrictive laws, long protected the Sabbath from profanation by "labour, business or work of ordinary callings . . . game, sport, play, or recreation." By the 1880s, however, great pressure had begun to mount, much of it based on the realistic needs of an urban environment. Reverend James Freeman Clarke urged churches to adopt a more "rational Sunday observance," and thereby attract the "multitudes who have abandoned church-going" by "offering them innocent recreation in the place of intemperance and its evil consequences." Carroll Davidson Wright, director of the Massachusetts Bureau of Statistics of Labor, issued a report that challenged the realism of the Sunday blue laws. Wright argued that while no one wanted a seventh day of *production*, certain services had to continue on the Sabbath, including transportation and the distribution of food, medicine, and information. The Sunday newspaper was "almost a necessity." From here it was but a small jump to a concluding question: "Is not the wearied worker fairly entitled to the opportunity of the rest that comes of recreation on Sunday, if it is not granted to him on other days?"[50]

In 1887, the General Court finally legalized a variety of Sunday services, many of which had been operating under a policy of benign neglect. Some of these included the manufacture and distribution of steam, gas, and electricity; the use of telephone and telegraph; the production and sale of newspapers or bakery products; and finally, the letting or use of vehicles for transportation. Sports, games, and amusements were still illegal on Sunday, but the application of the law led to some glaring inconsistencies. Oarsmen and yachtsmen could ply the waters, bicycle clubs could tour the city and its suburbs on hundred-mile "century runs" with impunity, but baseball players, golfers, and cricketeers ran the risk of police harassment or arrest. In 1897, nine Harvard students were arrested for playing golf in nearby Waverly, on the same Sunday that saw thousands of cyclists whirling on their wheels! A few years later, Brookline police invaded The Country Club to arrest over thirty surprised Sunday golfers.[51]

The parks commissioners, who were forced to prohibit Sunday ball games on parks and playgrounds, frequently complained of this absurd situation. In 1910, they noted that Sunday patrons

Tobogganing
Franklin Park

Tobogganing in Franklin Park—A Legal Sunday Sport
Courtesy of the Frederick Law Olmsted Museum

could skate and toboggan in winter on grounds where they could not play ball in summer. "The logic of all this is a little hard to follow," they declared, "but it appears that skating and tobogganing as 'forms of locomotion' fare better than anything that can be called a game." The commissioners hoped that Yankee ingenuity could invent additional "forms of locomotion."[52]

Reformers like Joseph Lee (see Chapter Five) joined the fight for Sunday sport. A central figure in the campaign for organized play, Lee put the Sabbath laws in first place "as an example of legislation enjoining idleness and producing crime." What good were parks and playgrounds if they couldn't be used to full measure on the day with the greatest amount of free time? Many people agreed with Lee, and in 1911 there was a major campaign to change the law. But it would be 1920 before the legislature allowed amateur sports and games on Sunday; the professionals had to wait until 1928.[53]

IN THE END, of course, there was no ultimate solution to the amusement problem, as later reformers painfully discovered. Certainly sport in general was never a panacea for the multiple evils which leisure time in the city presented. Some traditional pastimes like boxing and horse racing appeared to many as a continued part of the problem, not the solution. The saloon and the dance hall yielded to the singles bar and the massage parlor, despite the growth of playgrounds and amateur athletics. Yet the record is not as important as the perception, developed a century ago, that organized recreation, play, and exercise might prove to offer an attractive asylum of wholesome and healthy activity within the hustle of drudgery and degradation that seemed to stamp the urban existence.

When reformers and social critics like Edward Everett Hale, Thomas Wentworth Higginson, and Robert A. Woods suggested that active and physical forms of recreation could fill expanding segments of free time with a positive force to empty the gambling rooms and the tippling shops, their calls found acceptance in ever-widening circles. To be sure, some organizations maintained an older, more authoritarian approach toward the problems of urban leisure. The New England Society for the Suppression of Vice (later the Watch and Ward Society) felt its time was better spent in shutting down the evil than in nurturing the good. But by the end of the nineteenth century, a stronger current of thought counseled a policy that Paul Boyer has labeled "positive environmentalism."[54] Operating within this framework, many Bostonians organized to advance the cause of parks and playgrounds, which they claimed would remedy a number of urban problems, including the misuse of leisure time. This line of reasoning was adopted by other public and private promoters, who also advertised the idea that sports and games were healthful and of noble purpose to the community and its residents. The acceptance of this argument by a wide range of Bostonians undoubtedly contributed to the tremendous boom of bats, balls, and bicycles that occurred after the Civil War.

The process was not a simple one, however, for it raised serious questions about the control of space and time in a city that was home to social classes, ethnic groups, and neighborhoods that were bound to disagree over issues from which only some could emerge as winners.[55] The tensions were multiple; it was not just a case of the middle and upper classes attempting to manipulate the interests and destinies of immigrant workers. The Irish had a number of active temperance societies. John Boyle O'Reilly directed his ardent pen against the gambler and the drunkard with prose that rivaled that of Robert A. Woods or Joseph Lee. Black ministers and white were equally concerned about vicious amusements. At the same time, the fight over Sunday baseball could find politicians like John F. Fitzgerald and James Michael Curley on the same side as Brahmin philanthropists, while the strongest voice favoring the Puritan Sabbath issued from Archbishop O'Connell![56]

The control of space, time, and behavior was central both to the amusement problem and to the proposed solution of organized recreation and sport. Each, in turn, related to a broader reaction and adjustment that I have termed a search for community. Two significant and closely related thrusts of this search were the movements for public parks and playgrounds. Both were very much an active search for community which hinged on the control of space and time. In both cases, the mediums for action were new political associations—civic organizations, pressure lobbies, mass rallies— developed expressly for the purpose.

Historians have typically linked parks and playgrounds to the efforts of middle- and upper-class reformers like those in this chapter. In so doing, they have tended to overlook the efforts of other urban constituents who were actively seeking to shape their communities on their own terms. Their tools for action were similar to those of the reformers, only they were far less visible in the historical record. As we shall see, however, they were no less effective.

Part Two

SHAPING THE CITY THROUGH RECREATION AND SPORT

4/Parks for the People

IN HIS 1847 INAUGURAL ADDRESS to the Boston City Council, Mayor Josiah Quincy, Jr., raised an issue that many American cities grappled with for the next half-century. This was the need to provide urban inhabitants with a New World blessing that was fading beyond their reach—namely, open space:

> We have also an inestimable treasure in the Common, and the lands adjacent. In monarchies, such pieces of ground are procured and ornamented at a great expense, for the benefit of the people; and why should we be behind them in a republic.

Quincy argued that Boston had a compelling obligation to provide her less fortunate citizens with "the means of obtaining some share in the glorious and beautiful aspects of nature, with which a beneficent Creator designs to minister to the physical and mental well-being of his children."[1] The mayor envisioned the establishment of public parks, but his dream was slow in coming; twenty years later, Boston's park land was still confined to the Common and Public Garden. By World War I, however, the city was surrounded by an "emerald necklace" of public parks. By 1920, her citizens had expended over twenty million dollars on the protection and operation of open spaces.[2]

The development of a public park system marks a significant chapter in Boston's sport history. For one, the parks represented the first major civic response to the amusement question. Indeed, parks provided much of the open space upon which Bostonians pursued their favorite sports. But the parks issue also embodied many of the philosophies and arguments aired in a city rudely awakened to the fact that urban growth was not all positive. Commercial and industrial success rested on top of a much denser population that included hordes of immigrants; the by-products of "progress" included an inexorable sprawl of housing, a choking pollution of the air, and the erosion of cultural homogeneity. In large part, public parks were first presented as a reform to many of these problems. But the record of park development reveals that simple solutions were not easily implemented. Urban growth was accompanied by widening divisions between social classes and interest groups within the city's boundaries. Residents in new and old neighborhoods sought to control the use of local space. New political machinery had developed to represent their divergent interests. The workings of this changing social and political order complicated, challenged, and transformed the park system in Boston. Their complexity argues against simple notions about the nature and process of this important urban reform.

Most historians have viewed parks and their close relation, playgrounds, as the creation of middle- and upper-class reformers who desired to provide order for both the urban landscape and its inhabitants. As a recent article on Frederick Law Olmsted, consultant and chief architect for the Boston park system from 1875 to 1895, maintains, "Olmsted's parks seemed to offer an attractive remedy for the dangerous problem of discontent among the urban masses. . . . By providing pleasant and uplifting outlets in the narrow lives of city dwellers, they promised a measure of social tranquility."[3] Historians differ, however, in their interpretations of the motives behind this "reform" impulse. An older, "progressive" interpretation holds that parks and playgrounds grew as the handiwork of philanthropic reformers who strived to create a more beautiful and livable city for all inhabitants. A more recent and cynical interpretation holds that these reformers' motives smacked more of social control than social uplift.[4]

Unfortunately, both interpretations have been anchored in the rhetoric of park advocates and planners. They have not examined the actual process by which plans were implemented. As a recent, more careful analysis of parks and playgrounds in Worcester, Massachusetts, argues, such an omission ignores the likelihood that other interest groups "might have taken an active part in conceiving or advocating parks." It assumes, instead, that they "uncritically accepted the park programs handed down by an omnipotent ruling class."[5] While the rhetoric behind Boston's early park proposals anticipated and received general acceptance, Olmsted and other early park advocates quickly and continually discovered that factional strife and class resentment could erupt and envenom debates on the placement, benefits, and beneficiaries of nature's blessings. In Boston, as in Worcester, the larger urban constituency—laborers and clerks, artisans and bookkeepers, natives and immigrants, men and women—expressed their interests, either directly or through their political representatives. Their pressure forced adjustments in the initial visions of genteel reformers like Olmsted and his supporters.

THE PARK MOVEMENT in Boston was part of an active, conscious search for order amid the environmental, political, social, and cultural dislocations we have already described. Much of the initiative clearly lay with established middle- and upper-class groups who designed their programs for all Bostonians. But it would be wrong to think that the remainder of Boston's population sat passively as major public policy filtered down from above. On the contrary, both the form and essence of public parks developed in ways determined by interest groups representing a wide range of citizens, as one discovers by comparing the early rhetoric with the later reality.

The main story begins in 1869, when the pressures of increased growth and a heightened awareness of the Common's inadequacies resulted in a series of proposals for public park systems. Unfortunately, the fear of higher taxes, coupled with the conviction that the nearby suburbs provided ample scenery, prevented the approval of such early legislation as the Park Act of 1870.[6] The debate over parks continued unchecked, however, and within five years Boston's citizens had swayed enough to approve the Park Act of 1875.[7] Accordingly, the mayor appointed three commissioners (approved by the city aldermen) who were charged to entertain citizens' proposals and examine possible acquisitions "with regard to many different points such as convenience of access, original cost and betterments, probable cost of improvements, sanitary conditions and natural beauty." The commissioners retained Frederick Law Olmsted as a consultant until 1878, when he was appointed chief landscape architect for the park system.[8]

Early park advocates claimed (convincingly enough) that the entire city benefited from and supported the movement. As one popular newspaper urged:

> A public park is now a great necessity and not an expensive luxury. It is the property of the people, rich and poor together, and the only place where all classes can daily meet one another face to face in a spirit of fraternal recreation.[9]

Another claimed on the eve of the park referendum:

> The moment anything is done under the act it will open a new field for laborers, and at the same time enlarge the possessions in which their wives and children will have an equal inheritance with the most favored. Indeed, the great benefit of public parks is gathered by those who are not rich.[10]

Park boosters, often among Boston's most prominent and established residents, felt their arguments represented those of all citizens, rich or poor. Their formula for reform was simple. Parks would offer both escape from and control of the traumas caused by the rapid spread of houses, factories, and people, with their congestion, noise, and pollution. Parks would provide something the much-revered small town always had offered; open space and rural scenery. Thus, while park proponents tended to revel in the prospect of a booming Boston, they also desired to brake its unchecked growth by imposing at least three qualities that the small-town community seemed to offer: fresh air and open space, healthy citizens, and pervasive morality.

It was not so much that park proponents wanted to make Boston a small town. They desired, rather, to balance urbanization with a form of ruralization. With parks the city would always retain part of what it had had in the past. Few denied the inexorable nature of the population's advance. A special committee of the City Council agreed that all experience indicated the nation's population to be concentrating in the cities; in their words, "centralization is the type of the age." Unfortunately, the congestion of humanity threatened the existence of open space and pure air, and so endangered the lives of individual inhabitants as to threaten the life of the city itself.[11]

During the heated debates of 1881, the critical year of parkland acquisition, one alderman emphasized the changes that had occurred in his thirty-seven years as a Bostonian. The city had been smaller, but at the same time, "the boys could go anywhere, the lands of all seemed to be public. . . . Now you will find a sign up, 'No trespassing'; 'Keep off the grass.'" He warned his colleagues that they voted not for their generation, but for "those that follow us, fifty or a hundred or perhaps a thousand years hence."[12] To opponents who argued that Boston's sleepy suburbs provided ample rustic scenery for city dwellers, the parks commissioners retorted: "Beautiful as these roads now are, they are, year by year, losing their rural character; their roadside hedges are giving place to sidewalks with granite curbs, and adjacent grounds are being cut up into house lots." Parks would keep a part of the country within the growing city.[13]

Shaping the city environment by means of well-planned open space was matched in urgency by the concern for health. It was a well-circulated belief that parks were the "lungs of the city." At a public rally, held in 1876 to promote parks, Dr. Edward H. Clarke reminded Bostonians that a city, like each house in it, needed proper ventilation. To this end, parks were more than the lungs of the city. As Dr. Clarke put it, "They are reservoirs of oxygen and fresh air. They produce atmospheric currents which sweep through and purify the streets." Parks would be part of a triad of services which, along with pure water and efficient sewage systems, would "make the cities in all ways healthful and beautiful."[14] The weight of the medical profession aided the momentum for parks. Physicians cited numerous statistics and studies to show that urban areas suffered higher death and disease rates, which could in large part be traced to foul air and insufficient sunlight. Particularly alarming were the facts disclosing high rates of cholera infantum and stillbirths in cities like Boston. The haunting conclusion remained that "unless open spaces of sufficient extent are provided and properly located, we shall create and shut up in this city the conditions, of which disease, pestilence and death will be the natural offspring."[15]

Others saw a different therapeutic value in parks. One alderman wove the sights and sounds of parks into a logical argument about the requisites of labor and wealth. Since wealth rested on labor, and labor involved expenditures of force, "it follows that without recuperation and recreation of force, the ability of each individual to labor is diminished and his power to add to the wealth of the community is lost." The catch was that the recuperation or recreation of force could only occur "by presenting to the senses and imagination scenes entirely different to those with which they are daily associated."[16] More than a sometime antidote to urban living, parks were thus a critical instrument without which the entire economic system might fail. The system's defect, of course, was that all laborers were not among the wealthy!

Physical health, or the lack of it, was delicately entwined with the issue of public morality. To those concerned with a degenerating social order, the benefit of public parks in this area was unrivaled. The classical maxim of *mens sana in corpore sano* took a new twist in the modern city. In romantic prose, Dr. Edward Crane outlined the link between public health and morality in a letter to a special joint committee of the City Council. Uncleanliness and impure air could intensify the evil in society and diminish the good, he argued. While foul air prompted to vice, oxygen promoted virtue, "as surely as sunlight paints the flowers and ripens the fruits of our gardens." It was, said Dr. Crane, the "close atmosphere" of his house and street that drove the tired workman to the saloon to seek relief. If only he had a park accessible to him, the poor laborer would seek it with his family "as instinctively as a plant stretched toward the light." The park would "educate him and his family into the enjoyment of innocent amusements and open-air pleasures." Somehow, by an association with nature, the workingman and his family would experience a florescence of morality previously stifled by the choking air of city streets.[17] Thus the parks would help resolve the nagging problem of urban amusements.

Actually parks had already been proposed to serve this purpose. When the problem had first caught the notice of concerned citizens, some had suggested such outdoor activities as flower gathering, horticulture, walking in the open air, and excursions for the study of natural history.[18] The catch was finding space. By 1876, as the speakers at a public park rally made clear, it was necessary for the city to provide asylums for these wholesome activities. The cost of parks would be far less than the cost of the jails, prisons, and police used in repressing wasteful indulgences like liquor and gambling. Parks would provide the blue sky, the gurgling brook, and the green trees that acted as immeasurable moral agents in the village. The country would elevate the minds and manners of the urban poor. If the masses could not get to the country, let the

Country Meets City—Franklin Park

city "bring the country to them, and give them a chance, at least, to experience its humanizing and blessed influence." Since parks belonged to all the people, rich or poor, all could mingle freely in a neutral cultural asylum. Fresh air would naturally improve the temperament of working-class men and women, for they would be induced "by public orders and public favor to elevate themselves and their condition in society" by associating with their betters through the medium of nature.[19]

Boston needed parks to preserve her environment, her health, and her morality. But she also needed parks to prove her legitimacy as a first-class American city. Other great American cities could boast of established park systems, yet in 1875 Boston still had not begun to implement one. The best public schools, art museums, conservatories of music, and schools of design could not ensure Boston's reputation as the Athens of America if she lacked the spirit by which public parks were developed. A City Council committee concluded that "if Boston cannot afford such an expenditure to secure the priceless benefit of parks, it must be because she has entered the ranks of cities like Newburyport and Salem, which have ceased to grow."[20] Civic boosterism clearly accelerated the growing demand for public parks. Boston's top business firms favored parks as a grand advertisement of the city's commercial health, and claimed that their beauty would attract wealthy merchants from around the globe. Moreover, these plush pleasure grounds would convince the prosperous classes to retain their homes within the city's limits and eschew the flight to rural suburbs. As Oliver Wendell Holmes maintained, parks would help provide the city "with the complete equipment, not of a village community, not of a thriving town, but of a true metropolis."[21]

The argument supporting public parks was clear. They would improve the physical environment of the city and, more important, elevate the living conditions of her inhabitants. Rich and poor alike would enjoy the benefits of nature, placed in perpetuum within the city limits. Families in the impoverished North End or in the elegant Back Bay could rest assured that fresh air would be forever available to their children and to their children's children. Finally, Boston, by displaying the spirit necessary for such a project, would reestablish her reputation as America's premier city.

There can be no doubt that a broad consensus supported the position of park advocates. By 1900, the park system surrounding Boston was, in large part, complete. The Parks Department could, and still does, proudly point to the evidence of popular participation by all classes of the city. By means of parkways, expanses of greenery were effectively linked throughout the city. A Bicentennial pamphlet could boast, "Together, they form a five-mile corridor of continuous park land that has long been recognized as a landmark of urban planning."[22]

But while Bostonians agreed upon the general benefits that parks could produce, they differed over answers to several specific questions that arose during the implementation of the plan proposed by Olmsted and the commissioners. These questions and their resultant friction revolved around three interrelated concerns. First, where in the city should parks properly be located? Second, for whose benefit were the parks ultimately intended? Finally, how exactly were parks to improve the leisure, and through it the life, of all citizens? Bostonians did not passively accept the answers suggested by genteel reformers like Olmsted.

They fought for their own solutions, in the context of their own adaptations to change. The debates and lobbying over these issues continued into the twentieth century, and their ultimate resolution demonstrates the manner in which the divergent elements of an urban community could partially reshape the initiatives of one group to meet their own interests.

THE TASK OF LOCATING A PARK or parks was not an easy one. While advocates stressed the benefits to be enjoyed by the entire city, politicians and citizens' lobbies were more concerned about the advantages or disadvantages of placing parks within their particular neighborhoods. One finds this parochial attitude early and often in the public record. For instance, in July of 1877 the Common Council rejected the initial proposal for a $450,000 loan to be used for buying land in the reclaimed Back Bay. This was to be the first park area, as determined by Olmsted and the commissioners.[23] One councilor from Ward 23 got to the very heart of the question. It was a matter neither of increasing the most revenues from property taxes, nor of decreasing the most nuisances from noise and foul air. These were secondary to the question of finding locations that would most benefit the mass of "clerks, bookkeepers, artisans of various kinds and laborers." Each section of the city concluded that all would be best served by locating a park within its boundaries.[24]

By 1881, the year in which the City Council considered the bulk of park bonds, this parochialism had become so acute as to threaten the very purpose of a park system. Olmsted complained to the parks commissioners:

> There is a habit now of looking upon the proposed parks of the city, each apart and independently of its relations to others of the system, as if it were to be of little value except to the people of the districts adjoining it. . . . It presents a difficulty which should be contended with; for unquestionably, if it is maintained and allowed influence in legislation, it will be likely to nullify half the value to the city of the properties now promised to be acquired for parks. . . . It is not uncommon to hear [the West Roxbury Park] referred to as if it were to be a special property of the West Roxbury Community and its chief value lie in what that community would gain from it.[25]

A City Council committee pleaded that "an end be put to sectional contentions respecting park lands."[26] Yet as the votes in the Com-

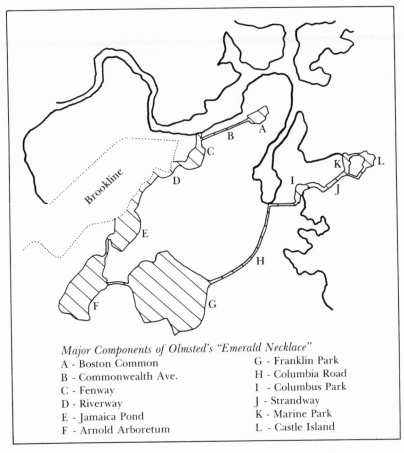

Major Components of Olmsted's "Emerald Necklace"

A - Boston Common
B - Commonwealth Ave.
C - Fenway
D - Riverway
E - Jamaica Pond
F - Arnold Arboretum

G - Franklin Park
H - Columbia Road
I - Columbus Park
J - Strandway
K - Marine Park
L - Castle Island

mon Council indicate, local interests rivaled general concerns. Every area of the city, from East Boston to West Roxbury, was represented by a politician who steadfastly maintained both the urgent need for a park in his district and the general benefits to be derived from placing one there.[27]

The voting patterns on two key proposals are illustrated in the maps. Each displays the type of parochialism that worried Olmsted. For instance, in 1877 the first proposal to purchase land for a Back Bay park failed because of negative votes from members of the Common Council representing the congested inner wards and the outlying suburban wards. The proposal succeeded only when it was reevaluated as a necessary instrument for the improvement of the city's sewage system. Second, and more clearly, one can view the local interest pattern in the December 1881 vote on the purchase of land for the West Roxbury (Franklin) Park, the linchpin of Olmsted's system. The map shows graphically that opposition to the suburban park came from congested wards in the inner city. At the same time, councilors from wards adjacent to the park were almost unanimous in their approval of the costly ($600,000) acquisition.[28] Although it is important to note that each proposal was approved on reconsideration, the message was clear. Many citizens viewed park benefits in local, not general terms. The debates and votes on the placement of public parks thus exhibited the polarity in urban politics so well described in historical literature: centralized reform groups at odds with localized political machinery. In this case one sees Olmsted's grand vision matched against legitimate neighborhood and ward interests. The parks commissioners were forced to deal with an ever-increasing parochialism that reared its head early and often, as when many Ward 3 voters qualified their rejection of the 1875 Park Act by voting "No, unless Copps Hill is taken."[29]

These attitudes continued even after the parks were completed. Some neighborhoods objected when "outsiders" availed themselves of local greenery. For instance, in 1892 a group of South Boston residents complained to the commissioners that Marine Park "had been an injury to South Boston on account of the rabble it had attracted there." Sunday arrests had involved far too many "Cambridge people"; they worried that the park had attracted "undesirable visitors to the neighborhood." Although these protests stemmed from fights against increased property taxes, they also illustrate the alienation from strangers that has typified life in the modern city. City people could continually refashion private communities in local neighborhoods, but in so doing they frequently exhibited a public posture of estrangement from outsiders.[30]

But despite Olmsted's fears, parochial interests never seriously threatened the success of the park system. On the contrary, they may have *ensured* success, by forcing central planners to accommodate local interests. Olmsted and the parks commissioners might have had more than topographical considerations in mind when they designed a *series* of parks spread about Boston's various districts. Perhaps they realized the growing importance of neighborhood communities within the larger city boundaries. The over-

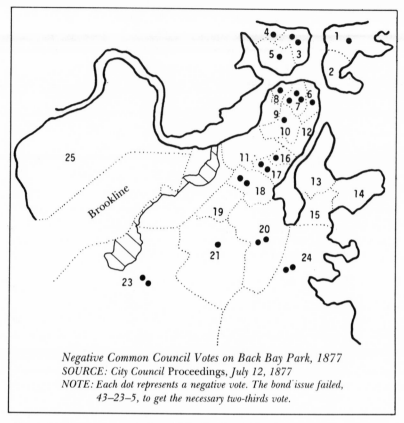

Negative Common Council Votes on Back Bay Park, 1877
SOURCE: *City Council* Proceedings, *July 12, 1877*
NOTE: *Each dot represents a negative vote. The bond issue failed,*
43–23–5, to get the necessary two-thirds vote.

all park plan succeeded politically in 1881 because it offered a chain or package, with a little something for everyone. Eventually, the local lobbies recognized this. The *South Boston Inquirer,* which pressed the case for Marine Park, told its readers that "retaliation voting" threatened their own interests. The paper ultimately directed local councilors and aldermen to vote for other parks so as to ensure the approval of their own.[31]

Local pressures continued, however, well after 1881. As the minutes of the Parks Department constantly display, ad hoc neighborhood lobbies were later the driving force behind the expansion of the system. Petitions from groups in areas like Brighton, Dorchester Lower Mills, and Roxbury planted the seeds for an extension of greenery by means of small parks and playgrounds.[32]

There was another side to the problem of locating parks. Most

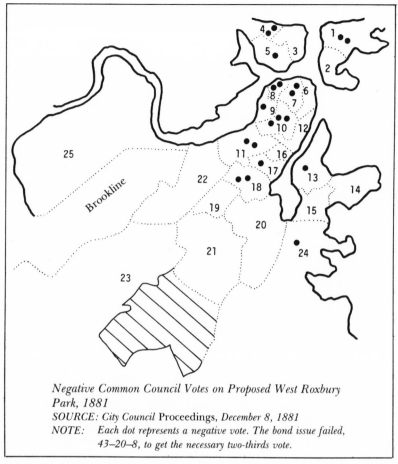

*Negative Common Council Votes on Proposed West Roxbury
Park, 1881*
SOURCE: *City Council* Proceedings, *December 8, 1881*
NOTE: *Each dot represents a negative vote. The bond issue failed,
43–20–8, to get the necessary two-thirds vote.*

of the acreage, as originally conceived and as expanded by local
pressure, was situated in less-congested wards. While land was
more available and cheaper here, the anomaly raised serious questions. For whom were parks really intended? The rich or the poor?
Some of the early citizen-planners had no doubts. As Charles
Davenport, self-styled "first projector" of the Charles River Embankment and Bay, concluded, parks would improve the city by
housing the residences of the rich. Here would be, he proposed,
the "widest avenues and streets of the metropolis." Here would be
the "finest residences in our modern Athens," the homes of "the
men of large capital and scholarly attainments and of public re-

nown, who give to the metropolis the character and enterprise for which she is famed throughout the world." In a similar vein, Uriel Crocker, whose proposal for a park system contained many elements of the parks commissioners' basic plan, believed that "it increases the enjoyment of those who walk, to watch the elegant equipages of those who ride."[33]

With such elitist sentiment lurking under the surface of public proclamations, it was no wonder that the *Boston Daily Advertiser* worried about approval of the Park Act of 1875, noting that "in some of the northerly wards there will be formidable opposition, the laborers and others having been made to believe that in some way the act will be against their interests."[34] Many had doubts. The councilors from inner-city wards realized that "the people" could not enjoy distant parks as easily as some believed. As one representative from Ward 7 reminded his colleagues, the poor workingman was not likely to march his family across town on a hot summer night just "to enjoy the benefits of the park which Boston, in its wisdom and philanthropy, has furnished for the laboring classes." He predicted that the plan, so grand on paper, "will not be so much benefit to those whom you propose to benefit, as it will those who can ride in carriages."[35] What good would "elegant equipages" provide, if working people could never reach the parks?

One clearly deduces from the public record a sense of working-class frustration with the outlying parks. One alderman who voted against the large appropriation for the Back Bay Fens suggested sarcastically that "the advocates of a park go down to the sickly district of the Back Bay and select a place for the poor man to eat his lunch and look over the $75,000 houses and envy the people who live inside of them." Many continued to regard much of the system as essentially "rich man's parks," to enjoy which required either a carriage, or, later, an automobile.[36]

But the changing political structure provided workingmen with more clout than they had previously enjoyed. Working through their local representatives in the City Council, the people of Charlestown effectively lobbied for a park in their area. During the mid-nineties, John F. Fitzgerald, the ward boss of the North End, continually pressured the commissioners for a park in his district. His unfailing energy and political savvy ensured the project's success despite the city's financial troubles. The North End park was thereafter his personal "monument." In like manner, the West End could count on strong political support to increase the capacity and facilities of its Charlesbank gymnasium. The inhabitants of the inner city did not reap the promised fruits of the outlying "emerald necklace," but they traded off support for rural parks in return for open space in their local neighborhoods. Much of this open space would take the form of small parks and playgrounds. These breathing spaces did not fit the classic model of an Olmsted park. They offered only limited foliage or serenity. But they did offer working people something tangible, and their development represented an important accommodation in the original vision of the park system.[37]

THE FINAL AREA OF CONTENTION was closely related and involved the question of appropriate activities for park patrons. Park advocates claimed that properly placed enclaves of "rus in urbe" would elevate the life of all citizens. Parks would provide true recreation for Boston's collective body and soul. The practical question, however, became whether or not the masses could be educated into the "proper" use of parks. Or would parks become simply an open-air emporium of commercialized amusements? To find the answer, one must again compare the rhetoric of a reform vision with the reality of its implementation.

The central figure in this issue was, of course, Frederick Law Olmsted, who guided the Boston Park System until 1895, when his failing health forced him into retirement.[38] The Olmsted firm, however, continued as the chief landscape architects. Throughout his career, Olmsted amply articulated his thoughts on the role of parks in city life. Because of his national influence and, of course, his position as chief architect, his views were indelibly stamped on the policies of the Boston parks commissioners. Yet, in the end, ideal philosophies had to make concessions to the realities of Boston's changing social life.

Olmsted believed that the city was the source of civilization's great advances, but he also saw that its population density could induce a reactive alienation, a "quickness of apprehension, a peculiarly hard sort of selfishness." As an antidote to this pejorative side of urban life, Olmsted, along with other urban reformers, looked to recreative amusements. Expanding the concept of recreation, he wrote:

All forms of recreation may, in the first place, be conveniently arranged under two general heads. One will include all of which the predominating influence is to stimulate exertion of any part or parts needing it; the other, all which cause us to receive pleasure without conscious exertion. Games chiefly of mental skill as chess, or athletic sports, as baseball, are examples of means of recreation of the first class, which may be termed that of *exertive* recreation; music and the fine arts generally of the second or *receptive* division.[39]

Olmsted obviously fashioned his views of parks around the notion of receptive recreation.

In outlining his plans for Franklin Park, the heart of his proposed system, Olmsted prescribed the form of recreation he envisioned within its boundaries:

A man's eyes cannot be as much occupied as they are in large cities by artificial things, or by natural things seen under artificial conditions without a harmful effect, first on his mental and nervous system and ultimately on his entire constitutional organization. That relief from this evil is to be obtained through recreation is often said, without sufficient discrimination as to the nature of the recreation required. The several varieties of recreation to be obtained in churches, newspapers, theaters, picture galleries, billiard rooms, baseball grounds, trotting courses and flower gardens, may each serve to supply a mitigating influence. An influence is desirable, however, that, acting through the eye, shall be more than mitigative, that shall be antithetical, reversive, and antidotal. Such an influence is found in what, in notes to follow, will be called the enjoyment of rural scenery.[40]

To Olmsted, then, action had little or no place in a public park. Boston's parks commissioners took Olmsted's views to heart and banned almost all active pursuits in the park system. There would be no "orations, harangues or loud outcries," no parades, drills, or processions, no individual music making. The rules allowed little legitimate activity beyond quiet picnics, meditations, and tours.[41]

This tranquillity would not last; the patrons had their own ideas about the activities that ought to occur in a park. They continually pressured for accommodation in the regulations, and, in Olmsted's view, constantly threatened the integrity of his receptive-recreation grounds. Perhaps some clerks and laborers were educated to the joys of nature-communing. But they, in turn, educated genteel Bostonians to the realities of urban leisure. In the end, this com-

Catholic Picnic on Franklin Park—Receptive Recreation En Masse
Courtesy of the Frederick Law Olmsted Museum

promise transformed, but did not destroy, the essence and value of public parks.

The growth of interest in athletic sports proved to be a major problem for the parks commissioners. While the wealthy could join suburban country clubs for playing space, the majority of the population looked to the new parklands for sports. The commissioners tried to suppress this appetite, particularly that of baseballers, and finally declared in 1884: "No entertainment, exercises, or athletic game or sport shall be held or performed within public parks except with the prior consent of the Park Commission." Olmsted was in full agreement, citing similar rules in Hartford, Baltimore, Chicago, Buffalo, New York, and Philadelphia. Only a corner of Franklin Park was allotted to active sports, and that for children only.[42]

Yet by the turn of the century, the City Council and public pressure had forced the commissioners to permit virtually every popular sport within the confines of the parks. Cricket clubs battled baseball interests for exclusive privileges. By the mid-1890s, several parks were the scene of scheduled football matches; tennis courts and a golf course were laid out in Franklin Park; the parkways whirled with wheels, many in procession and in parade! At the turn of the century, "horseless carriages" began to intrude; by 1902 they had received full privileges. Although certain sports were restricted to particular places and times, and much of the sporting activity was funneled to the related playground system, the evidence in the Parks Department minutes clearly indicates that the concept of public parks in Boston was altered, by special-interest groups, to include provisions for active sports. The Olmsted firm had hoped that the local "pleasure grounds" for active pursuits, such as North End Beach, Charlestown Heights, the Charlesbank (West End), and Franklin Field, would relieve the pressure being put on "receptive" recreation areas. This was not to be. The firm could only warn that park ground was being "put to a use quite inconsistent with its purpose."[43]

Athletic sports were probably eventually accepted as legitimate park recreations because they represented a less severe encroachment than commercial amusements. As soon as the parks neared completion, the commissioners were inundated with license petitions from operators of hurdy-gurdy machines, merry-go-rounds, photo tents, refreshment stands, and amusement theaters, to name but a few. The operator of one theater argued that "the purpose of amusing the public is a public benefit entirely consistent with the use of the public parks." Further, the operators claimed that they desired only to satisfy an overwhelming demand for their services.[44]

Alderman Martin Lomasney, the powerful boss of Ward 8, accurately voiced one attitude of the inner city when he opposed a rule outlawing mechanical "flying horses" or similar commercial amusements on the Sabbath:

> I don't believe we should be activated by the same spirit that prevailed in the days of the old Blue Laws, when on Sunday you would have to walk down Washington Street carrying a Bible in your hand and not speak to anybody on the street. . . . Certain people in the North End and in South Boston can reach these parks Sundays who cannot reach them any other day, and I don't believe they should be deprived of going on the flying horses if they wish to do so.[45]

The laborer who found his relief in a nickel beer and free lunch at the saloon, or in a 25-cent seat at the Columbia Theatre, might

Mass Tennis on Franklin Park—Exertive Recreation Creeps In
Courtesy of the Trustees of the Boston Public Library

well expect similar offerings at the parks. Olmsted's vision had to accommodate Lomasney's. Working through their connections on the City Council and even on the Parks Commission, commercial amusements operators succeeded in placing merry-go-rounds, photo tents, refreshment stands, and vending machines among the elm trees, brooks, and beaches.[46]

By World War I, "receptive" recreation was no longer the rule in public parks. The Olmsted firm had to admit that "for most of the population, the enjoyment of scenery is in a more or less embryonic state." They suggested adding certain "feature" attractions to draw people to Franklin Park: band concerts, a zoo, animal rides. Beyond this, active sports and commercialized amusements had secured guaranteed, if restricted, privileges. Conservative reformers like the Olmsteds and Boston 1915, a private reform group of prominent citizens, did not agree in principle with serious compromise in park use. But they wisely realized that they had to yield to popular attitudes toward leisure if the parks were to have any reforming value.[47]

THE DEVELOPMENT OF A PARK SYSTEM involved an active and conscious attempt by Bostonians to shape and control the physical aspects of their community. In this respect, the Parks

Department can arguably be described as the city's first municipal planning board. Olmsted and his successors successfully blended the available topography to reconcile beauty and space for recreation with basic needs like adequate drainage and traffic flow. Beyond all else, the park system was a farsighted response to a prevailing belief that the city was fast gobbling up both open spaces and a way of life; it was what Olmsted called a "self-preserving instinct of civilization." The islandlike quality of these parks today is testimony to the accuracy of that instinct.[48]

If the Boston case is at all representative, however, it cautions the historian to take special care in categorizing urban park systems as a vehicle of genteel reform or social control whereby an elite class, whatever its members' motives, could readily manipulate the behavior of inferiors. Considerable evidence suggests this as the intent of many park advocates, but its basis lies largely in the arguments of early proposals. Herein parks were envisaged as large expanses of water, woods, and dales where all social classes might mix and be elevated in a fraternal communion with nature. An equally compelling body of evidence, the public record, displays the active role which the "popular mass" took in altering this vision. Special interest groups—neighborhood citizens' lobbies, athletic clubs, amusement operators—all representing a wide range of social classes, continually worked directly and through their political representatives to influence major decisions in park placement and policy. These groups succeeded in getting parks where they wished them; they pursued their own choice of recreation on the park grounds. Thus, the park movement in Boston was a reform that issued from the "bottom up" as well as from the top down. Because of this, the ultimate product of reform differed from the intended product. Only by an examination of the long implementation process can we hope to discern the difference.

5/ *Playgrounds for Children*

IN DECEMBER OF 1869, a group of amateur baseball players met in the clubroom of Boston's Lowell Baseball Club. Their purpose was not to discuss past or future seasons, but to plan a dramatic protest of the gradual exclusion of recreation from the Boston Common. The result was the "Red Ball" ticket in the aldermanic elections held that month. In describing their platform, the Red Ballers claimed that their purpose was to foster outdoor sports in general, not just baseball. "The Common has been taken and nothing left in its place as a playground," they complained, "and the main object is to elect men who will grant our youth some spot for recreation."[1] The system operated like present consumer lobbies, which endorse candidates according to their records on nuclear power or no-return bottles. Rallying committees marshaled support in every ward and passed out "Red Ball" tickets at each polling place. The results were heartening; eight of the twelve elected aldermen were on the Red Ball ticket. The following spring, the lower end of the Common was reassigned to boys' sports.

Play space had not seemed such an urgent problem before the Civil War. Descriptions of antebellum Boston by men like Edward Everett Hale portray an uncongested town. The Common was but a central play area, large enough for games such as baseball; but indeed, all of Boston seemed a playground for Hale and his friends.[2] These childhood memories of a pastoral environment made the diminution of open space even more intolerable.

So the advocates of playgrounds became more vocal after the Civil War. We can trace their cause as it was pleaded in City Hall. In 1881, an alderman reminded his listeners that twenty-five years before there had been plenty of open land in South Boston. "You could go across the land," he claimed, "and there was no trouble about the boys playing on the ground." Things had changed quickly, however; now there wasn't a "fit place in South Boston where the boys can go and play football without being ordered off the grass."[3] This was not an isolated complaint. Petitions had been circulating since the Red Ball ticket. Play areas were needed with great urgency, if the instincts of youth were not to be subverted to baser activities.

For a variety of reasons, Boston responded to this need. Within thirty years, both public and private forces combined to conceive a comprehensive playground system, one of the first in the country. By 1915, the city operated forty playgrounds of varying sizes and uses. The fortieth *Annual Report* of the Board of Parks Commissioners boasted that all residents of the city, young or old, could find ample space and activities to suit their recreational fancy. Every section of the city provided some facility of "full advantage" to its residents. Including the special areas in the parks, one could find scores of ball fields, one hundred tennis courts, two golf courses, three toboggan slides, dozens of skating areas, eight beaches, twelve bath houses, and nine gymnasia. All were public facilities. Some KEEP OFF THE GRASS signs still existed, but Boston was confident that she was meeting her citizens' desires for active play. The beneficiaries of this response included men and women of all ages, but the main focus of concern was the child and the youth, in particular the boy.[4]

The Red Ball ticket had signaled the beginning of a chapter in Boston's history that stands out as far more than an addendum to the movement for public parks. The parks represented a grand scheme, radical surgery to implant a new arterial system that would push the lifeblood of fresh air, health, and morality throughout the urban system. Playgrounds attempted to address many of the same issues, but in a smaller, localized manner. The rhetoric of parks, while grandiose, was also general and vague; the arguments of playground advocates stressed concrete, local, specific remedies. Parks were designed as an antidote, a refuge from the hectic, congested conditions of life in the city. Playgrounds were too small for such a purpose and, moreover, were often located in the very heart of the problems. Rather, playgrounds quickly came to provide a solution of direct control and organization of social life in

A Playground Movement Success—Baseball on Marcella Street
Courtesy of the Trustees of the Boston Public Library

the city. Parks offered an escape for all ages, playgrounds a counterattack through the impressionable substance of youth. And both parks and playgrounds represented active attempts to develop community in the city.

The links between parks and playgrounds were important. The major initiative for public playgrounds came from neighborhood lobbies who were sold on the simple proposition that outdoor exercise was wholesome, a deterrent to crime and disease. One of the principal sources of this position was of course the parks debates. The early playground advocates wanted "breathing spaces" or mini-parks for children; their support came from a broad-based, unsophisticated belief in the importance of open space. Only when the drive for playgrounds was well under way did genteel reformers exalt the movement with sophisticated theories about play, child development, and social behavior. In other words, we find elites reforming a process begun by a wider constituency—just the reverse of what we found in the parks movement.

Most research into Boston's playground movement has unfortunately overemphasized the role of private, philanthropic, and progressive organizations, such as the Massachusetts Emergency and Hygiene Association or the Massachusetts Civic League. Historians in this tradition see playgrounds as the fruits of voluntary reform groups who closely analyzed the plight of their social inferiors. As one such historian has put it, they "formulated tentative approaches, and finally, through experimentation, evolved successful techniques for dealing with [the problem]." Only when proven by experience did the "techniques" become "public property."

One should be careful, however, not to slight the important impetus that public officials and "uninformed" citizens' groups gave to the playground movement. The fact is that elite, philanthropic organizations simply refined the concept and purpose behind playgrounds.[5]

A major reason that scholars credit voluntary reform groups with the establishment of organized playgrounds lies in the fact that the most available source material was written by members of these very groups. Thus works by Luther Gulick, Joseph Lee, Everett Mero, Jacob Riis, or their disciples are commonly used as basic source material for understanding the role that playgrounds played in answering historical urban problems.[6] This is not to say that private organizations were minor contributors to the development of playgrounds, nor that leaders like Joseph Lee deliberately warped the historical record in order to aggrandize their own role. By consulting the public records, however, we can better understand that all elements of Boston's social environment played roles in the development of her playgrounds, and that these various groups, both public and private, offer insights into the ways Bostonians and all Americans responded to urban growth. Irish politicians were as concerned about the need for playgrounds as were Brahmin philanthropists. All groups involved in the playground debate were anxious about the changing nature of community in Boston. It is the divergence in their approaches to playgrounds and to change that is of special interest. For this reason, the efforts of one group cannot be highlighted to the exclusion of another's.

THE *ANNUAL REPORTS* of Boston's Auditor of Accounts (see the accompanying table) unveil an interesting trend in the appropriations earmarked for playgrounds from 1869 until 1898, when

CITY APPROPRIATIONS FOR PLAYGROUNDS, 1869–1898

Year	Appropriation
1869–1877	$ 0
1877–1878	2,000[a]
1878–1879	0
1879–1880	1,000[b]
1880–1881	250
1881–1887	0
1887–1888	200
1888–1889	1,200
1889–1892	1,000[c]
1892–1893	2,780
1893–1894	41,400[d]
1894–1895	22,200
1895–1896	30,000[e]
1896–1897	124,000[f]
1897–1898	180,000

SOURCE: City of Boston, *Annual Reports of the Auditor of Accounts*, 1869–98
NOTES: [a]spent $740 of appropriation
[b]spent $582 of appropriation
[c]spent none of appropriation
[d]$40,000 of total earmarked to Franklin Field, a 77-acre tract adjoining Franklin Park
[e]figure represents authorized loans
[f]figure represents authorized loans

a major bill passed in the State House, ensuring a "comprehensive system of playgrounds for the City of Boston."[7]

Several obvious patterns stand out in need of explanation. The first is the lack of appropriations from 1869 to 1877. The debate that the Red Ball ticket incited in 1869 seems to have had little real effect on the problem of open space for playgrounds. The next is the sputtering start of appropriations from 1878 to 1881, followed by the six-year drought from 1881 to 1887. The last important trend one notices is the steady, then tremendous growth of appropriations in the ten-year period beginning 1887. After 1898, spending on playgrounds continued at a very high rate as the city engaged in building a comprehensive playground system. The events that occurred within these patterns illustrate the public phase of playground growth.

Let us return to the beginning. The debate over baseball on the Common resumed in 1873 when the Beacon Baseball Club petitioned the aldermen to appropriate more Common space to baseball. The ball club claimed to represent not only the two thousand persons who directly backed their petition but also the estimated "25,000 to 30,000 young men who must have some games to play."[8]

The petitioners began the debate on a harsh note, accusing the Committee on the Common of perpetrating class discrimination. In their words, the committee had paid too much heed to the objections of "a few wealthy citizens, most of whom pass the summer months, when the playground is in requisition, away from the city." The aldermen, they claimed, had neglected the interests of the young men who were "unable to afford expensive recreations, nor have the time to go to the outskirts of the city to obtain exercise."[9] Although the baseballers backed off this harder line, real class resentment could fester below and occasionally surface to envenom subsequent debates.

A number of other advocates of this measure decried the gradual shriveling of open space and the exclusion of play areas. They further cited reports from school and health authorities stressing the need for schoolchildren to exercise, or as one put it, the desire "to have his children come out of school with a good constitution [rather] than to have their brains crammed with debilitated bodies [*sic*]."[10]

Opponents of the measure were able to call upon other health authorities who stressed the dangers involved in baseball playing. Citing a number of actual cases, these remonstrants pointed out that innocent passersby would be wounded, maimed, and otherwise injured by flying baseballs! The old baseball had been soft; the newer version "more like a grape shot, or a paving stone." This, coupled with the control of fields that older boys exerted, led one opponent to maintain that "the present game is to that of our school days almost as a rifle to a pop gun."[11]

The aldermen denied the request for increased baseball grounds on the Common. Public authorities did not feel acutely enough the need for special allocations of play areas for children. Besides, the debate on public parks was currently raging, and park advocates stressed the improvement in recreations that these acquisitions would bring to young and old alike.[12]

By 1877, however, the issue of play space for children surfaced again. There seem to have been several reasons for this. The Committee on the Common, in an effort to beautify the area with more lush grass, had further restricted the section for open recreation. The councilor from nearby Ward 9 pointed out that grass might be beautiful, but so would the sight of "two or three hundred boys playing there who would otherwise be back in the slums, or perhaps in saloons, and other places qualifying themselves to be criminals, and entailing expense upon the city in reforming them."[13] Many playground advocates also sensed that the parks commissioners, newly appointed in 1875, were not going to offer solutions to the problems of inner-city space. The second report of the Parks Board offered a detailed plan that proposed the placement of most parks in an "emerald chain" on the suburban perimeter.[14]

In the interests of city children and in the spirit of compromise, the Common Council and the aldermen voted in May of 1877 to appropriate two thousand dollars to provide "playgrounds for boys in the several sections of the city." During the debate over this issue, however, several comments indicated the total novelty of this concept. One councilor from Ward 10 requested a reconsideration of the vote:

> The City Council have never made an appropriation of that kind before, as I am informed. It is something new; it might be considered a new departure for the amusement of the people, or instruction—whichever you please to call it; and therefore we have not any experience to look to by which we can gain any information in regard to exactly what the character of these playgrounds is to be.

A colleague, equally bewildered about this new concept, admitted that if the proponents had stated their desire for a park he could have understood them "perfectly." Likewise, if they meant a baseball ground. But if they meant neither, he despaired, "I do not know what a playground means."[15]

The uncertainty over playgrounds as a special use of urban space underscores a point made by Dominick Cavallo in his recent study of the organized play ideology. A sophisticated rationale for

91

children's playgrounds rested on top of a general "rediscovery" of the child as a special type of human being, demanding special forms of moral and physical education. This current of thought flowed strongest from 1885 to 1910 in the works of G. Stanley Hall, John Dewey, Mark Baldwin, and others. Our city fathers were ten or more years ahead of all this! They had heard much about parks and baseball fields, but virtually nothing about playgrounds. A majority of them, however, had a sense that play space was a worthy appropriation, and so they set aside two thousand dollars for the summer rental of private property.[16]

As it turned out, only two areas were rented, for a total cost of $740. The choice of locations triggered a round of parochial bickering that typified the early debates over parks and playgrounds. The following year, stiff opposition awaited a request for another appropriation of playground rental funds, as councilors from inner-city wards protested the locations of the past year's playgrounds: Brighton, Jamaica Plain, West Roxbury—all "suburban" areas. As a councilor from Ward 8 (who had voted against the Back Bay park) complained, these were of no "benefit to the boys of the North and West Ends." A counterpart from South Boston said, "I fail to see why the boys of South Boston should have to go to Roxbury or to the Back Bay."[17]

There were, then, no special public playgrounds for fiscal year 1878–79. As the table shows, however, the city reacted with a two-year spurt of modest rental appropriations in 1880 and 1881. The City Council *Proceedings* indicate organized pressure from citizens' groups in Dorchester, West Roxbury, and Brighton. Neighborhood newspapers like the *Charlestown News* or the *East Boston Argus* vigorously asserted the need their local boys had of playgrounds.[18] These parochial lobbies would become an important ingredient in later playground development. But the parks commissioners appeared to be hearing these early rumblings as well. Their fourth annual report contained an elegant lament for the lost central playground that the Common had provided, comparing the city's youth to the Indians; both were forced to move "steadily westward."[19] Thus, 1878 to 1881 witnessed a cautious response to public discussion about the need for playgrounds. More important, two key ingredients of the entire movement surfaced during this early phase: the activity of localized interest groups, and the focus on play for children.

The next six years saw a lapse in momentum. To begin with, the parochial bickering over the placement of playgrounds in particular areas hindered the development of playgrounds in any section of the city. This problem illustrated a dilemma that had slowed the growth of parks. On the one hand, neighborhood citizen lobbies provided the key impetus for the development of playgrounds. Petitions for local play areas spurred the City Council and parks commissioners to action. On the other hand, the same local, neighborhood attachment caused city councilors and aldermen to delay voting to build playgrounds in neighborhoods too distant from their own.

The other reasons for the hiatus in playground growth stem from the heavy financial and emotional commitment that Boston made in the early 1880s to the public park system. After six years of study and debate, in late 1881 the City Council voted over one million dollars in bonds for the development of a park system. And as we have seen, this grand design initially appeared as a panacea to the recreational ills of a growing city.[20]

On the other hand, as the parks commissioners deferred increasingly to the views of Frederick Law Olmsted, it became clear that public parks would not provide the answer to playground needs. Olmsted's opinions on recreation for the urban masses carried great clout with city officials, and unfortunately, active play was not a primary ingredient in Olmsted's scheme. His control of park policy, coupled with his philosophy of passive recreation, proved a hindrance to the development of playgrounds.

We know, however, that many park patrons were not interested in the enjoyment of rural scenery. To them, Franklin, City Point, Wood Island, and Marine Park offered open areas for the pursuit of active sports and games. The initial response of the parks commissioners was repression! The first "Instructions" for park patrolmen, issued in 1883, noted that "games of ball and similar sports are to be allowed upon the greensward."[21] Yet one year later the regulations indicated that "baseball and other games are prohibited on Sunday and will be restricted on other days of the week to such grounds as are from time to time designated, under penalty of a fine not exceeding $20."[22] If there had been too much baseball and active recreation in 1883, there was more in 1884, for the commissioners continued to retrench. In September of 1884, the new park rules noted that no athletic games or sport would be allowed within a public park except with the prior consent of the commissioners. Not only the days and grounds, but also the very activities now were restricted.[23]

At this point, the parks commissioners were squeezed between Olmsted's principles and the demands of neighborhood groups, who were pressing the City Council for play space.[24] Again, the emphasis lay in the needs of children, particularly boys. Well-organized lobbies from East Boston, Dorchester, and Brighton pressured their representatives to carry the playground banner. One alderman summarized the compelling theme of the playground proposals. Private land development was fast enclosing the old play areas, he said, "and the consequence is you find them on the corners insulting passers by, and presently the police take them to the station houses for their first petty crime, and from there they go to something worse." It was a matter of law and order, said a colleague in the Common Council. Since the boys had no playgrounds in the denser areas of the city, like the South End, South Boston, and Roxbury, they were "forced to play on the public streets, thus violating the city ordinances."[25]

Since it was clear that Boston needed a concerted effort to develop playgrounds, the City Council determined that the Parks Department should be a major party in the process. In view of the department's stance toward "active play," there was little wonder why some councilors desired the Health Department to control playgrounds. But the city wisely stayed with the Parks Department, as it carried significant clout with the public. Furthermore, it was far better to ally with Olmsted, and thus gain the benefit of his genius for design.[26]

In the end, the Parks Department slowly responded to the challenge. Its next report asked whether it would not be wiser to *appropriate* the play areas that the city had rented in the past.[27] Even Olmsted reasoned that the flat "Playstead" area of Franklin Park could be properly used for "youthful" sports.[28] After this beginning, the next decade witnessed a unified public response to the need for play space in the Hub.

Two permanent play areas for children were added to the city's roster in 1889. The first was the Playstead, a flat, grassy portion of Franklin Park's north end, designed specifically for children from seven to sixteen years of age. The Playstead opened in June of 1889, with much fanfare. Schoolchildren had the day off and were provided free transportation on the West End Street Railway to the festivities, which included a dramatic flag raising, a salute by the school regiment, and patriotic renditions of the national anthem and "America the Beautiful." In that year's annual report, the parks commissioners admitted the need to provide more play space to the many thousands of children "living in the denser part of the city," whose only arenas of activity were the "more or less filthy street pavements." If Franklin Park offered all citizens an asylum from the hustle of Boston, the Playstead was the children's ward.[29]

The second new play area, the Charlesbank Gymnasium, was located on a half-mile embankment of the Charles River, within easy walking distance of the West End slums. It included separate gymnasiums for men and women, as well as play areas for children. Olmsted designed the Charlesbank, shielded by mounds and trees from excessive street noise. A blend of park and playground, the Charlesbank contained more vegetation, shrubbery, and trees than running tracks, vaulting horses, or sand gardens. But it must stand as the first attempt to provide active play space within a recognized "slum" area. Its popularity was beyond question. The *Boston Journal* applauded its creation. There was cause for thanksgiving, it said, among the hundreds of poor men and women who struggled daily from morning to night only to face the prospects of "some wretched tenement house, whose poor drainage and close and often stifling atmosphere, lay the foundation for malarial and other complaints." This class of citizens, "who scarcely know the meaning of a summer vacation," would find in the Charlesbank some compensation for their inability to enjoy the "beauties of nature."[30] When (for lack of funds) the City Council delayed the Charlesbank's opening in 1892, a huge public uproar ensued. One councilor claimed he had "never heard so much clamor in regard to anything of the kind since I have been a member of the government." The Council unanimously appropriated the necessary five thousand dollars.[31]

The popularity of these local pleasure grounds underscored the limitations of distant parks; even if poor children could reach Franklin Park, they might never appreciate the quiet and serenity of meadows or forest groves. As South End settlement workers knew, the "sights and sounds of the street" were the "recreative resources" of inner-city youngsters. Why not combine the benefits

Fellows Street Playground—A Breathing Space
Courtesy of the Trustees of the Boston Public Library

of open space with the familiarity of local surroundings?[32] In this vein, neighborhood lobbies kept pressuring their representatives and the parks commissioners for playgrounds "for youth." The city, in turn, responded by renting or constructing playgrounds in all sections of the city, as the figures of the city auditor indicate.[33]

This surge of pressure culminated in 1898 with "an act to provide for a comprehensive system of playgrounds for the city of Boston." This bill authorized half a million dollars in city bonds to be used in building "playgrounds in such different locations, not exceeding twenty in number, as they may deem best adapted for such purpose."[34]

In 1897, Mayor Quincy had joined hands with the parks commissioners to push for passage of such a comprehensive playground package. The mayor reasoned in his annual address for 1897:

> I know of no direction in which the expenditure of a few hundred thousand dollars will do more for this community through the healthful development of its children than by the judicious provision of properly located and equipped playgrounds. So much public

attention has been given to the advantages of extensive park areas that the equally great need of comparatively small open spaces, particularly in the thickly settled districts, for use as playgrounds, has been overlooked. If one-twentieth of the sum expended for park systems could be devoted to playgrounds, in my opinion there would be a still larger percentage of return in healthful physical development and social well-being.[35]

The mayor's remarks typify the overblown rhetoric that led later researchers to believe that a serious neglect of public playgrounds existed to this point.[36] In fact, as the parks commissioners outlined, the city already had more than twenty playgrounds either in operation or currently under construction. But there was no doubt that Boston needed more.[37]

The inferences about past neglect of playgrounds do bear some meaning when one remembers that Olmsted had retired in 1895. While Olmsted had included playground areas in some of his parks, he clung to the very principle that Quincy wished to overturn—that is, that one large park area was more beneficial than a number of small, scattered "breathing spaces."[38] Perhaps it is no coincidence that the small-playground concept flourished only after Olmsted's ideological grip had loosened.

The passage of the 1898 bill ensured a commitment to public playgrounds. Support continued to grow and money continued to flow, and by 1915 the city had constructed twenty-six playgrounds for full-time operation. These were playgrounds proper, not simply attachments to parks or public gymnasiums. Further, every section of the city enjoyed the blessing of one or more playgrounds.[39]

It is worth reemphasizing the fact that, at their core, all playground arguments represented a reaction to industrial-urban growth that surfaced in most late nineteenth-century cities. Like parks, they were a medium for the control of space, time, and behavior. In the early proposals of city fathers and neighborhood activists, the playgrounds were but a simple mechanism—they would get the children off the streets. This argument had clout, however, and so it continued to surface; its logic was hard to refute. As one Common Council committee put it, a playground was necessary in South Boston's northern ward because, without one, the boys naturally played their athletic contests in the streets. Peace, quiet, and windows suffered. The alternatives seemed to be either a playground or a mass arrest! Neither the police nor the residents desired the latter, so both put up with "a great deal of annoyance, hoping all the time that the city will come to their relief, provide a playground for the ward, and thereby take the children off the streets." And so went the principal argument, from 1869 to 1915.[40]

Playgrounds as a relief for children had been a public issue since the days of the Red Ball ticket. The major lobby behind the acceptance of playgrounds had not been private philanthropic or reform groups, but the local neighborhood citizenry. These coveys of community sentiment successfully pressured city politicians for local playgrounds. Who were these groups? Their composition, and their motives, varied. Many were residents in the "streetcar suburbs"; basically middle and upper classes who desired to avoid the congestion of the inner wards. As Sam Bass Warner has demonstrated, "each homeowner wanted to believe that his new house was in the country, or at least near it." The tone of their petitions suggests that they viewed playgrounds as a safeguard to the financial and emotional investment that they had made in their flight from the city's center. This fear of loss led to a surge of requests for local playgrounds that poured into City Hall in the 1880s and 1890s.[41]

It was not just the more prosperous neighborhoods that pressed for open space; the "zone of emergence" was also represented in the petitions recorded by the City Council and the Parks Department. In 1899, forty-one residents of Ward 18 requested a playground in their district of Roxbury. Thirty-three of the petitioners could be positively identified in the city directory. They were a decidedly working-class group, albeit skilled workers. Their common bond lay not in protecting the future, but in salvaging the present.[42]

To these early lobbyists, playgrounds were a simple response to *physical* changes in the community. Playgrounds would keep the children off the streets, out of the haunts of dissipation, and in good health. They had no theories to explain why this would happen; only a gut feeling that open space was a moral elixir for youth, and that parks were not effectively serving this purpose. This basic contention was to be quickly transformed by genteel reformers into a sophisticated manifesto on the relationship of organized play to child development and social engineering. When

one considers the backgrounds of these later reformers, this transformation becomes understandable. If early groups revealed the
existence of *local* neighborhood community sentiment, reform
groups lamented the breakdown of an older *city-wide* community.
Playgrounds became to them a scientific means of slowing this
collapse.

THE DIFFERENCE BETWEEN the old and the new philosophies of playgrounds can be seen in the following recollection
of Joseph Lee (1862–1937), sometimes called the "father of Boston's playgrounds." The son of Colonel Henry Lee, a prominent banker, Joseph Lee had graduated from Harvard College in
1883 and Harvard Law School in 1887. After a continental tour,
he began a lifetime in local and national social work, including a
long tenure as president of the Playground Association of America.
An associate of Mayor Quincy, Lee's interest in playgrounds began
when he sensed that the fruits of the 1898 legislation were not
being utilized. Here there were thousands of boys, he said, "thirst-
ing for a chance to play and getting into all kinds of mischief for
lack of opportunity." At the very same time, the new playgrounds
were lying empty. Why? A boy in the North End told him, "Oh,
dere's a tough crowd down dere who would knock the stuffin out
of yer." Play space itself was not enough, Lee concluded. What was
needed was supervision! Lee was perceptive, for the early advocates had been more concerned with providing playgrounds than
with organizing the activities within them. More than a plea for
organized play, however, these later demands for supervision
within the playgrounds were very much rooted in anxiety over
changes in the social fabric of the entire community.[43]
  Although several reform groups sporadically sponsored vaca-
tion-school play areas after the Civil War, the first organized and
well-articulated argument for supervised playgrounds came from
the Massachusetts Emergency and Hygiene Association, which
during the second half of the 1880s had successfully operated
"sand gardens" for young children.[44] Ellen Tower, chairwoman of
the association's Committee on Playgrounds, was among the first
to cite the moral effect of *supervised* play. Her report of 1889 noted
that "the moral influence of the playground and the steady, kind
treatment of the children are of large service in the formation of
their character."[45] In 1891, the MEHA convinced the parks com-

Columbus Avenue Playground—Organized Play
Courtesy of the Trustees of the Boston Public Library

missioners to let them run a supervised play area at the Charlesbank Gymnasium. The reports of this committee continually stressed the "refining influence," the "moral or civilizing work," and the obedience training emphasized by supervisors. The greater the diversity of ethnic groups, the greater the need for the work:

> The happiness and at-home feeling of the children has been strongly in evidence. Their little bows and courtesies on entering and leaving the classes, their shy friendliness or their more boisterous regard has proved their affection for the city enclosure, which to so many of them is the only steady summer resort they know. The more the population in that part of Boston has changed in nationality, the plainer has become the hygienic and moral necessity for just such a playground as Charlesbank affords.

And so the delight that Jews, Germans, Russians, Irish, and negroes came in large numbers.[46]

The Massachusetts Emergency and Hygiene Association played an important part in the development of Boston's playgrounds. Its members successfully petitioned the Boston School Committee for the use of schoolyards during the summer months. Under the leadership of Kate Gannett Wells, the children's playground at the Charlesbank Gymnasium was both popular and successful. But their influence on major playground development was limited, for as we have seen, the great surge of public support for playgrounds at this same time was due more directly to the successful lobbying of unrelated neighborhood citizens' groups. Beyond this, the MEHA did not clarify the importance of supervision to the extent where the public clearly understood its value. For instance, although the MEHA deserves credit for introducing the playground idea into the school system, it did not successfully convey the gospel of supervision. One senses this in a school committee report of 1902 which expounded a philosophy of playgrounds little different from that of earlier city councilors. Playgrounds were destined to be a "blessed success," said the committee, "as a factor which helps to keep away much that is vitiating in the lives of these children." But for all this, the school committee still talked of playgrounds as but a substitute for the "noisy, dangerous streets."[47] It remained for Joseph Lee and the Massachusetts Civic League to popularize the importance of supervised playgrounds as a weapon of social order.

Joseph Lee had founded the Massachusetts Civic League in 1897 as an organization suited to the careful study of Boston's social problems. In 1899, the league's Committee on the Prevention of Juvenile Law-Breaking had determined that the crime rate for ten-to-fifteen-year-olds increased 119 percent in August, while the crime rate for the city as a whole increased by only 30 percent. The committee concluded that these juveniles turned to crime for want of other activities.[48] The playground committee coincidentally reached the conclusion that the city's existing playgrounds "were not used to nearly their full capacity and that the principal reason was the lack of supervision." Without supervision, it seemed, the bigger boys broke up constructive play by carrying off the bats and balls of the younger boys.[49]

Proceeding directly, the league requested and received permission from the Boston parks commissioners to organize and oversee supervised play at the North End Park and the Columbus Avenue

Playground.[50] As the league's Playground Committee noted, their principal aim was to provide organization and structure to the spirit and energy of boys between the ages of eight and sixteen. But they hoped that the result would be more far-reaching:

> Popular support is essential for every reason; not only to get the playground used, to make it a true popular and neighborhood institution, affecting social life and ideals as well as individual health and muscle, but also for the very practical reason that *our object is to get the city to introduce similar work in all the public playgrounds, our function being merely to carry the work through the experimental stage* [their emphasis].[51]

Through private and public appeal, Joseph Lee raised both money and consciousness in support of more supervised playgrounds. He stressed that, to be successful, Boston should provide enough playgrounds for every child in the city to have one within a quarter of a mile of home.[52] In this effort, the league enjoyed much success—by 1913 it could point to seventy-three equipped and supervised playgrounds in Boston.[53]

But the growing *ideology* of supervised play was the greatest success of philanthropic societies like the Massachusetts Civic League, and this could be measured by more than sheer numbers of supervised playgrounds. Within this philosophy lay the groundwork for altering the concept of sport so that it would become a tool by which urban youth, the victims of a fragmented community, might fit into the new industrial order.[54]

To Lee and other play theoreticians, the traditional structures of social stability appeared to be in serious trouble. The "greatest menace to civilization," he said, was "the weakening of the family relation," but to this he added the shredding of wider community ties, in the face of wholesale immigration, and rapacious economic individualism. Playgrounds and supervised play might, in Lee's plan, prove a source for reweaving the social and moral fabric of neighborhood, city, and nation.[55]

Lee believed that the teenage years represented an "age of loyalty," a disposition that lay at the heart of the urban gang. Through supervised play and organized team sports, he believed, this loyalty could be redirected toward the larger community. Lee described the process on many occasions. "In playing these games," he said, "the boy is not going through the forms of citizenship—learning parliamentary law, raising points of order and moving the previous question—he is being initiated into its essence, actually and in a very vivid way participating in the thing itself." While a boy played football, he subordinated his individual aims to the common purpose, and thus became "part of a social or political whole."[56] In Lee's opinion, the playground's greatest function was to transform this "budding loyalty," which was being "perverted by lack of opportunity," into the foundation of the future citizen.[57] Lee did not invent this philosophy, but he was by far its greatest salesman. Indeed, he was a major force in the Playground Association of America, so his success reached beyond Boston's city limits.

Yet the picture of Lee is often incomplete. While he is often portrayed holding out his hand with playgrounds to urban youth, he is seldom revealed as a prominent supporter of the Immigrant Restriction League. In *Ancestors and Immigrants: A Changing New England Tradition,* Barbara Miller Solomon demonstrates that many Brahmin reformers like Joseph Lee could delicately balance their philanthropy with financial and ideological commitments to immigrant restriction.[58] Lee should not be considered a hypocrite. To be sure, when forced to accept the gloomy vision of "a medieval empire of autonomous groups in which the newer stocks would live side by side with the old American remnant without fusing into a single nationality," he decided that the time had come to cut down the surge of immigrants flooding into the country.[59] Yet this did not prevent him from fighting against slums, delinquency, or corruption. It did not prevent him from leading the battle for civic improvements.

Therefore the campaign on the playgrounds was directed at *preserving* a cherished community that was once dominated by Brahmins and was now splintered by the pressures of immigration and urbanization. As Lee put it, "The idea is not that we, the rich, out of our great goodness and kindness of heart, should help you the poor, but that we . . . insist on being proud . . . of the sort of citizen we produce; for the honor of the family we cannot have rags and drunkenness."[60] It is not surprising that the Massachusetts Civic League actively sought Harvard students as football coaches, or that of sixty volumes in its North End playground library, ten were copies of *Tom Brown's School Days.* It also becomes clearer why the Playground Committee exuded such euphoria in reporting that its "hockey and football teams ignored, to a great extent, the race lines between Irish, Jews, and Italians, which are so marked at the North End."[61]

Lee and the Massachusetts Civic League were influenced by the communitarian themes of Charles Horton Cooley and of Josiah Royce, his old Harvard mentor. Concerned about the social effects of laissez faire industrial capitalism, Royce and Cooley stressed the need for humanizing society and restoring the fellow feeling and identity that had seemingly vanished from American life. Along similar lines the Massachusetts Civic League concluded its report for 1913. The playground movement assumed a "new and added significance," its members noted, in view of Royce's "discovery" that the "salvation of the individual can be effected by cultivating the spirit of loyalty to the 'blessed community,' or social group." In their words, "it makes our work seem indeed consecrated."[62]

If playgrounds could contribute to what Lee saw as a traditional communitarian moral order, they could also prepare workers for a modern productive system. When the Massachusetts Civic League barnstormed the state to drum up support for a referendum on playgrounds, they found a ready audience among businessmen who agreed that organized play promoted qualities that were fundamental to the successful worker. Among them were the "capacity for teamwork, good health, enthusiasm, observation, ability to play a losing game, honesty, clean play, temperance and imagination."[63] As the reform group Boston 1915 put it, with the optimism typical of contemporary progressives, playgrounds were an integral part of the "great business of making a community."[64]

REFORMERS LIKE JOSEPH LEE and his Massachusetts Civic League had discovered some consecrated ideals for the playground movement. But what was actually happening on the playgrounds? Were they successfully transformed into training grounds for a genteel notion of elevated and purified American "community"? Or did they remain as they began in the 1870s—simply breathing spaces in the heart of the city's congestion? These are very difficult questions to answer, since the ultimate sources would be the children themselves, and they have left little record of their feelings about organized play. Nor did settlement workers conduct long-term studies comparing the lives of those who were touched by the mysterious qualities of a sand garden or a team game with those who were not.[65]

The playgrounds and the organized activities on them doubtless achieved a mixture of success and failure, but the measure depended on the perspective of the measurer. While the reformer hoped that playgrounds would sweep the streets clear, it is doubtful that the young immigrant held a similar wish. In the tightly knit ethnic enclaves, the playground was at best a supplement to street life, which the settlement workers realized was at the core of "life's amenities." In the North End or West End, the playground was a temporary substitute not a permanent replacement for the sights and sounds of street pianos and organ grinders, holiday processions, and vegetable carts. As one Boston reformer recognized in 1915, it was the "unbridled freedom" of the street that attracted children. Nor did the playgrounds eliminate street games. As Joseph Lee recognized in 1913, nine-tenths of the city's play was still done in the streets. But it was not just because there weren't enough playgrounds. Despite the dangers and disruptions of trolleys and, increasingly, automobiles, the streets could be exciting arenas in their own right, readily adaptable to games like hoop-rolling or stick ball. As North End "corner boys" told William Foote Whyte in the late 1930s, their intergang athletic contests were often nothing more than races around the block. By contrast, the playground was often the scene of "rallies" (fights).[66]

This was hardly what Joseph Lee and his contemporaries had in mind. Indeed, this was why they argued for *supervised* play. Even good supervision, however, could not help the "incorrigibles" who preferred to hang out on the corners or in their clubhouses. As a 1930s study, *Juvenile Probation,* had to conclude, the preferred recreations among Boston delinquents were in the "poor" category. The problem of delinquency was not a lack of facilities but a preference for "poor" recreations "when more desirable ones are available."[67] Similar disappointments awaited the opinion that team games could overcome ethnic or racial differences. If the Irish, Italians, and Jews played together on the playgrounds of the Massachusetts Civic League, they fought one another with equal vigor in gang fights or "rallies."[68]

Even if playgrounds and organized play failed to achieve all their intended goals, the *belief* in supervised play met with increasing acceptance. Saloon-fighters looked to the playgrounds to teach children "order, decency and fair play."[69] But the greatest influence was in the school system. Following the prodding of the Massachusetts Emergency and Hygiene Association and the mayor, Joseph Lee convinced the city and the state that the School Committee should have greater control of all public playgrounds. Lee's point, which found its way into state law, was that as professional supervisors teachers were obviously the most qualified at their job, whether in the classroom or on the playground.[70] Subsequent School Committee reports stressed the emphasis on discipline, which included having the students line up each day to receive instruction and salute the flag. At the same time, the Parks Department restricted the use of its playgrounds to adolescents during the "prime time" weekday afternoon and weekend hours. By 1913, the city had appointed a director of playground athletics who organized competition that culminated in a city-wide interplayground championship. The city hired physicians as medical examiners for the playgrounds. The parks commissioners were even prepared to fight the state's blue laws to ensure that their efforts might be sustained on the Sabbath.[71]

Playgrounds were obviously different things to different people; no one concept ever prevailed. But at their core, playgrounds always stood as evidence of an active and conscious attempt to shape and reshape the physical and social dimensions of community in the city. Throughout the late nineteenth and early twentieth centuries, the expansion of playgrounds was due to the insistence of neighborhood lobbies concerned with protecting their local environs from suffocation by urban development. This fact stands in partial opposition to the lament of some reformers that Boston suffered from a lack of "local attachments . . . concerted action for a better social life . . . watchfulness over common interests."[72] It remained for reformers with a broader perspective to determine how playgrounds might fit into an overall scheme of social order in Boston. The two visions did not always mesh. Their fusion or their conflict was determined by the peculiar conditions of life in the neighborhoods around the city.

6/Exercise & Sports for the Schools

GEORGE WRIGHT, captain of the Boston Red Stockings during the 1870s and later owner of Wright and Ditson sporting goods, was ever the promoter. Realizing the importance of cultivating a youthful demand for baseball, he inserted the following criticism in his 1874 tribute to the champion Red Stockings:

> Our school management—we are very sorry to say—has, in too many melancholy instances, exhibited the *mens sana in corpore sano* rule as a practical fallacy; but the time is close at hand, we hope, when it will be otherwise, and when a schoolboy expert at baseball will have his marks of merit regularly and properly assigned to him on that account.[1]

Wright could not understand why public school officials stressed the importance of gymnastics and military drill while treating sports and athletics with benign neglect.

We might find it hard to believe that sports have not always played the important role in the overall school program that they do today. But gymnastic drill had the eye of Boston's educational leaders until the turn of the century, and it was only a concern for abuses in student-run sports that led them to regulate and control activities like baseball, football, basketball, and track. Students had initially organized their own teams in order to ensure regular competition in baseball and football. By the 1880s they had begun to recognize the value of promoting an athletic team as a vehicle for building loyalty and attachment to their school community. In this regard, the early organizations were similar in function to the clubs and interest groups examined in Part Three. Three decades later, however, administrators took control of the athletic programs, and broadened their purpose. Sports would now remedy the disruptions of modern life by developing efficient workers and effective citizens, loyal to a wider community, including city, state, and nation. In the minds of school authorities, then, exercise and sports were quite related to the same goals as parks and playgrounds.

AS EARLY AS 1833, the Primary School Committee of Boston included daily class exercise among its rules and regulations, reminding all instructors that it was their duty "to attend to the physical comfort and education of the pupils under their care." To this end, fifteen minutes were set aside, "each part of the day," for use "in such a manner as each instructor shall judge best adapted to relieve weariness, strengthen the physical constitution, excite love of order, and associate with the school ideas of cheerfulness, as well as of improvement."[2] The concern for exercise was part of a larger desire to ensure that public schools provided an adequate bulwark for the impressionable bodies and souls of children exposed to the perils of the growing city.

In his study of Boston's school system, Stanley Schultz has demonstrated that by the 1840s, "educators and reformers in Boston and New England had come to agree that the social role of the public school was to assure social stability in a time of change." Reflecting an antiurban, pastoral bias, schoolhouses were to provide students a "community in miniature," with the proper ventilation and play space that already seemed to be fading from sight in the city.[3] As Horace Mann, secretary of the State Board of Education, sarcastically concluded, "to walk through the streets of a city, without striking or being struck, is an act for which one needs to be as limber as an eel, a rope-dancer or a party-politician."[4] From the beginning, then, organized exercise was but a tactic existing within an overall strategy of utilizing public education to confront and control the pejorative aspects of urban growth.

As urbanization continued, so too did the calls for gymnastic exercise in the schools. In his report for 1857, George Boutwell, a successor to Mann on the State Board of Education, reminded his readers that "a pernicious change will be wrought in the character of the Commonwealth" as more of the population gathered in cities and as "an increasing proportion of the people are employed in sedentary pursuits." Boutwell's solution was to provide more play areas and gymnastics programs in the schools. Recall that the late 1850s saw a general increase in the popularity of organized exercise—Dr. G. B. Winship and his promotion of heavy lifting; Dr. Dio Lewis and his "New Gymnastics"—and it is no surprise that the Boston School Committee rekindled the fires for fitness.[5]

In 1860, a City Council committee examining physical training in the public schools warned of the physical deterioration that had beset urban schoolchildren. Airtight houses, poor diets, and over-emphasis on mental life had all contributed to the ill health of young and old alike. The committee noted the current interest among adults in skating, riding, boating, ball playing, and gymnastics; their special concern of course was the child. To this end, they considered "the preservation of health and the cultivation of the physical faculties as the foundation of the whole edifice of education." They defined this "care and cultivation" of the body as *physical* education. In elevating the goals of physical education, they asserted that "its object is to favor as much as possible the development of the strength and activity of the body—in the first place for the sake of moral and intellectual culture and next for the labor to which man is destined."[6] To physical education the committee attributed great powers, including the ability to inculcate "courage, perseverance, self-control," and the power to "foster a disposition, and excite a desire to assist our fellow creatures in danger."[7] Superintendent of Schools John O. Philbrick joined the chorus the following year, distinguishing between the rural child, who enjoyed a "natural" form of physical training, and the city child, whose "eminently artificial" existence made systematic physical education a "prime necessity." Philbrick recommended the creation of a standing committee on physical training, the appointment of an instructor of gymnastics and calisthenics, and the adoption of a mandatory exercise period in all public schools, not just at the primary level.[8]

The School Committee was quite receptive to the idea, but wished to move with caution. Indeed, only acute urban disorder prompted the adoption of a comprehensive plan for physical training. Following the draft riots during July of 1863, a group of concerned citizens, including Edward Everett and Charles Loring, who were "interested in the preservation of public order, and the protection of property," suggested the formation of a quasi-military force of high-school students.[9] Physical education in the guise of military drill and gymnastics had great significance to Yankees yet unsure of victory over the Confederacy. In its annual report, the School Committee noted assuredly that "it is this preliminary training of the body, systematically and persistently followed up, to which, no doubt, the Duke of Wellington referred when he said it was Eton that gave him Waterloo."[10] Buoyed by this promise, the School Committee created a standing committee on "gymnastics and military drill," and hired an instructor to carry the program out. Though the program through the years was sporadic, the schoolboy regiment proved to be quite popular, and its drills on the Common always spurred public enthusiasm.[11]

During the next two decades physical training was sometimes under the aegis of a superintendent of "vocal and physical culture" who trained schoolteachers in the rudiments of exercise instruction. But the city had no regular, systematic program of physical education, and it is doubtful that the earlier regulations were strictly enforced. The year 1889 brought great changes, however. Mrs. Mary Hemenway, whose son Augustus had donated $115,000 for a gymnasium at Harvard, opened the Boston Normal School of Gymnastics in order to train instructors in the Ling or "Swedish" system of exercise. She was also instrumental in staging a major conference on physical training, held at M.I.T. in November. The U.S. Commissioner of Education presided over the sessions, which featured presentations of the various "systems" of gymnastics, including the Swedish and German "light" exercises, and the more strenuous regimen of Harvard's Dudley A. Sargent.[12]

The members of the Boston School Committee were among the audience. Based on the conference presentations and the urging of Mrs. Hemenway, the School Committee announced the following year that the Ling or Swedish gymnastics would be introduced in all the city's public schools, and that a director of physical training and four assistants would be hired to implement the program. Mrs. Hemenway's Normal School provided a continuous flow of qualified instructors, as Boston finally settled on a regular system of exercise for school students.[13]

Physical education or physical training was recognized early in the nineteenth century as an urgent necessity in the urban school curriculum. Regular exercise would provide both reinforcement and release from the mental stress within and without the classroom; many educators believed that physical education would go beyond this, by nurturing a sense of order and discipline. Thus, physical training was incorporated as a compulsory part of the daily experience of Boston's schoolchildren. We should not be surprised that sports and athletics did not figure prominently in the antebellum discussions; after all, few team sports were organized at any level before the 1850s. But why was there such a disregard of sports during the debates over exercise "systems" during the 1880s?

Actually, there had been some recognition of "athletic sports," doubtless because of the increasing popularity of college teams in football, baseball, and, more important, rowing. In fact, Baron Pierre de Coubertin, the man who would found the modern Olympic Games, addressing the 1889 Boston Conference, steadfastly asserted that dumbbells, vaulting horses, and light exercises not withstanding, no "system" stood higher than the "English athletic sport system." Of course he meant interschool competition in baseball, football, and the like. Coubertin was politely applauded, and school authorities did recognize the "character-building" values of athletics. Despite this, they preferred to encourage and compel students to participate in gymnastics, which they believed would result in a more "uniform and harmonious development of the entire frame." Besides, gymnastics were cheaper, less time consuming, and lent themselves more readily to the structured, class-based systems necessary in the school curriculum. Thus, students were left to their own athletic devices.[14]

FROM THE BEGINNING, it was football, baseball, and track that captured the enthusiasm of students, not drills with Indian clubs. As an editorial in the student magazine at Boston Latin School concluded, "Surely a baseball game or a tennis match is far more interesting both to participants and spectators, than the efforts of a gymnast to jump half an inch higher than his opponent." Gymnastics were tolerated by these athletic promoters only as a supplement to outdoor sports.[15]

Even before the Civil War, schoolboys had competed against each other on their acknowledged playground, the Common. One old-timer recalled, "No policeman or signboard in those days told us to 'keep off the grass' . . . and those who were annoyed by our games were expected to keep away." [16] In the fall of 1862, one group of boys, principally from the Dixwell Private Latin School, formed the Oneida Football Club, the first organized football club in the United States. Led by "Gat" Miller and R. Clifford Watson, who frequently labored long into the night planning new formations and strategies, the lineup was dotted with the names of Boston's most prominent families, including a Bowditch, a Forbes, a Wolcott, a Lawrence, and a Peabody. Inspired by Miller's motto, "Defeat with Honor Is Better than Victory with Dishonor," the Oneidas were ever honorable and ever victorious. Their goal line on the Common field was never crossed, as they defeated teams from Latin, English, and Dorchester high schools. The Oneida Club lasted only three years, but informal clubs from public and private secondary schools continued to compete in football and baseball. Doubtless they were emulating the activities of the men at Harvard, for which many of them were "preparing." Their early competition was not rigidly structured or scheduled, but organized leagues of school teams were not long in coming. [17]

In June of 1888, students from Boston Latin, Roxbury Latin, Cambridge High and Latin School, and several smaller preparatory schools formed the Interscholastic Football Association. English High School joined the association the following year. Harvard students acted as team advisors and also donated a "valuable cup," to be awarded to the championship team. In order to ensure the availability of playing space for their regularly scheduled games, the association successfully petitioned the parks commissioners to reserve a spot on Franklin Park "for schoolboys only." [18] Within several years, the association had developed a written constitution and had sired an offspring, the Junior Interscholastic Football Association, which included Dorchester High, Cambridge Manual Training School, Newton High, and several private schools. [19]

Football had set the stage, but other sports were quickly organized into league competition. Within two decades, baseball, track, basketball, and ice hockey leagues operated among the city's secondary schools. The enthusiasm quickly spread to the suburban areas, affording successful teams the opportunity to compete for and lay claim to Greater Boston and even New England supremacy. In 1911, more than a hundred thousand people watched the area schoolboys compete in Thanksgiving football. It is worth repeating that these initial leagues were organized by the *students*

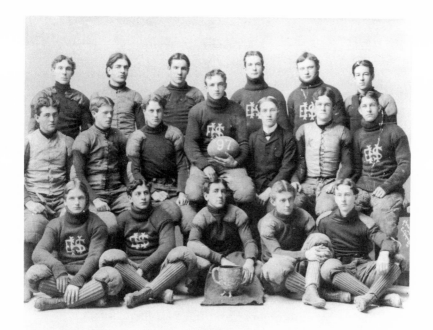

English High School Defenders of the Interscholastic Football Association's Challenge Cup, 1897

Courtesy of Boston English High School

themselves, with encouragement and assistance from collegians who were probably school alumni. Like their college counterparts, their efforts were largely ignored by the faculty and administration, at least for the time being.[20]

The growth of organized leagues and the popularity among both participants and spectators were symptoms of the great value that students placed on sport. Indeed, students were quick to develop a "team" concept which involved the entire school community in the athletic program. Unfortunately, their enthusiasm fueled the excessive demand for victories and championships, which in turn corrupted the original values of their sports. It was only at this point that grownups stepped in.

The editors of the Boston Latin School *Register* quickly saw the importance of sport to the growth of school unity:

> The feeling of school unity or school loyalty, so strikingly exhibited
> in college life, should be developed in the preparatory schools.
> Especially is it valued in the latter, since most men, on graduating,

break off into business life. . . . Athletics more than anything else, can foster this spirit of unity; for on the campus all class distinctions are done away with, the men gather about actuated by a common motive, cheer with a common impulse, and develop a better and more generous fellowship.[21]

These schoolboys were animated by the school-wide spirit they saw evident at Harvard when its nines or elevens matched brawn with teams from Yale or Princeton. Even at the colleges, "school spirit" was a relatively recent phenomenon, born along with intercollegiate athletics at mid-century. Prior to this, emphasis had revolved around class spirit, nurtured by the hardships of hazing and "class scraps," such as had occurred annually on the Cambridge Delta, when Harvard's sophomores and freshmen squared off in a raucous, shin-splintering version of mass football. But with the advent of intercollegiate competition, school spirit quickly overshadowed class spirit. Schoolboys were fast to follow suit.[22]

These students were, in effect, promoting athletic teams as the catalyst for a form of community, a bond that would quickly cement batches of newcomers with upperclassmen and alumni. This could be particularly important for the Latin School or English High, whose students were likely to come from several different sections of the city. But athletics could be equally effective in a new neighborhood high school, like that in South Boston.

South Boston High School had opened its doors only in 1901, yet the athletic virus hit the school immediately. No wonder; for while there were hundreds of years of tradition and glory separating her from the Latin School or English High, a few victories on the football field would provide equal glory for "Old Southie." Athletics could make the difference between the successful school and its "sleepy" counterparts, as the school newspaper readily understood:

There are not many schools, happily, that do not have athletics. Those that do are always superior to those that do not; to a great many this seems strange; they think that so small a matter can not make any great difference. If they compare the two, however, they will see that a school that does not have athletics is always made up of slow, sleepy students. Why? Simply because athletics are the means of quickening the senses. To be a successful athlete, one must be able to see, think, and act quickly and intelligently, and above all, to be able to concentrate the mind on the subject.[23]

The *Chandelier*'s editors stressed the ethical values of athletics, the strict discipline, unquestioning obedience, and control of temper, which all served to transform the individual schoolboy into a "loyal and valued member of the organization."[24]

All students were encouraged to join the school athletic associations, which sprang into existence to provide spiritual and, more important, financial assistance to the school's varsity athletes. To some degree, the competition among schools to organize bigger and better athletic associations rivaled the struggles on the field. Individual students paid only a small annual fee (fifty cents to a dollar) to join the athletic association, so it was necessary to enlist as many members as possible.[25] While advocates often chided their mates on the need to further the cause, it sometimes became clear that athletics provided the *only* basis for school spirit.

The concept of school unity was quickly linked to the quest for victory. Students were encouraged by their peers to turn out and cheer the team to victory. One of the reasons for organizing a school's contingent of spectators was to assure the tactical advantage of ordered, timely cheering. The cheerleader had not yet been relegated to a glamor–only role, but was rather an important instrument of victory through unity. The fields echoed with school cheers:

Hurrah, hurrah, we'll be the champion yet,
Hurrah, hurrah, for all the boys who sweat,
For we're the boys from the English High
And we'll get there, just you bet,
Rah, rah, rah, boys for High School.[26]
[sung to chorus of "Marching through Georgia"]

The quest for victory through unity, however, led to abuses. And it was only these abuses that moved school authorities to take an interest in athletics.

By the turn of the century, interscholastic sports had become a fixture. The daily newspapers carried not only regular coverage of the competition, but also feature articles on the prominent schoolboy stars and the prospects of each team for the upcoming season.[27] Student editors pressured their peers with continual appeals; the *English High School Record* called for support of all athletic teams because "such support will be the means of furthering the fame of our school; insofar as it will further one institution of it, athletics."[28] Woe to the laggard who did not do his part:

> There are a number of big fellows in the school who refuse to go
> out for the team. What is the matter with them? Do they lack school
> spirit or are they afraid of spoiling their good looks? A first class
> eleven could be turned out of the school if these fellows would only
> show up with a determination to make the team and not quit when
> their nose bleeds or they are scratched.[29]

This was the tyranny of school unity. It had once been fun to play
football with classmates and friends. Then with the growth of
organized leagues it became an honor to seek glory for the school.
Finally, however, it became an obligation, at least for all those who
looked strong and able.

If a team could not find enough players from its own school, it
often looked elsewhere, to another school or to a big husky boy
with no academic inclination. The "tramp" athlete was a sore in
schoolboy sports, a source of irritation and criticism among schools.
Upon their inception, the Interscholastic Football Association and
the Interscholastic Athletic Association drafted eligibility rules that
limited a player's age and years of competition, and demanded
that he be a bona fide student at the school he represented. But
the rules were not totally effective. The South Boston High School
Chandelier printed a homiletic short story about a heroic football
captain who resisted the temptation to use "ringers" against an
arch-rival which had armed itself with two stars from "Audley
Academy." The hero beat the villains, but the moral fell on deaf
ears. A year later, the paper admitted the use of tramp athletes as
a matter of course.[30]

Athletic stars became the demigods of school corridors, as this
poem witnesses:

> E'er his brief life he'd kicked away,
> E'er he had changed to worthless clay,
> He had played many a well fought game,
> He had been tired, sore and lame,
> But death one day to claim him came,
> And everlasting is his fame.
> Put tombstones at his head and feet,
> And on them grave these few words, meet:
> "Freely his young life did he offer up,
> For the school's glory and the silver cup."[31]

Though not quite a cavalier attitude toward another's death, the
poem suggests the ease with which abuses could overwhelm a

philosophy that exalted victory as the sine qua non of athletic performance.

ADULT EDUCATORS had quite early been concerned about the rapid growth and spread of athleticism in the schools and colleges. In the 1897 report of the United States commissioner of education, Edward Mussey Hartwell lamented that the meteoric rise of school sports had left most adults unqualified in either experience or insight to serve capably as advisors to young athletes:

> Hence our athletes have been left in the main to their own crude and boyish devices, which tend, when unchecked, toward extravagance and professionalism. The powerlessness of our educational leaders to originate, and their failure to adopt effectual measures for evolving order out of the athletic and gymnastic chaos over which they nominally preside, constitutes one of the marvels of our time.[32]

Earlier in the decade, Hartwell had served as director of physical training for Boston's public schools; he had witnessed firsthand the growth and chaos at which he marveled.

Even critics of school athletics, however, recognized the positive values of team competition. As we have seen in the arguments of urban reformers and playground advocates, this was a social form of the old "muscular Christianity" of Edward Everett Hale and Thomas Wentworth Higginson. Emphasis and benefits now focused on the group. The lessons of sport went beyond individual health and endurance to include "the spirit of working together earnestly, enthusiastically, and intelligently for a given end, which is the spirit of our democracy," and "the desire of working for one's institution with one's whole mind and heart and strength, which in the world outside we call Patriotism." At the theoretical level, then, students and adults agreed on the social values of sport.[33]

But the question remained: What to do about the obvious problems? And of problems there were many, as Dr. Dudley Sargent, director of Harvard's Hemenway Gymnasium, pointed out to the Massachusetts School Superintendents' Association at its meeting in 1900. Sargent's opinions carried great weight; he had been at Harvard since 1879, and had concurrently directed both the Sargent Normal School of Physical Education and the Harvard Summer School. A prolific author and organizer, widely recognized in physical education and health circles, Sargent had also devised the gymnastics and training program at the Charlesbank Gymnasium.[34]

Sargent, too, acknowledged the benefits of school athletics. They provided "a subject of immediate interest to discuss, rally around and enthuse over." They afforded a release of surplus energy in many young boys; they promoted and measured an individual's success on the basis of deeds, not promises. But Sargent stressed that these benefits could exist within a program of intramural games. On the other hand, only danger lurked for the interscholastic program. The desire to win led to excess training that could strain the developing heart and frame. Excess adulation could make the athletic star less likely to concentrate on academics. Coaches, fans, and players were ever tempted to sully sportsmanship and honor for the sake of victory. To Sargent, however, the answer lay not in abolishing interscholastic sports. "Will our secondary school authorities have the good sense," he asked, "to realize that athletics cannot be eliminated from school life, and unite with others in trying to check the abuses and direct the use of this important adjunct in education?"[35] This was Sargent's challenge; it did not go unheeded. Strengthened by over a half-century of growing control over health and fitness, the Boston School Department needed only a little prodding before it quickly absorbed the students' games.

In 1903, the director of physical training, James B. Fitzgerald, reported to the superintendent what Sargent and others had long been warning; that high school athletics were in a "generally unsatisfactory condition." Although Fitzgerald had already instituted mandatory physical examinations for all competitors, he urged that the various headmasters organize to create their own code of regulations controlling, among other things, physical, mental, and moral requirements for competition, all other questions of eligibility, financial considerations, the selection of competent officials, and the proper policing of grounds. The School Committee responded by ordering its committee on high schools to consider the formulation of just such a code.[36]

For the next two years, pressure for adult regulation increased. The superintendent of schools reported that star players who had been disqualified for grievous fouls committed in previous games were, "by agreement," allowed to play in order to "swell" the gate.

He told of headmasters and school officials barely able to hold fast under the lobbying of students and parents who demanded they cover up the ineligibility of certain players, or allow disqualified players to return to action immediately.[37] He reported that athletic activities, "modelled after those of the colleges," had become "factors of such magnitude in most of the high schools as to interfere seriously with the regular work." The influence which star athletes exerted among their schoolmates was "vastly out of proportion to their real merit." Although encouraged that the headmasters had enacted a set of rules, the superintendent urged that the state legislature authorize the School Committee to draw athletics into their custody.[38]

From this point things moved quickly, with little or no opposition. In 1906, the General Court invested the School Committee with the right to "supervise and control all athletic organizations composed of pupils of the public schools and bearing the name of the school." Further, the School Committee could "directly or through an authorized representative determine under what conditions such organizations may enter into competition."[39] In 1907, the School Committee appropriated twenty-five thousand dollars for its expanded program of physical training, and in a significant step, directed that all high school athletic coaches be appointed only by the School Committee, from the city's list of certified instructors. Previously coaches had been hired and paid by the student associations. By 1911, the director of physical training had become the director of physical training and athletics, with three assistants. Further, the School Committee had begun to regulate all revenues and expenses for schoolboy athletics. Students were no longer controlling the management of their own contests.[40]

Was this a coup d'état? A plot? Part of a master plan by school administrators which, as one recent article suggests, included school athletics in a program that would "relieve the monotony and tedium of work in an industrial society, end social unrest and crime, provide worthy use of leisure time and build a corporate bureaucracy"?[41] In short, did the School Committee embrace the games of high school students in order to transform them into a vehicle of social control?

In Boston, at least, this was not quite the case. School authorities were hesitant to become involved in the regulation of schoolboy athletics. Only after continued prodding and complaining (sometimes by the students themselves) of the growing evidence of abuses and cheating did the administration enact reform and regulation from above. To be sure, the chance to nurture such values as patience, obedience, self-control, loyalty to leaders, cooperation, and teamwork must have been appealing; and all were stressed to the School Committee by the likes of Dudley Sargent and Joseph Lee.[42] But one must recall that the students championed these same notions when they promoted sports among their schoolmates. Moreover, the athletic teams gained invaluably from a more equitable administration of eligibility rules, centralized officiating appointments, better medical supervision, and a more stable financial structure.[43]

Schoolboy sports were not co-opted by the bureaucracy as part of a grand plan of education for social control. Rather, the philosophy underlying the educational value of athletics was broadened only after school authorities made the choice to assimilate, not abolish, athletics. Two ingredients made this ideological adjustment both possible and necessary. One was the existence of a growing profession—physical education—which was expanding its own horizons to include sports and games with gymnastics. The other was a gradual shift in educational philosophy. Where antebellum educators had sought to preserve an earlier social and moral order, their twentieth-century counterparts tended to accept the new industrial order; they concentrated rather on preparing their charges to fit neatly into productive roles.

By the turn of the century, professional physical education organizations (like the American Association for the Advancement of Physical Education) and individual schools of professional training (like the YMCA Training School in Springfield, Massachusetts, and the Boston Normal School of Gymnastics) had begun to prepare instructors to direct sports and games as well as gymnastics. Naturally, it was not long before physical educators considered themselves best suited to convey to students the character-building values of sport.[44] This trend paralleled that of the larger education bureaucracy. Stanley Schultz discerned this sense of "professional" prerogative among Boston's school administrators even before the Civil War. The professional educator claimed to have indispensable knowledge that was critical for the well-being of the community. "He also demanded a degree of authority," said Schultz, "for if his knowledge was vital to the community, it was necessary that he possess control over the application of his skills."[45] The director of physical training and athletics had realized expanded control in 1906–7, with the addition of three assistants and as many instructors as he deemed necessary. By 1910, the physical educator's specialized knowledge included athletics, as sports and games were incorporated as mandatory elements into the physical education curriculum of boys and girls.[46]

At the same time, the visions of education's broad role in society had changed. No longer secure in the hope of using schools to preserve the social and moral characteristics they felt existed in an earlier period, educators gradually accepted the notion that schools should convey to students the specific skills, behavior, and values necessary to a productive life in the new industrial order. Physical educators could count on reformers and philosophers to support their contributions to these goals of education. In this respect, the lessons of teamwork, self-sacrifice, and discipline were seen to be transferable from the playing field to the business world or the factory. The philosophy was virtually identical to that of playground leaders; the target was an older age group, one on the verge of entering the work force.[47]

But there were even loftier goals for athletics. In 1907, Josiah Royce delivered the quarter-centennial address at the Sargent Normal School. Royce, professor of philosophy at Harvard, believed that "loyalty" and "loyalty to loyalty" were the foundations upon which society must be based. He encouraged the teachers in attendance to believe that their work helped cement the masonry of the "Great Community." If a man was but loyal to the loyalty he had seen expressed "on the playground, the gymnasium, and the athletic field," said Royce, he ought to be able to sustain the "loyalty to unseen loyalty" which stood at the core of American business and at the "heart of honor in our national and international enterprises." Ultimately, Royce reminded the teachers, "you are all working to combine in your pupils, skill, devotion, loyalty of the individual to his community. . . . Whenever you have an opportunity to insist upon fair play in difficult situations, you are teaching loyalty to loyalty."[48] The lessons learned in free time on the supervised playground were now a compulsory part of structured education. The "team" was no longer simply the baseball nine or the football eleven, it was the wider community—city, state, or nation.

Never before—or perhaps since—were the goals of physical education so openly embraced by educational reforms. Social activists like Jacob Riis maintained that, through the benefits of athletics, the young man who emerged from the school "does not drop the interest aroused there in manly pursuits for kicking his heels in front of the corner saloons. . . . He has acquired certain principles that help keep him on an even keel." His colleague Luther Gulick, who helped found the New York Public Schools Athletic League, believed the same spirit of loyalty and morality extended to all students, not just the actual competitors. That wholesome sport would encourage the virtues upon which to build city, state, and country, Riis had no more doubt than he had "that the sun will rise tomorrow."[49]

The lessons learned on the athletic field fit well into the prevailing belief that public education must provide the moral, social, and vocational talents, which in less turbulent times the family and church had helped instill. By the same token, physical educators were quick to realize the importance of drawing sports and athletics under their aegis. As Boston's director of physical training and athletics reminded his teachers, they now had "exceptional opportunities for instilling into the minds and the habits of pupils, who come to them for physical exercises, lessons of personal hygiene, self-restraint and moral righteousness."[50]

BOTH THE STUDENTS and the central school authorities had embraced sports teams as an epoxy with which to bond fragments into wholes. Both groups realized that the process must involve all students, whether they played or not. But there were important differences in the two visions. The students saw interscholastic sports as a vehicle only for school unity and pride. In their view, the team and its supporters would be but an extension of the family or the neighborhood, wherein everyone contributed, albeit in different ways, to a common but localized goal. As the Latin School *Register* reminded its readers, the teams needed assistance in three ways: large numbers for squad tryouts, financial assistance, and massed, organized cheering at games. No one was absolved from helping in one way or another. "Be Patriotic," urged the South Boston *Chandelier*. "Keep up the standard. It is only by support of the school boys and girls that we can succeed."[51]

When the students could not control the abuses that school spirit bred, administrators took command. At the same time, however, they broadened the promise of sports. Both on and off the field, the disciplined and unified effort required to produce a winner would help train students for assuming roles *outside* their family, neighborhood, or school networks. As Luther Gulick and Josiah Royce expressed it, the loyalty, social morality, and social conscience that school sports developed were *transferable*. What is more, they were the very qualities upon which rested the greatness of America's cities and corporations, and the nation's indomitable progress. In 1895 a City Council committee requested a nine-hundred-dollar appropriation for an interscholastic trophy, in the hope that competition in athletics and academics might foster civic unity and municipal responsibility by creating bonds of interest among the schools. Seen in this light, school sports were in the same tradition as public parks and playgrounds, since each represented an attempt to control the city's physical, social, or moral environment and thus help integrate individuals into a changing order.[52]

As with the parks and playgrounds, however, one suspects that the grand vision was never quite realized. Schoolboy teams cemented the schools and neighborhoods they represented. But by the turn of the century, Boston had a dozen secondary schools in her fold; their schedules emphasized *intra*city competition. Boston was not a one high school town, like Muncie, Indiana, where a classic sociological study in the 1920s found the "Bearcat" basketball team to be a principal source of civic unity.[53] In Boston, the Thanksgiving gridiron clashes turned Eastie against Southie and Latin against English, sometimes with a vengeance. City-wide spirit developed through sports only when a team or an individual competed as *Boston's* representative against an external challenger. As we shall see, this occurred with regularity only at the professional and top amateur levels.

Students were able to nurture a community bond. Unlike their elders on the school board, however, they were not interested in confronting the urban conditions that surrounded them. Rather, they sought only to establish the ties of association and identity that the city's reality presented to them. In this respect, the school and neighborhood spirit that interscholastic sports could foster represented what we have called a *receptive* mode of community formation. The chapters that follow trace a similar pattern in the history of Boston's sports clubs, bicycle booms, and athletic heroes.

Part Three

NEW FORMS OF COMMUNITY

7/ *The Fellowship of the Sporting Club*

THE NEW STADIUM, financed by a wealthy Alexandrian, teemed with spectators and patriotic excitement as the first modern Olympics began in Athens during the spring of 1896. Following the program developed milleniums before, when heroes and demigods competed on the sacred plains of Elis, the first event was the dash, now measured at one hundred yards. Two Americans burst from the starting line and led the field all the way—American domination of the modern Olympics had begun. But the Greek spectators were more baffled, and amused, at the victory cry bellowed by a group of the athletes:

> BAA rah rah rah
> BAA rah rah rah
> Boston! Boston! Boston!

"It is the yell of the wild Indians!" the crowd reacted.[1]

Not so—it was the cry of the Boston Athletic Association, whose athletes comprised a major component of the American contingent to this first modern quadrennial athletic spectacle. Fellow Americans would not have wondered at the importance of the private club to these athletes. A decade earlier one observer had noted: "Athletic clubs are now springing into existence in the United States in such profusion as to baffle the effort to enumerate them." Scarcely a city could be found, he said, that had over thirty thousand people and not at least one athletic club. "In the large cities, there are from five to twenty-five; sometimes even more."[2] Boston was representative of this trend. In Boston, as elsewhere, the sporting club was very much a product of the urban environment. Clubs, or voluntary associations, depend for their existence upon a sizable population base, adequate communication among members, reasonable accessibility (in travel time), and steady financial support. The city was the richest source for all these necessities.[3]

Voluntary associations have long been a source of interest to observers and analysts of American culture. The sagacious antebellum visitor, Alexis de Tocqueville observed, "Americans of all ages, all stations in life and all types of dispositions are forever forming associations." Not just commercial or industrial associations, he went on, "but others of a thousand different types." They were formed for any reason: to establish institutions, to promote causes, to proclaim truths, or to "propagate some feelings by the encouragement of a great example." Since then, other scholars have credited clubs with a variety of attributes, including the ability, at various times, to socialize members into modern roles, to provide avenues of upward mobility, to establish cultural and social networks for dominant groups, and to sort groups by social class, ethnicity, or political persuasion. Typically, the club's role has loomed larger in urban areas.[4]

Had Tocqueville written his account after the Civil War, he no doubt would have included sporting clubs as a glaring example of the American penchant for associations. Indeed, in large part the growth of American sport in the second half of the nineteenth century lay in the growth of private sporting associations, from clubs to leagues to national governing bodies like the Amateur Athletic Union. Private clubs were necessary for the promotion of sport. As we have seen, city government was slow to sponsor these activities. Public parks and playgrounds won support as issues of space; little municipal planning was directed at the activities within them until much later. Schoolboys sensed this and organized their own clubs. Their elders were no different. Like-minded sportsmen banded together to lease or purchase playing space, to erect clubhouses and storage facilities, and to purchase equipment for group use. The size and scope of these endeavors varied from club to club, but in any case, collective action was a financial necessity in an environment wherein open space was diminishing while property values were surging. Beyond this, clubs ensured the regularity and reliability of teams, the focus of most competition. Finally, it was typically the organized clubs that championed the cause of outdoor sports to the sometimes reluctant parks commissioners.[5]

Sporting clubs did more than promote athletic activities. They served less obvious but equally important social functions for their members. One recent historian argues that these voluntary associations represented the quest by Americans for a new form of community, elicited by the decline of "earlier communities based on small geographic areas—typically agricultural villages." In sports clubs, he adds, men might "counter the impersonality of the burgeoning cities."[6] Along similar lines, a study of early amateur baseball clubs in Chicago suggests that their popularity lay in their ability to promote a sense of "healthfulness" and "gentlemanly virtue" among their young middle-class patrons.[7] These were men "on the make," and baseball clubs were training grounds for their roles as future leaders.

Boston enjoyed a similar experience with her sporting clubs, some of which began even before the Civil War. These voluntary associations played an obvious and important function in promoting a wide variety of activities, from yachting to cricket. Long before philosophers or politicians fully articulated the values inherent in gentlemanly, sporting competition, there existed clusters of individuals who joined together to pursue baseball, football, tennis, or gymnastics simply because they were immensely enjoyable pastimes. But sport demands more than players; so the clubs addressed the need for equipment, rules, playing space (remember the Red Ballers), regular game schedules, and competent officiating. In this way, they clearly contributed to the rise of organized sport.

One must not, however, overlook the latent functions that the sporting clubs served. Whether located in a "three-decker" in Charlestown, in a lavishly paneled brick house in the Back Bay, or in a converted farmhouse in the suburbs, the club and its activities offered a source of group identity and solidarity to collections of sportsmen determined by locality, ethnicity, race, sex, and social class. Sport helped to define the expected roles for these groups; it was a cohesive force. Moreover, the association and its activities helped countless individuals, at various positions on the social ladder, respond to the forces of disruption and change so intensely at work in the city.

THE MOST OBVIOUS SOURCE of organization lay in devotion to a particular sport. We can't fully explain why people chose crew over cricket or bicycling over baseball, but regardless of one's athletic persuasion, it was not difficult to find a club existing for that purpose (membership might be a different matter!). So many sporting clubs existed in Boston that it would be an endless task to enumerate them all. Indeed, many undoubtedly lived and died without leaving so much as a trace in the historical record. Nonetheless, a brief look at some representative organizations is instructive.

Yachting and rowing clubs claim the earliest ancestry in Boston, quite fitting for a seaport whose maritime history brought prominence equal to that of her politics and literature. New as a leisure pursuit of merchants, yachting turned to club form in 1834, when a group of young men of maritime business and inclination formed a short-lived group under the leadership of their "commodore," Robert Bennet Forbes, famous in the China trade and possessed of "the most original brain, and the most attractive personality of any Boston merchant of his generation." A year later, many of the same associates, again under Forbes's leadership, reorganized around the purchase of a thirty-ton schooner, the *Dream*. This early venture fizzled during the economic panic that began two years later, and a thirty-year hiatus intruded before the founding of the next yacht club.[8]

The sport continued to grow in popularity, however, through informal races off coasts from Marblehead to Woods Hole. The first regatta off Nahant, in 1845, helped ensure that peninsula's popularity as a summer resort. By 1866, a younger generation of wealthy sailors organized the Boston Yacht Club. Two years later the South Boston Yacht Club opened its doors, followed closely by the Eastern and the Dorchester (later Massachusetts) yacht clubs in 1870. These pioneers were joined in the years to follow by a host of others, like the Mosquito Fleet, Savin Hill, and Atlantic clubs, founded as the upper-middle classes invested income and leisure in sail and halyard.[9]

Rowing has a long history on Boston's harbor and on her bays, so much of which have yielded to landfill and housing. Harvard boys and longshoremen's sons alike learned early the secrets of releasing and feathering an oar, as they pulled on the Charles River, South Bay, or the Mill Pond. In 1851, Daniel Webster Rogers and eleven other gentlemen purchased a boat and formed the Union Boat Club. Located at Braman's Bath House on the corner of Chester and Brimmer streets, the club had "no object other than that of making passible oarsmen and the enjoyment of rowing excursions." A hardy lot, the members began their excursions on Fridays at 5:00 A.M.! Twenty years later, the Union Boat Club's membership had swelled to 150, and in the meantime, rowing had become the most popular sport in Boston. The city regattas, which had begun on July 4, 1854, provided exciting challenge matches between Irish longshoremen, such as the Fort Hill Boys, and Brahmin "Beacon Street swells" like the Hurons or the Volants. The Irish-crewed *Maid of Erin* swept to many a victory in these years, but the older stock was by no means outdone. By 1855, the amateur rowers had joined to form the Charles River Amateur Boat Club Association, complete with its own regatta. New clubs continued to form after the Civil War: the Avenue, Chester, Dolphin, Enterprise, Lafayette, Shawmut, West End— many are long since forgotten. Through the years, however, clubs have made rowing an integral part of Boston's sporting heritage. Its popularity continues to this day, as witnessed by the throngs of rowers and spectators who take part in the annual fall classic, the Head of the Charles Regatta.[10]

Political revolutions aside, Anglophilia has long been a mainstay in Boston's cultural life, and so it is not surprising to find cricket in the city's sporting annals. A Boston Cricket Club existed as early as 1809, although it was short-lived. By the 1850s, cricket enjoyed a small flourish with the organization of several clubs, including the Bay States, the Star and Thistle, the Young Bostons, and the Mount Vernons. In 1857, the Star and Thistle was transformed into the Boston Cricket Club, which grew in size to nearly two hundred members. This club continued strong through the century, and continually badgered the parks commissioners for increased playing space and special privileges. In 1877, the Boston club gave birth to an offspring, the Longwood Cricket Club, which had immense success in the years that followed. The Longwood Club enjoyed the services of George Wright, who returned to his native game after his retirement from baseball. As a British-American, Wright was not alone in the local cricket clubs. The enthusiasm in Boston, at Harvard, and in other New England cities was clearly fueled both by immigrants from the British Empire and by natives who emulated the British sporting ideal, of which cricket was a prime example.[11]

Cricket could not match the popularity of baseball, however, as

Americans flocked to play or watch their national pastime. For one thing, cricket was too slow a game. As James D'Wolf Lovett, Boston's early sport historian, observed, an office boy could occasionally take a few hours off for baseball by fabricating the funeral of a relative—but the excuse was no good for a cricket match, which normally ran two days!

The Boston Olympics were organized in 1854 as the city's first baseball club. Followed closely by the Elm Trees (1855) and the Green Mountains (1857), these clubs played the "Massachusetts game," which featured a rectangular arrangement of bases, the batting box being located halfway between first and home. The Tri-Mountains, formed in 1857, were the first to champion the "New York game," a diamond version and forerunner of the modern game. By the 1860s, the New York game reigned supreme in Boston, although as late as the 1880s one finds exhibitions of the "old Massachusetts round ball." Amateur clubs continued to form in the decades after the Civil War, with more than twenty appearing on Hallock's club list of 1878. As we shall see, the enthusiasm for baseball was not confined to white-collar clerks. Boston's working class also organized baseball clubs. Indeed, it was the wide representation in amateur baseball, as much as the success of professional teams, that nurtured the game's popularity in Boston.[12]

A number of other sporting crazes hit the country during the last three decades of the nineteenth century, and representative clubs were always formed in the Hub. In 1878, as the bicycle was first attracting patrons, fourteen men formed the Boston Bicycle Club, the nation's first. Located six flights up a Devonshire Street building (those who eschewed use of the elevator were known to be the best hill-riders!), the club toasted itself in rare Latin form:

Bibamus ad primum Bicyclicum Club;
In urbe eorum cui nomen est Hub;
Et floreant, valeant, volitant tam,
Non Peircius ipse enumeret quam.

As we shall see in the next chapter, the 1880s and 1890s saw the emergence of dozens of bicycle clubs throughout the city.[13]

Track and field athletic clubs emerged during the 1870s. Doubtless their organization was due in part to the current interest in college athletics and professional "pedestrianism." The college

Boston Bicycle Club—1878

boys had begun their races as mere appendages to the annual intercollegiate regatta on Lake Saratoga. In 1873, James Gordon Bennett had offered a cup for the winner of a two-mile run. The following year there were five events; by 1876 the collegians had formed their own organization, the Intercollegiate Association of Amateur Athletes of America, which to this day conducts championships in cross-country, indoor, and outdoor track and field.[14]

Pedestrianism, however, held the audience during the 1870s. These long-distance affairs, usually "go as you please," walk or run, had enjoyed sporadic popularity back to the 1830s. Boston herself had been the starting place for the famous walk by Edward Payson Weston, who left the State House steps on February 22, 1861, with the goal of reaching Washington in time for Lincoln's inauguration on March 4. Weston was paying off an election wager; he had bet on Breckinridge to win the presidency. Weston was thereafter a popular athlete in Boston (he arrived in Washington in time for the inaugural ball), but there were other standout performers. In the summer of 1875 Hugh Donahue of Springfield completed 1100 miles in 1100 hours at Mystic Park, although he needed rifle volleys and the Lynn Temperance Drum Corps to keep him awake! Running and walking contests expanded in the next few years under the sponsorship of individual promoters and new organizations like the Boston Athletic Club, which held its first indoor games in December of 1879 with a program that included a seventy-five-yard dash, quarter-, half-, and one-mile runs, and the shot put. The Boston Athletic Association, formed in 1887, was essentially an effort to pool the interests and finances of these smaller clubs so that Boston might have a building to rival that of the New York Athletic Club.[15]

Other sports had clubs as well. Racing adherents formed driving clubs and trotting associations throughout the second half of the century and raced their trotters at the South End Driving Park, at the Riverside Riding Park (later Beacon Park) in Allston, and at the Readville Race Course.[16] By the turn of the century, golf, tennis, lacrosse, and curling were all represented in newspaper coverage, in the city's "official" club lists, and in the city directory.[17]

Clubs were crucial to the development of all these sports. But it was not just for the obvious (albeit important) reasons, like collective finances for purchasing or leasing facilities, equipment, and playing space, or the establishment of playing rules and competitive leagues. The early clubs also provided critical psychological support to their members; the fellowship among members could bolster the spirit of individuals who might otherwise hesitate to partake in "oddball" activities. When the Boston Yacht Club petitioned the General Court for a charter in 1866, they were initially refused on the grounds that a yacht club "might lead to immoral and ungentlemanly conduct and be prejudicial to the public good." Think of how "deviant" the first baseball clubs must have seemed; after all, baseball grew out of "rounders," which was essentially a child's game. Consider the wheelman of the 1880s, high atop the front wheel of his "ordinary," clad in colorful uniform and cap, at any moment bound to crash on his head; or the knickers-sporting golfer thrashing away at a small ball in the bushes. The pioneer sportsmen and sportswomen needed emotional support. They found this in the club, a group of like-minded deviants who formed a subculture based on enjoyment of a certain activity. The initial club introduced the organized activity to larger publics who, in turn, organized other clubs. As similar clubs multiplied, they formed leagues and associations that furthered the legitimacy of their chosen sport. With its wide range of cultural types, its effectiveness of communication, and its ability to tolerate unconventionality, the city was the natural spawning ground for these clubs.[18]

Name a sport—it had its share of representative clubs. Thus it was that common interest in a particular activity was a primary force behind the organization of these sporting clubs, which multiplied to the hundreds in the half-century after the Civil War. Sports themselves, however, were not the only fertile ground for club growth. Neighborhood attachment, ethnic identity, and social status were also compelling bonds.

Numerous clubs represented the interests of a particular neighborhood or section. The choice of a name often highlighted the sectional aspect—the South Boston Athletic Club, the North End Athletic Club, the Bunker Hill Yacht Club, the Roxbury Cricket Club, the Savin Hill Yacht Club. Other clubs might have less local names, but their members were often from small areas. The Columbia Rowing Association (East Boston), the Lafayette Athletic Club (Ward 7), the Atlantics Baseball Club (Charlestown), and the Peninsular Athletic Club (South Boston) were similar in this regard.[19]

Frequently these clubs pressed the parks commissioners for improvements in their own locale. A typical lobby was the Roslindale Baseball and Athletic Association, which in 1903 urged additions to the Roslindale Playground. What they wanted was seating to accommodate the "3800 to 4000 people" who occasionally viewed their games, including the hundred or so ladies, who they felt ought to have a special grandstand.[20] The other local clubs, established by the citizens of particular districts, pressed just as vigorously for special treatment. Their actions were similar to those of the neighborhood lobbies urging the creation of nearby parks and playgrounds. One club might appeal for more tennis courts on Wood Island Park; another for preservation of marinas near Old Harbor; yet another for football-playing privileges at Charlestown Heights. The Savin Hill Beach Association was formed in 1877 explicitly "to restrict certain abuses, to improve the beach and surroundings and to build a wharf or landing." These clubs helped quench the growing thirst for sports; equally important, they helped nurture and promote neighborhood and district identity. If sports clubs are any indication, then, perhaps reformers like Robert A. Woods were too alarmist in their fears for the collapse of "local attachments" and "watchfulness over common interests."[21]

Sporting activities also helped provide a sense of community for many of Boston's immigrants who often strove, in Oscar Handlin's words, "to reweave on alien looms the sundered fabric of familiar social patterns."[22] Boston's German community numbered only a few thousand before the Civil War; yet before 1850, they had established a Turnverein. The Turnverein was an association founded in 1811 outside Berlin by Friedrich Ludwig Jahn. Jahn hoped that through a combination of gymnastic training and the inculcation of German nationalism, he might lift his homeland from the disorganization and disgrace so evident when Napoleon routed the Prussians at Jena. His ideas caught hold, and quickly Turnvereine were organized throughout the country. The "Turners'" nationalism and free-thinking posed a threat to the autocratic Prussian regime, and so the societies were officially suppressed from 1819 to 1842. Frederick William IV lifted the ban in 1842 and the Turner societies mushroomed again. But because of their very active role in the ill-fated revolution of 1848, many Turners were forced to flee the country. The "Forty-Eighters" who emigrated to the United States brought their organization with them.

The Boston Turnverein was founded by Karl Heinzen, a Forty-Eighter who had been active in the revolution in Baden. A radical intellectual, Heinzen also edited the local German newspaper, *Der Pionier,* which influenced not only his own kinsmen but also native Bostonians like Wendell Phillips and William Lloyd Garrison. By 1850 the Boston Club was sufficiently organized to send delegates to the founding convention of the United Turnvereine of North America. Through gymnastics and cultural activities, the club members maintained their German identity. Describing a picnic in Jamaica Plain, the society's secretary applauded the "festival of brotherhood," highlighted by the initial unfurling of the Turner flag, the gymnastics exhibition, the dinner under the open sky, and the stirring speeches:

> What impression the blue ether and the glorious sun shining through the tips of the oak trees made upon me, what memories and what hopes crossed my mind at the sight of the charming green of the forest only a German heart can fathom. With the same pleasure I viewed the company in whose faces gay happiness was mirrored.

The Turnverein encouraged its members to keep their hearts German even as they accepted the ways of their adopted land. Indeed, they were later described by Boston's director of physical training as too "chauvinistic and distant" to have great influence on the school system's debate over physical training.[23]

The Germans were not alone in their devotion to their own pastimes. The city's Scottish immigrants held annual summer festivals of Highland games for several years before founding the country's first Caledonian Club in 1853. The club's stated purpose was to perpetuate "the manners and customs, literature, the Highland costume and the athletic games of Scotland, as practiced by our forefathers."[24] These "Games of the Agile Scot" became a regular feature of Boston's sporting scene. Crowds watched the procession of clansmen "in full regalia" stride down Washington and Principal streets to the garden at Park Square, where athletes from all over the country competed for prize money. The viewers also marveled at the drone of the bagpipes and the farrago of tribal kilts which accompanied the caber toss, the pole vault, the races, and other athletic events. The annual Scots picnic at Caledonian Grove in West Roxbury remained an exciting attraction into the early twentieth century. As one resident recalled in 1976, "*Everybody* would go to the Scots picnic."[25]

Irish sportsmen were probably the most active of all. Irish rowers competed against each other in races reminiscent of regattas in Ireland. Their sense of identity was clearly jarred when a newspaper described the *Maid of Erin* as a "Protestant" crew. The Boston *Pilot* quickly received a letter from the indignant group:

> They embrace this opportunity to inform the public through your talented, widely diffused and useful paper, that they firmly adhere to their religion which stood the ordeal of English tyranny and prosecution for nearly four centuries, and which their forefathers professed and they believe to be the only way of salvation, namely, the Roman Catholic religion.

No assimilationists here—these oarsmen were Catholic, Irish, and proud of it![26]

The desire to nurture an interest in distinctively Irish sports led to the creation of the Irish Athletic Club in 1879. The club's initial meeting featured Hibernian activities like goaling, trapball, stone throwing, and the Geataidhe Aoda. John Boyle O'Reilly's *Pilot* and

Patrick Maguire's *Republic* followed and promoted with great care the meetings of the Irish Athletic Club, the Irish-American Athletic Club, and the Ancient Order of Hibernians. The *Pilot* jubilantly announced in 1881: "A large number of the Irish people in Boston are becoming interested in the exhibitions of the games and pastimes of their ancestors."[27] Hurling, the national game of Ireland, enjoyed a definite surge of popularity during the eighties and nineties, with the Boston Hurling Club, the Shamrock Hurling clubs of Boston and Lynn, and contingents from the South Boston Athletic Club and the Irish Athletic Club playing on a regular basis. While it is difficult to trace such commonplace names as "John Donovan" or "Daniel Murphy," the players who appear in lineups were clearly of Irish descent, were basically working class, and were probably of second or third generation immigrant stock.[28] John Boyle O'Reilly reminded them that it was their responsibility to reestablish the Irish genius in literature, art, and all the "earliest known fields of the human race." It was clear that he included athletics among the lofty accomplishments of humanity. Irish Bostonians might enjoy American baseball, but as late as 1895 they actively sought to organize a Gaelic Athletic Union for "those interested in the revival of Irish sports."[29]

Along similar lines, Boston's black community, which might appear a homogeneous mass to the white outsider, sorted itself in groups that were reflected in sporting associations. The native "elites" of long standing or the young "smart set" might emulate their white counterparts by forming a tennis club. The newer migrants from the South found a common bond in social networks at neighborhood gymnasiums, where the latest boxing news might be discussed. West Indian immigrants formed cricket clubs. The West Indian, the Zingari, and the Caribbean cricket clubs appear with regularity in the newspapers and Parks Minutes at the turn of the century. A settlement worker complained that such associations "do not aim to Americanize their members, but rather to have them retain their British citizenship and their distinct affiliations." To a degree he was correct, but much of the desire to maintain distinct affiliations stemmed from the exclusionary practices of the native population, both black and white.[30]

Sporting and gymnastic activities provided the basis for forming and maintaining ethnic clubs that reflected both the segregative and assimilative forces at work among immigrants and natives alike. Competition and participation often brought immigrants in closer contact with their adopted countrymen. Turners and Caledonians were successful in promoting their activities in Boston and elsewhere. In this way, sport helped to break down some of the barriers between cultures. On the other hand, the ethnic clubs and their sports served to remind their members that they must not totally forsake the ancestral heritage. Boston was their city; it was not, however, their all-encompassing community.[31]

SPORTING CLUBS, finally, helped to define and strengthen interest communities based on social and economic status. Social status is largely a perceived quality, and as many social relationships in the growing city became broader and shallower, immediate knowledge of another's social status became increasingly difficult. City dwellers were forced to assess their fellow citizens by means of superficial evidence and visible symbols of status. Three of the most common were residential address, occupational title, and club memberships.[32]

Sporting clubs were important in Boston for similar reasons. Their role in determining and maintaining status was of particular importance to middle- and upper-level status groups. An 1891 directory of Boston's clubs described this sorting function:

> The early clubs of Boston were considered a gathering of certain cliques, classes or parties, with no pretense of being representative of the metropolitan life of the city. But this was to be expected of a place that from its settlement had pursued such conservative methods in its social, political and business affairs, and only during the past decade has it been able to support a club in which no specifically defined qualifications were necessary to entitle one to membership. . . . But the transformation of the city from a provincial to a metropolitan state, created a demand among her businessmen for clubs devoted to the masses, those having a liberal policy in which any respectable person possessing the means and acceptable in the best sense of the word would be welcome.[33]

The confused equation of "businessmen," "masses," and "respectable persons" and the restrictive membership policies in most clubs leads one to conclude that few were open to all classes or all groups. Indeed, as one contemporary noted, "It has always been possible to test the state of Boston's best society by the touchstone of its recognized aristocratic clubs."[34]

To be sure, sporting associations were not at the very top of the club ladder. That spot was reserved for the older, men's clubs like the Somerset and the Union. But sporting clubs were important supplements.[35] A prime example of this was The Country Club, founded in 1882 and located in suburban Brookline. Though not the first sporting club in the Boston area, it was the prototype of all later country clubs, as a well-known Boston guidebook realized. "Though its house and grounds are situated without the city limits," said Edwin Bacon in 1892, "it is composed of Bostonians almost exclusively, members of several of the leading clubs in town."[36] Conceived in the Back Bay home of J. Murray Forbes, a wealthy railroad magnate, The Country Club served the sporting interests of local men of prominence who desired a permanent rendezvous for their hunts, steeplechases, coaching excursions, and later their golf, tennis, squash, and curling. But they were indeed a special group of sportsmen who gathered in the refurbished Clyde Park (Brookline) farmhouse.[37] Forbes and several of the other charter members had attended the famous Round Hill School in Northampton, Massachusetts, where they developed a lifelong interest in outdoor sports.[38] But high social status was a more prominent bond among club members. A perusal of the membership lists reveals names like Adams, Saltonstall, Peabody, Cabot, Lowell, and Bowditch. Of the 403 original members, 199 were Harvard graduates, 123 were or became members of the Union Club, and a full 281 were or became members of the Somerset Club. No ordinary sporting club, The Country Club was part of an interlocking "constellation" of financial, cultural, medical, and industrial institutions that Ronald Story describes in his recent study of the Boston upper class.[39]

The Country Club itself has always been an exclusive proposition. As its first member-historians readily admit, its spirit has been partially "a denial of the spirit of democracy, since a small group sets itself apart from the majority, building, as it were, a wall around its pastimes, and making admission thereto more or less difficult according to the temper and social requirements of its members."[40] But if a club expected to maintain its position as a symbol of status, it naturally would ensure that any new members were of the same ilk. With this in mind, many clubs, including The Country Club, the Eastern and Boston Yacht clubs, the Union

Boat Club, and the Tennis and Racquet Club, created strict procedures for the induction of new members. These included the necessity of obtaining sponsorship by a number of club members, approval by an executive committee, posting of an application that sometimes included place of residence and occupation, and often ultimate approval in open or secret ballot by the entire membership. Almost all clubs had "blackball" provisions, in which a minority of negative votes would spell doom for a person's candidacy. Because of their exclusiveness, membership in these clubs was an important symbol of attainment, especially for the newly rich.[41]

As one might expect, however, exclusive sporting clubs were not universally popular. The Independent Lacrosse Club discovered this when it petitioned the city aldermen for permission to play matches on the Common. The club's hopes were dashed when one alderman complained, in a burst of outrage, that he was familiar with these kinds of organizations whose policies excluded many of Boston's residents. "Some of these organizations," he grumbled, "are made up of people who do not care to associate with some people who like to be members and take part in the exercises of the organizations."[42] A similar sentiment was later echoed by Mayor John F. Fitzgerald, who groaned, "What this city needs is a lunch club where the blue-bloods will eat with the rest of us." The mayor would certainly have included The Country Club or the Tennis and Racquet Club in this criticism.[43]

The sports many of these clubs were formed around also served to symbolize a member's status. Many, such as coaching, were far beyond the means of most Bostonians. Others, like tennis and golf, which hit the country clubs in the eighties and nineties, took decades to attain popularity with the masses. In either case, status clubs took pains to protect their sports from commercial or professional interests. A document signed in 1860 by 117 of Boston's most prominent citizens outlined the sentiments and plans that came to fruition twenty years later when many of the same men founded The Country Club. They noted their desire to establish a course "under the direct control and supervision of Gentlemen," where they would train, exhibit, and race their horses, "freed from the presence or control of those persons who have made this sport objectionable to Gentlemen."[44] The same desire to protect the status of their favorite pastimes led the elite clubs to support and promote the amateur principles of the United States Golf Association, the United States Lawn Tennis Association, and the Amateur Athletic Union.

Restrictive membership policies and the exclusive nature of their activities ensured that many of Boston's sporting clubs occupied prominent positions as symbols of elite social and economic status. But there was a wide range of clubs, representing many steps on the socioeconomic ladder. The salesman, the tobacconist, or the theater manager had little chance of membership in The Country Club or the Tennis and Racquet Club, but if he had an interest he might well join the Boston Athletic Association, to which many a Country Club member also belonged. If the BAA's forty-dollar entry fee and thirty-dollar annual membership dues proved too steep, he might join a small local club like the Peninsular or the Lafayette Athletic Club.[45] Likewise, the South Boston plumber harbored no hopes (and perhaps no desire) of joining the elite Union Boat Club, but the *South Boston Bulletin* reminded him that it was not just the "swell club men" from Back Bay mansions who made up the rowing clubs of Boston; there were also "those who walk the humbler paths of life—yet are oarsmen and prize winners."[46] Skilled workers organized a number of trade baseball teams. In 1874 the printers at Rockwell and Churchill's challenged counterparts from any and all rival firms to a contest. In 1888 the YMCA hosted a tradesmen's baseball championship between the Boston Leather Associates and the Shoe and Leather Drummers' Association. Workers could count on City Council support in their desire to have one of Franklin Park's baseball fields reserved for their teams on Saturday afternoons.[47]

The subjective nature of status meant that the importance of a given club varied with the perceptions of different social and economic groups. Thus, John F. Fitzgerald and James Michael Curley had little use for The Country Club, but they held great stock in their affiliation with the Dorchester Gentlemen's Driving Club, which was organized in 1899. Each, while mayor, reveled in his winning appearance at the Dorchester Day trotting races on the Franklin Field Speedway. Fitzgerald entertained the fifteen thousand spectators with his classic rendition of "Sweet Adeline," and Curley, in khaki suit and jockey cap, joked with the crowd that trotting beat any political race he had ever run.[48]

Many sporting clubs, but especially those that sought status, developed a prominent "social" side to their activities. Four years after its inception, the Boston Bicycle Club had increased its membership from 14 to 140 and had moved into a sumptuous five-story brick clubhouse on the corner of Union Park and Tremont Street. The club had also increased its activities to include whist, pool, chess, and special "entertainment" nights. Country clubs increasingly hosted debutante and charity balls. While some critics lamented the growing emphasis on social life at the expense of sporting interests, these aspects of club life were important to the promotion of group solidarity.[49]

Women were partial beneficiaries of the social approach to club life. It was typically in these elite sporting clubs where women made the greatest progress in the athletic arena. To be sure, there was important work being done in several gymnasiums that specialized in female "fitness" classes. The Boston YWCA building, which opened on Berkeley Street in 1884, had a complete facility on the fifth floor. Miss Mary Allen's "Ladies' Gymnasium" had opened in 1878; by 1891, when it moved to a new location on the corner of St. Botolph and Garrison, its proprietor was recognized as an expert in physical training. But like Mary Hemenway's Boston Normal School, these programs stressed calisthenics for health and symmetrical development. The sports-minded woman found her fullest opportunities elsewhere.[50]

Tennis, golf, and country clubs usually allowed women privileges in both the social and the sporting aspects of club life. As one contemporary reported, "out-door life, delight in action, the spirit of sport, have taken hold of American womanhood."[51] The *Boston Herald* complimented the "prowess and untiring devotion" of the golfers who competed in pelting rain for the 1897 U.S.G.A. ladies' championship at Essex County Club. Liberation on the links or the tennis court, however, was not to be a threat to male domination in social life. As one article on the "golfing woman" put it, the man could use the mixed foursome as a perfect test of a woman's character. It was no longer necessary to take a six-week voyage with a prospective spouse—"he simply invites her to take part in a mixed foursome, and knows it all within the short space of two hours."[52] Sports of all kinds could improve the physique, the health, and the character of the woman; but not for an equal role in society. Lucille Hill, director of physical training at Wellesley College, summed it up in 1903. "Our everpresent ideal should be

Health and Beauty," she said, "and during this early stage of our experience in athletics our watchword should be 'Moderation.'"[53] The athletic women could rightfully scorn the effete male, but the radical feminists of the day directed their energy toward suffrage, not sports.[54]

The country club, with its emphasis on family activities, contributed to the development of class consciousness by bringing prospective spouses together. "Here this new race of clear cut, manly, modest, athletic young men," said one analyst, "learn to make companions of these bright-eyed girls, to associate with them in frank *camaraderie* and to win their friendship and respect." On the courts, on the greens, or in the ballrooms, the elites could fuse themselves into an aristocracy.[55] As one observer remarked, the country club brought together "persons of similar tastes and means." By nurturing common social traits, the club could bring "order to the chaos created by sudden prosperity." Further, it could stratify social development and assure its permanence.[56] Thus, if the whirlwind of urban opportunity blurred older distinctions of social status, many sporting clubs developed and maintained them.

A final appeal of many clubs, especially those in the suburban areas, lay in their ability to act as asylums of relaxation and diversion away from the stress and anxiety of town life and business. Observers of country club life, much like Thomas Wentworth Higginson forty years before, urged the need for businessmen to find refuge from the "nervous strain of living," and the "stress and tension of new century town life, so generally condemned."[57] The Country Club itself was established with the idea of providing a pleasant "Park or Drive" near the city and within easy driving distance, where members could be "free from the annoyance of Horse Railroads."[58] Caspar Whitney aptly summed up the club's qualities as a convenient sanctuary. It could be reached from Boston "without going off pavement," he said, but "in its immediate neighborhood none of its rural effects have been marred."[59]

Descriptions of golf courses in suburban Boston likewise stressed the beauty and serenity of winding brooks and broad valleys, mingled with "the whistle of quail" and the "music of the kennelled hounds." Though considered "hazards" to the hapless golfer who found his ball within them, these forests, brambles, and brooks were welcome retreats from the clanging of streetcars and the logging of ledger books. In this respect, clubs were like parks, only they were privately controlled and existed to serve the needs of a homogeneous minority.[60]

We have seen how perceptions of a changed and deteriorating community struck Boston's most established families hardest. It is no surprise, then, that these same groups first began the drive to the suburban sporting clubs. Having the time and money, they also possessed the powerful inclination during the last decades of the nineteenth century to preserve traditions and values which, as one historian put it, "were good enough to have been taken for granted when the community was more homogeneous, socially speaking, when there had been more interplay between employer and employee, between workman and scholar, between farmer and manufacturer."[61] Justice Brandeis recalled the time, at the turn of the century, when wealthy Bostonians advised their sons that the city held nothing in store but "heavy taxes and political misrule," and that their best plans lay in quitting the city for suburb, joining the country club, and centering their life around "your club, your home and your family."[62]

YET ALL CLUBS offered a similar refuge from urban life—a similar sense of community—to other classes, in other sections of the city. Social analysis of voluntary associations suggests that they occupy important positions in times of change. They can mediate between stability and innovation, between the individual and the wider world. They are schools for developing valuable social skills and attitudes. In the club the individual commingles with role models. But the behavior and values learned in the club are not always of the mainstream. They might be avant-garde or they might be extremely traditional; they might be a mix. Regardless, the club has the ability both to prepare individuals to face a changing world and to harbor them from the effects of change.[63]

Sporting clubs were important in Boston for similar reasons. Whether formed around neighborhood ties, ethnic inheritance, or social status, sporting clubs and their associated activities, be it tossing the caber or sinking a birdie putt, helped develop a sense of identity and cohesion among their members and families. At the same time, the club member could enjoy a temporary haven from the strains of work and taxes, and enjoy the "jolly fellowship" and "sympathy of tastes among those who love the open air, the

145

sensation of fine health, and the recreative exercise of mind and muscle."[64]

One historian of American sport has suggested that the last half of the nineteenth century was in many ways the age of the athletic club.[65] This was certainly true in Boston. Organized clubs led the way in promoting the sports and games that became so popular during these years. Our generation is so used to the presence of municipal and national governing bodies in sport and recreation that we have lost sight of the initial impetus for organization. Indeed, small clubs pressured city agencies into providing more athletic services; representatives from local clubs organized state and national governing bodies. Ironically, their success at promotion and organization ensured their ingestion and digestion by the larger bodies who now control and dominate the sporting scene.

Perhaps, as Tocqueville concluded, it was a commonly "American" trait to nurture an activity, a cause, or a philosophy by forming a voluntary association. But the widespread growth and success of urban sporting clubs was due in part to their ability to serve the social and psychological needs of city dwellers. The club was more than a building or a roster; it offered more than facilities or games. These associations gave countless residents a sense of identity and belonging, a source of social unity and stability amid the fast pace of city life. Club flags, uniforms, songs and cheers—all were symbols of a form of community that grew in the new reality of urban life. Indeed, the city's heterogeneous population, its improved communications, its toleration of unconventionality—all of these gave the sporting club a fertile ground for growth. Clubs were receptive developments; new ties of affect, made possible by urban amenities. Sports clubs did not confront the city. They were a rapprochement with its new order.

8/Bicycle Crazes

IN 1895 BOSTON WAS BEGINNING to feel the first major swell of the bicycle craze that swept the country during the middle of the Gay Nineties. The public parks were a favorite haven for drivers of the "wheeled steed," and a popular park guide reported that swarms of bicyclers, "representing all sorts of conditions," filled the park roads on the weekends, presenting "one of the great sights of Boston." The author continued: "Men and women eminent in the social life of the city may be pointed out on their wheels as they once were on horseback or in their carriages."[1] The parkways provided good surfaces for riding at any speed, but the "scorchers" (bicycle jargon for a speedster) wanted more. To this end, the City Council delivered an order that the Parks Department should develop a special bicycle speedway in Franklin Park or the Back Bay Fens.[2]

Here was a case of the "machine in the garden"; technology encroaching on nature. The Olmsted firm, consultants to the parks commissioners, quickly pointed out that parks existed to provide pleasant scenery and vistas in striking contrast to those found on the city streets. The parks were no place for the bicycler's "scorching track." Building such a track would mean putting park ground "to a use quite inconsistent with its purpose." There was an irony in this antagonism, for bicycles, like parks, existed as an antidote to the normal routine of city life. As a recent article persuasively argues, "the bicycle was both a mechanism of progress and a vehicle of flight." And although the Olmsteds won this round against the "scorchers," they and the parks commissioners learned to live with the bicycle and accommodate its interests.[3]

The bicycle's history in Boston offers many insights into the way the city reacted to its own growth and change. One may profitably investigate the very basic question that contemporary observers asked: Why the boom? Beyond this, one might ask, what did the bicycle offer? To which groups did its attractions appear most compelling? What problems, if any, did it address or resolve?

Ultimately, the bicycle was the basis for a new form of receptive community building—the consumption community—in which men and women joined in a shared attachment to a product designed and promoted to serve their interests. Clubs were the inner core, but one did not need them to belong. Membership required only the ownership of a bicycle. This meant that the consumption community was at once more widespread, more democratic, and more tenuous.[4]

IN FACT, there was more than one passing bicycle rage. At least four different forms of two-wheeled cycles caught the fancy of Bostonians during the nineteenth century.[5] It was the fourth and last of the breed, the "safety" bicycle, that furnished the boom in the nineties. The paterfamilias of the line, the "draisine" (also called the "hobby horse" or "pedestrian curricle"), first appeared in Boston in 1819. Designed by Carl von Drais, baron of Sauerbronn, and exhibited at Paris in 1818, the machine was improved in England by Dennis Johnson. The draisine was an aid to walking, for there were no pedals. The rider perched himself on a saddle, suspended by heavy springs between two equal-sized wooden wheels, and pushed along with the balls of his feet. A wheelwright named Salisbury began making them in Boston, where the contraption "attracted the gaze of the crowd from the rapidity of its motion and the singularity of its shape."[6] Charles E. Pratt, a Boston lawyer who promoted the popularity of the bicycle in the 1880s and nineties, claimed that "with them many a study-worn Harvard student took his moonlight stroll across the long bridge over the Charles into Boston."[7] But the draisine held no wide popularity and quickly passed into oblivion. Roads were simply not smooth enough for speed and the financial panic of 1819 precluded capital investments in its manufacture. The machine was uncomfortable; its riders prone to ridicule.[8]

Fifty years passed before the next form of cycle entered Boston's sporting annals. This was the velocipede, and with it came the first real bicycle craze. A young Parisian mechanic named Pierre Lalle-

A Draisine—Ca. 1818

ment had experimented with an old draisine by adding foot-pedals to the front axle. His employer, Michaux et Cie, took out a patent and displayed a number of the devices at the 1865 Paris Exhibition. In 1866, Lallement emigrated to Ansonia, Connecticut, and brought his idea with him. There, he and an enterprising local man named Carroll received an American patent and began producing "velocipedes." This wooden-framed cycle weighed between fifty and one hundred pounds, and had wheels approximately forty inches in diameter (the front slightly larger than the rear), stout wooden spokes, and iron tires.[9]

The velocipede attracted little popularity until the Hanlon brothers, a famous acrobatic troupe, introduced a modified version in their act at Selwyn's Theatre, Boston, during August of 1868. It proved such a popular part of the act that the acrobats decided to give public demonstrations of their prowess on the Common. The curious crowd was so large that the Hanlons had a difficult time giving one exhibition.[10] These superb athletes naturally made the vehicle look easy to ride; people were enchanted by the grace with which the Hanlon brothers sped along the Common's pathways. Others were delighted in the business opportunity they saw.

Early in 1869, W. P. Sargent & Co., a carriage firm, opened a velocipede riding school in the basement of a building on Tremont Street. The craze began in earnest. Within a few weeks the school had 150 pupils, and the demand continued. By February, the city had a sizable number of indoor riding schools and several outdoor "arenas." Manufacturers met the demand at seventy-five to a hundred dollars per bicycle.

The indoor rink at 155 Tremont Street had a long, smooth floor with wooden pillars down its length. The pillars were wrapped with carpeting—designed to protect the bicycles, not the bones of the hapless neophyte! Approximately fifteen laps to the half-mile, traffic proceeded one way, "to the left, cavalry fashion." Usually two to four dozen riders packed the floor at once; nearly all, claimed the *Advertiser*, "from the wealthier classes of our society." Initiates could take lessons at a dollar an hour in a private room, where they crashed and fell "with about as much grace as a flock of ducks whose wings and legs have been broken."[11]

The velocipede enjoyed this craze during 1869 as a source of amusement and entertainment for the curious. But ultimately it proved to be a short-lived fad. Its nickname as the "bone-shaker" was truly descriptive. Heavy, clumsy, unable to absorb shocks, it was impractical for all surfaces but the hardwood floors of the riding schools and arenas. Even before its quick demise after 1869, the *Boston Advertiser* had predicted the brevity of its popularity:

> The right machine for our roads is not the present two wheeler; whether it has yet been made at all, I cannot say. But I advise all enthusiastic and hopeful velocipedists, who dream of long excursions into the country, of pleasant toddlings on time, of trips to their office, etc., in so many minutes and seconds, to reserve their money and enthusiasm for the rinks and wait for the machine which will stand alone, as a faithful velocipede should, and which can be made to run up a hill and over frozen ruts with a little less exertion than what is necessary to a man running at full speed on his own legs.[12]

Bostonians and urbanites elsewhere waited for a more practical and efficient means of self-propelled transportation, one that

A Velocipede—Ca. 1865

would convey them easily through the streets of the city and, better yet, to the suburbs beyond. Within a decade, many had found the answer.[13]

By the mid-1870s, English mechanics had designed a new form of bicycle called the "penny-farthing" or "ordinary." This machine was centered on an enlarged front wheel, usually forty to sixty inches in diameter, depending on the length of the driver's legs. The larger wheel yielded greater speed than was possible with a velocipede, despite the fact that the pedals remained on the front axle. The rear wheel was reduced in size to minimize weight. The frame was made of wrought iron, and total weight varied from twenty to sixty pounds, depending on whether the bicycle was designed as a "racer" or a "roadster." Wooden wheels gave way to steel, iron tires to "cushion" India rubber. A much-improved vehicle, the ordinary first caught American attention at the 1876 Centennial Exhibition in Philadelphia.[14]

One of the interested viewers was a native Bostonian named Albert A. Pope, a Civil War veteran who retained his colonel's rank in formal address. Early the following year Pope had an ordinary made under the supervision of an Englishman who was staying at his Newton home. Although Frank Weston had organized Boston's first bicycle importing firm—Cunningham, Heath & Company—in 1877, Pope also saw the machine's potential and began importing English cycles through his new Pope Manufacturing Company in Hartford, Connecticut. A visit to England, however, convinced him that the import trade was too limited a venture, greater profit lay in manufacture. In 1878 he began making Columbia bicycles. The first fifty were made at the Weed Sewing-Machine Company in Hartford; by 1895 his group of factories in the Connecticut Valley employed twenty-five hundred, and his three thousand sales agencies covered the entire country.

A large, strong, physically vigorous man, with prominent brows and a "deep, modulated and vibrant" voice, Pope was a shrewd businessman and an ideal bicycle promoter. He purchased all of the available American patent rights to the bicycle, an expensive proposition that later give him great advantage in the industry. He helped organize the Boston Bicycle Club in 1878, and later founded the Massachusetts Bicycle Club. He was a guiding force behind the League of American Wheelmen, ever pressing for the cyclist's legal rights and for improved roads. He promoted and subsidized bicycling newspapers, pamphlets, and journals. Indeed, in many ways, his Pope Manufacturing Co. and its Columbia bicycle were to the industry and sport what Henry Ford and the Model T were to the automobile. Not the first or the only, both were the most responsible for transforming a novelty into a popular vehicle.[15]

As proved by its enduring, although limited, popularity, the ordinary was a vast improvement over the velocipede. It gave America its first cycling sportsmen; proud of their devotion to the wheel, happy and quick to promote its benefits and usefulness.

Although there were only five hundred cyclists in 1879, by 1882 the *Wheelman* estimated that twenty thousand plied the roads, mostly in the Eastern cities.[16] When Boston hosted the sixth annual meet of the League of American Wheelmen, two hundred cyclists took part in the major "run about town." More than a thousand cyclists from all over the country merrily wheeled about in their club uniforms, with shades of gray, blue, and brown predominating. The *Boston Journal* noted, "The absence of any flashy uniforms shows how cycling has come to be a part of the rider's everyday life and not a means of display." The early clubs chose drab colors, grays and khakis especially, for practical reasons as well—to hide the dirt that soiled the rider thrown from his wheel.[17]

Cycling on the ordinary revolved mainly around membership in a bicycle club. As *Bicycling World*, a Boston-based journal, maintained, the chief fascination for racer and roadster alike was the "jolly fellowship . . . the sympathy of tastes among those who love the open air, the sense of fine health, and the recreative exercise of mind and muscle." This sense of common interest gave rise to "a freemasonry among bicyclers."[18] The Boston Bicycle Club, the first in the country, had begun operation in 1878 with 14 members; by 1882 its rolls had increased to 140. The Massachusetts Bicycle Club opened its doors in 1879, and by 1883 had 70 active members.[19]

Other clubs quickly followed suit. By 1886 Boston had so many small clubs that the League of American Wheelmen's *Bulletin* referred to them as "numberless, some of which are occasionally heard from, and others never." Denied membership in other clubs, a group of blacks from the West End—boot-polishers, elevator operators, waiters, and singers with money enough to purchase the machines—formed their own, the "Hubclinians."[20] To a greater or lesser degree, all clubs followed the model of their first forerunner, which had formally stated its twofold purpose: to enhance the "mutual enjoyment of its members in the pursuit of bicycling as a pastime," by means of clubmeets, tours, excursions, and races; and to promote "the use of the bicycle as a practicable and enjoyable aid to locomotion, by the general public."[21] Of course the earliest clubs provided their members the emotional support so necessary for these "deviant" activities. As Pope's corporate lawyer recalled, the general public had little use and much scorn for the ordinary. "If they did not take them for toys and

playthings," he wrote, they were just as apt to "look contemp-
tuously upon the men who put on again the short breeches of
boyhood and disported themselves upon these acrobatic
contrivances."[22]

Undaunted by criticism, members of the Boston Bicycle Club
rendezvoused regularly in front of the Museum of Fine Arts,
"where the wide and smooth avenues offer excellent facilities for
assembly and procession, and for access in several directions to the
country." These excursions would often lead to the Chestnut Hill
reservoir or to the outlying suburbs. Wheelmen especially loved
the reservoir, the *Herald* reported, "where the smooth roadway,
with its broad sweep and gentle declivities affords superb facilities
for fast and enjoyable riding."[23] Clubs sponsored road races of up
to a hundred miles through Boston's neighboring cities. Unfortunately, the courses were sometimes so difficult to follow that
many of the racers became hopelessly lost.[24] By 1889, the clubs
were strong enough to gain the support of the City Council in
petitioning the parks commissioners to allow July Fourth races on
the Playstead Road in Franklin Park. After some debate, the commissioners were forced "to accede to the wishes of the City
Council," although they deliberately added, "We think it proper
to say that we fear that such uses of the park are not wise." The
races were a success; despite foul weather, several thousand spectators turned out to marvel at the "scorchers."[25] The July Fourth
bicycle races became a regular feature of the city's annual patriotic
celebration, and other races soon followed along other parkways.[26]

Bicycle clubs successfully nurtured the love of wheeling among
a small but growing segment of the city's sportsmen. They were
not successful, however, in promoting the use of the ordinary as
a widespread, popular means of transportation. Purchase prices of
one hundred dollars up were extremely high for a machine that
was still quite difficult to master and manage. Although its cushion
tires were infinitely superior to the iron plate of the velocipede, a
rock or a sharp bump on the road would quickly jar its rider out
of any sense of comfort and ease.

In 1881, *The Bicycling World* extolled the availability of good
roads in the Boston area; but it had to lament that "there are only
about one thousand bicyclers in Boston and its suburbs! Can any-
body tell why there are not ten thousand?"[27] Indeed, there was
really little wonder. The ordinary was not only uncomfortable, it

was also very dangerous. Sitting almost directly above the front axle, the rider had great difficulty stopping and, worse yet, was prone to take a "header." The common surprise was that more cyclists were not killed! Bicycle advocates themselves knew that fear kept most people off the ordinary, but there was no way to convince the "shuffler" otherwise. A safer machine was needed.[28]

Despite its shortcomings, the ordinary performed invaluable service in laying the groundwork for the real bicycle boom of the 1890s. It proved that engineering technology could create a self-propelled machine that would satisfy the desires of city dwellers longing for outdoor exercise, speed, and long-distance travel. The ordinary's devotees carefully argued all of the benefits of cycling that analysts of the later boom treated as something new. Indeed, in this regard the marketing of the bicycle proceeds from 1877 on an unbroken course. Finally, although its high price and awkwardness limited its appeal to upper- and middle-class sportsmen, the ordinary set in motion several components of promotion that were critical in nurturing the immediate acceptance and universal popularity of the safety bicycle.

To begin, riders of the ordinary organized the first bicycle clubs. As Charles Pratt maintained, there were few charms in solitude; "Unity was strength, and concert of action was necessary to conquest."[29] When antagonism to the ordinary surfaced in 1878 and policemen began warning riders off the street, clubmen successfully lobbied in City Hall to ensure that bicycles received the same legal standing and treatment as other vehicles common to the roads. Pope himself invested thousands of dollars in legal fees at the city, county, and state levels, in Massachusetts and other states.[30] The national lobby was the League of American Wheelmen, formed on May 31, 1880 at Newport, Rhode Island. None other than Charles E. Pratt of the Boston Bicycle Club found himself elected president. The league performed local club services at a national level, protecting the rights of wheelmen, encouraging and facilitating bicycle tours, promoting the improvement of roads, and regulating the sport of bicycle racing. Within a year, the league had sixteen hundred members, and Massachusetts provided more than a third of them. Without question the local clubs and the national league had made the roads smoother, the laws fairer, and the sport more organized and enjoyable by the time hundreds of thousands took to the wheel in the 1890s.[31]

Of equal importance, the ordinary spawned individual promoters and entrepreneurs who, for love and money, published articles, magazines, and books, organized meetings and political lobbies, established sales dealerships, and advertised, advertised, advertised the bicycle's merits. Frank W. Weston edited the *American Bicycling Journal*; Charles Pratt edited its successor, *The Bicycling World*, which a local stockbroker financed; Albert Pope invested sixty thousand dollars in *The Wheelman*; soon after its inception, the LAW published a regular *Bulletin*. All were aimed at convincing the middle and upper professional classes to take up and sustain a love of cycling. Reinforced by club and league organization, bolstered by expanded advertising in magazines and newspapers, cycling manufacturers continued to grow steadily. By 1890 there were twenty-seven in the United States, of which seven were in Massachusetts. The ordinary had set the wheels in motion for widespread interest. Unfortunately, it was not the cycle upon which a real boom could perch.[32]

During the 1880s, bicycle manufacturers on both sides of the Atlantic had revised the vehicle's design in order to improve both its practicality and popularity. In 1880, James K. Starley of Coventry, England, invented the "Rover Wheel," which closely resembled the structure of present-day bicycles. Interestingly, its dimensions made it more like a velocipede than a penny-farthing. Front and back wheels of equal size, attached to a diamond-shaped frame, the machine was propelled by pedaling the chainloop that connected the crank with the rear chainwheel. The driver sat above the middle of the frame, between the wheels. This design provided greater balance without sacrificing any of the leverage needed for speed. Hence its name, the "safety" bicycle.[33]

The safety failed to attract widespread interest, however, until it was featured at the 1885 Stanley show in England. Two years later, A. H. Overman of Chicopee, Massachusetts, patented the Victor safety bicycle. By August of 1888 the *Globe* declared that local dealers were not able to meet the demand for safety bicycles. Some, including Pope, stubbornly stuck with the ordinary. But the following year he relented, with his own safety version of the Columbia bicycle. The big boom had begun.[34]

Additional improvements accelerated the safety's popularity. The pneumatic or air-filled tire, ball bearings, and suspension wheels all improved the speed and comfort of riding the safety bicycle. Frame weights continued downward until, by 1893, many bicycles weighed less than thirty-five pounds. Popularity increased, and so did production. From 1890 to 1896, the number of bicycle manufacturers increased from 27 to 250; output of new machines from forty thousand to over one million. While approximations vary, the national population of bicyclists increased during these years from several hundred thousand to several million.[35]

Analysts advised that the bicycle was here to stay:

> It is quite the custom to speak of bicycling as a "craze," and there has been much speculation as to whether it would prove permanent or would pass away like other "crazes" after a brief period of feverish popularity. It has been compared to the passion of a few years ago for rollerskating, and prophets have not been lacking who were confident that within five years it would run its course, leaving behind it the wrecks of innumerable bicycle factories and tons upon tons of unsalable machines. "Only wait," say these prophets, "and five years from now you can buy all the wheels you want, and of the best makes too, for five dollars; you may even get one with a pound of tea, or have it thrown in like a colored picture with a copy of a Sunday newspaper." The error in calculations of this kind lies in treating the matter as a "craze." It is something very different from that.[36]

With the continued growth in sales and use, surely there were reasons to feel that "its stay will be permanent." In 1892, Boston's Irish-Catholic newspaper, the *Pilot*, worried of the danger of too many wheelmen, adding that "verily, the bicycling has come to stay."[37]

Spring thaws in Boston found cyclers impatiently waiting for the roads to dry up. By April, the weekends whirled with wheels. The bright, clear sun on one Sunday in 1895 shone down on twenty-five thousand cyclers from early morning until late afternoon as they traveled the streets to and from Franklin Park and the reservoir, their favorite haunts. An almost continual line passed by, on new and old safety models, broken only by the clank and clatter of a high-wheeled ordinary, by now scorned as another "bone-shaker."[38]

In mid-decade, the demand for bicycles was as great as manufacturers could bear, and perhaps more so. The *Journal* estimated that one in twelve Bostonians desired "to supply themselves with a wheel."[39] By 1896, the *Herald* estimated the city's cycling population at one hundred thousand. Several local developers publicized a plan to erect a giant indoor sports complex in the Back Bay. The domed structure, to be called the "Colossic," focused around a high indoor bicycle track, three hundred by two hundred yards, with seating for five thousand and accommodations for checking two thousand bicycles. The venture was based on projections of unlimited growth for the sport, growth which "the most skillful statisticians cannot foretell." As the *Herald* concluded, "people will have the bike, even though they may have to deny themselves of almost the necessities of life."[40]

"Everyone under fifty learned to ride," Samuel Eliot Morison, Boston's preeminent historian, wrote in his autobiography, "either at Colonel Pope's bicycle rink on Columbus Avenue or on a quiet side street like ours [Brimmer]." Springtime brought hundreds of couples by the door, the young men often running beside the bicycles of their ladies fair. "From dusk to about ten p.m.," he concluded, "the street was filled with the young people learning to ride the bicycle, and resounded with tinklings, crashes, squeals and giggles."[41] But cycling was not limited to the young. Prominent members of the city's literati were seen wheeling about, including Kate Sanborn, Edward Bellamy, Sylvester Baxter, Thomas Wentworth Higginson, Charles Francis Adams, and Harvard professor Albert Bushnell Hart. Although Charles Eliot Norton did not ride, his son did, prompting one local paper to refer to the famous academician as "Professor Norton, better known as the father of young Norton, the bicycle rider." Even a house on Beacon Street and a lot in Mount Auburn Cemetery were not enough for Brahmin rank, said local lore, unless at least one family female was an expert "wheelwoman"![42]

Bicycle racing increased in popularity. In 1892 more than five thousand enthusiasts watched the July Fourth affair at Franklin Park. As the parks commissioners held out against a track in Boston, promoters looked to the suburbs. In 1893, W. D. Bradstreet of Waltham agreed to build a speed track in that city. Fifteen thousand people turned out for the opening, and when the original gravel surface gave way to "metalithic" cement, national champions like the legendary John Johnson ventured to Waltham to set record times at Bicycle Park.[43]

Much of the recreational touring revolved around the bicycle clubs, which burst forth by the dozens. Clubmen organized the early spring tours that signaled the start of the cycling season. Each club tried to outdo the distance records set by others, using as a benchmark the early tours of the Boston and Massachusetts clubs—over one hundred miles in a day, on the old ordinary! Local papers listed the rendezvous for each club, and its itinerary. Club runs and club news were standard features in the wheel-oriented newspapers. Here is a partial list of clubs that reported news in mid-decade: Berkeley, Bostonian, Mona Road, Mattapan, Bunker Hill, Roslindale, People's Institute Wheelmen, Alpha, Eagle, Mazzepa, Fellsmere Road, Tremont, Riverside, Woodbridge, Middlesex, Massachusetts, Lechmere, Mt. Pleasant, Orient, Roxbury, Noddle Island, Press, Commonwealth. As early as 1893, the various clubs had banded to form the Associated Cycling Clubs of Boston.[44]

Through their clubs and larger organizations, wheelmen continued the fight for better roads and equal treatment under the law. In 1887, cyclists in the greater Boston area created the Eastern Roads Association to promote Albert Pope's "Gospel of Good Roads." Their continued lobbying helped convince the General Court to create a permanent State Highway Commission six years later. Composed entirely of LAW members, the commission enjoyed an initial appropriation of three hundred thousand dollars.[45] Boston's roads received the highest accolades of the country's wheelmen, as the *Journal* proudly noted:

> No other city in the United States can boast of a greater incentive to cyclers in respect to delightful runs than can the city of Boston. Today the wheelman can start from the heart of the city, and, via Beacon Street, can, in a short time, reach the park system; there he can take a run of 28 miles over the most perfect of roads.[46]

By 1898 the Commonwealth had expended two million dollars in 125 different municipalities, under the supervision of the State Highway Commission's sixty resident managers.[47]

Bolstered by officers of the state's chapter of the LAW, cyclers remained ever vigilant of their legal rights. In 1894, George Perkins prevailed upon the parks commissioners to rescind a regulation requiring lanterns on the bicycles of night riders.[48] Three years later, Sterling Elliott, editor of the *LAW Bulletin,* hastened the defeat of a similar state law by exposing the fact that the politician who introduced the bill was scheming with a near relative to "make hay" on the manufacture of bicycle lamps. Successful lobbying ensured that state road laws applied equally to all vehicles, in all cities throughout the Commonwealth. The wheelman was assured that his rig and his habits were as legal in Brockton as they were in Boston.[49]

The ordinary had paved the path for the safety bicycle's ascendance, and the mid-1890s witnessed the reign of the bicycle:

> The great body of riders find in the bicycle a new pleasure in life, a means of seeing more of the world, a source of better health through open-air exercise, a bond of comradeship, a method of rapid locomotion either for business or pleasure, and many other enjoyments and advantages which they will not relinquish.[50]

The constituency of the reign, however, was basically urban, as Gary Allan Tobin points out.[51] But the ordinary's appeal had been confined to the city as well, and with good reason. The bicycle addressed a number of desires of city dwellers to remedy the deficiencies of urban living. It was a machine that combined the blessings of exercise, practical transportation, and travel. The safety bicycle simply exposed a wider population to these benefits.

Bicycle enthusiasts claimed that it met the needs of all social classes, including "the artisan, the millionaire, the professional man, the laborer, the rich merchant, the lady whose name appears in all the 'society movements of the day,' the shop-girl, the banker and his clerk."[52] The bicycle was "the people's carriage," the "crowning luxury of the common people and the necessity of the well-to-do," the "destroyer of caste and the annihilator of age." Prowess on the wheel brought anyone self-respect.[53]

Bicyclists did include a wide range of Bostonians; the bicycle was never the province of the elite only. From the beginning of the renaissance of wheeling with the ordinary, bicycling took on a decidedly middle-class stamp. The safety bicycle and the "drop" or open frame meant that women could easily enjoy the sport. In 1896 the *Herald* described the different types of women cyclists: the stout matron, out to lose some weight, in black skirt and heavy sweater, "so warm that it really makes one hot to see it"; the attractive young beauty, in "divided skirt and white waist," using the wheel as a machine of courting; the serious "scorcher" who "much prefers to wear bloomers that resemble as nearly as possible the attire of the sterner sex, and who dotes on riding a diamond framed safety with the speed of a racing man." Indeed, one can find reports of races for women.[54]

It is harder to wax euphoric about the bicycle's ability to annihilate class distinctions. In 1892 the *Pilot* described the cyclists as professional men, "brain workers," clergy, or women. And while secondhand bicycles could be purchased as cheaply as fifteen dollars by 1896, one finds no evidence to suggest that the unskilled laborers in the North or West Ends ever wheeled merrily in the parks. When newspapers reported the numerous "working class" taking to their bicycles, they doubtless meant skilled workers.[55]

The bicycle's appeal, however, was universal. To begin, the ordinary and the safety bicycle offered a pleasurable form of healthy exercise, a means of enjoying the fresh air. Like all active sports, bicycling was perceived as a tonic for the mental stress of business life in the city:

> The man who goes through ten hours' daily mental fret and worry will in an hour of pleasant road-riding throw off all its ill-effects, and prepare himself for the effectual accomplishment of another day's brain work.[56]

No wonder a ride through the parks was so popular; it combined the virtues of fresh air and exercise. In this sense, the bicycle can be linked with the underlying drive of park and playground advocates to redress the physical decline of the city and its inhabitants. As Sylvester Baxter maintained, universal acceptance of the quiet-riding bicycle would not only improve the health of the rider; it would also reduce or eliminate the "exasperating noise and confusion of city life" which proceeded from the "harsh rattle and clatter of vehicles in the streets." Even better, the new, silent steed of steel was not likely to dump manure![57]

The bicycle was the temporary release needed for full enjoyment and employment of the city's demanding business opportunity. This theme continually runs through the wheelman's literature:

> "Whither, on the whirling wheel?
> Whither, with so much haste,
> As if a thief thou wert?"
> "I have the wheel of life;
> Soiled from my city's dust,
> From the struggle and the strife
> Of the narrow street I fly

To the road's felicity,
To clear me from the frown
Of the moody toil of town."[58]

As one rider explained, when rolling along the smooth, hard driveway through the Back Bay Fens, he lived "on the borderline of Utopia." Nothing stood between him and "the realization of perfect happiness," except perhaps the clatter of horses' feet.[59] *Bicycling World* admonished wheelmen that the intoxicating effects of shady elms, exhilarating air, quiet, winding roads, and jolly companionship could consume all psychic and physical energy, to the detriment of family and business obligations.[60]

The improved roads for which clubs and the LAW fought were the arteries for this great escape. Weekend spins to the outlying suburbs remained a central feature of club life throughout the eighties and nineties. Medfield and Dedham were within easy reach. So was Waltham, where Prospect Hill offered a panoramic view of city and country alike. One must remember that these areas were still quite rural. Magnificent oaks, elms, and maples protected the cyclists from the hot summer sun, where "the fresh country air and picturesque landscape of green fields dotted with farm houses and haystacks" added attraction to the run. Summer also brought whirls to the North Shore and its beaches, where, along with good opportunities for cycling, wheelmen found "the seldom-combined enjoyments of cool sea breezes, fragrant whiffs from the pine woods, deep-sea fishing and shady avenues."[61]

But the bicycle's popularity did not represent a renunciation of the city. It was, rather, a medium for melding the best of all worlds. The bicycle produced a de facto expansion of the public parks; for all the suburban roads were public. Echoing the earlier views of park supporters, the *LAW Bulletin* noted that the bicycle "brings city and country close together, and places 'green fields and running brooks' where once there were but smoky walls and a heavy atmosphere."[62] But conversely, as with the parks, urban cyclers demanded that the city's amenities accompany them on their treks to the suburbs. Thus the fight for better roads and clearer road signs, the provision of bicycle tour maps and guides to identify the best routes, and the promotion of runs that encompassed inns, hotels, and shops.[63]

Further, the bicycle was not just a means of leaving the urban environment. Wheelmen actively promoted the machine's value as a practical means of transportation within the city. As early as 1881, *Bicycling World* claimed that the cycle was used "by all classes as an ever-ready and inexpensive horse, a car at one's own command, a 'quick transit' held to no arbitrary rails, available with the utmost of freedom and exhiliration for social and business purposes."[64] Capable of easily doubling or tripling the speed of a horse, the bicycle needed much less time and expense in upkeep and care.[65] Little wonder that the parks commissioners equipped their police with brand-new Columbia cycles.[66]

Some felt that the bicycle would make the streetcar superfluous, claiming that company profits had suffered considerably "since thousands of persons travel to and fro between their offices and their homes on wheels."[67] The early wheelmen looked with scorn on the horse railway:

> Go not with the crowd that crawls
> Where the rattling horse-car hauls,
> Sit the quiet nag of steel,
> Like together wheel and weal.

In the 1890s cyclists fought against the spread of trolley-car lines. But after receiving several complaints and calls for action, Boston's Sterling Elliott, the editor of the *LAW Bulletin*, replied in 1897 with a plea for conciliation. His argument was both realistic and ominous:

> If all people were wheelmen and always rode wheels, the street railroads, that are already made, wouldn't pay a dividend once in a hundred years. . . . The fact is, however, that since the successful introduction of electricity as a means of transmitting power, stock in street railway companies averages to be a good investment. Such roads carry a very large number of passengers who, because of age or youth, cannot be riders of the bicycle, while a very large percentage of the fares are paid by people who own bicycles, but who still find the electrics a great convenience.

Unaware that the bicycle boom was almost over, Elliott was offering a partial analysis of its demise![68]

By the turn of the century, the bicycle was no longer in vogue. Membership in the LAW had dropped 50 percent in two years. In 1901, the League *Bulletin* changed its name to simply *Good Roads Magazine*, and contained little news on cycling. By 1904 the Bostonian secretary-treasurer of the LAW lamented that "the enthu-siasts among wheelmen today are the old-timers." In the spring and summer of 1902, local newspapers carried almost no coverage of the pastime. Gone were the lengthy columns of club news and club runs.[69]

Society embraced new vehicles for temporary release from the strains of urban life; among them, the automobile and the sub-urban golf club.[70] But greater competition probably came from the improved efficiency in mass transit. The country's first subway had opened in Boston in 1898, and an estimated fifty million people used the line in its first eleven months. The revamped Boston Elevated Company bought out this and other lines from the West End Street Railway, and consolidated its new elevated lines with older street lines by way of transfers. By 1901 it was operating a unified streetcar and rapid transit system servicing most of the metropolitan area on three hundred miles of track. For a nickel fare, more than 222 million passengers annually rode its rails.[71]

NO ONE HAS DEFINITIVELY ANALYZED the rapid decline of the craze. Perhaps no one will. Nonetheless, the bicycle's brief but amazing ascendancy, both in sales and interest, provides rich insights for the curious historian. It tells us much about the reac-tions of urban residents to the growth of their cities; for the bicycle was not only a vehicle for release from the congestion, the strain, and the pressure of urban living, it was also a means of improving the quality of transportation and life within the city itself. And it helped convey urban tastes further and further into the suburbs and beyond.

But this was not an instinctive or natural process. The bicycle crazes, especially the boom in the 1890s, illustrate the interpene-tration of production and consumption in the capitalist economy of which the cities were centers of exchange. Bicycle manufacturers created the machines which city dwellers could "consume," i.e., buy and use, to satisfy their desires for an instrument for exploiting and escaping the city. At the same time, manufacturers like Albert A. Pope worked hard, in advertisements, articles, and apostleship, to create and nurture the need which their products were designed to fill. As Pope himself admitted, it was necessary "at the outset, to educate the people to the advantage of this invigorating sport, and with this end in view, the best literature that was to be had on the subject was gratuitously distributed."[72] It is clear that to this extent the bicycle boom was artificial; its demise would occur rapidly when a competitor, such as trolley, auto, or golf club, could sell itself as better suited to fill the need, or as servicing a slightly different, more *important* need.

The social appeal of the bicycle was very much related. While the ordinary's popularity had been restricted to clubmen, and while the safety bicycle had spawned countless clubs, the bicycle crazes especially in the 1890s had also created a much wider network of association, which transcended club membership. Bicycle advertising and sales created a new community of consumption, the cement of which was a commodity, the bicycle. As Daniel Boorstin has described it, the consumption community was in many ways like other communities; it "consisted of people with a feeling of shared well-being, shared risks, common interests, and common concerns." At the same time the ties were "thinner" and "more temporary."[73] The requirement of kinship in this community was merely the ownership of a bicycle, for which one needed only the common denominator of capitalist society—money. Although never a threat to basic distinctions of class and status, the bicycle community had its own system of stratification. The expert rider had higher status than the novice; a new Columbia rode above the level of a used Overman. But status could be topsy-turvy from that in the outside world—a Roxbury salesman might well have a more stylish bicycle than the Beacon Hill banker.[74]

Ultimately, however, the critical distinction lay between the cyclist and the noncyclist. Of course, in the end this was a tenuous tie, for it lasted only as long as manufacturers could sustain the consumer's desire for the commodity. By the turn of the century the boom was over; so was the wide community of cyclists. The network shrank to its beginning size. The bicycle was less a social machine, more a practical means of exercise and transportation for diehard enthusiasts. Pope turned his attention to the automobile, but it was too late. His conglomerate fell into receivership; shortly thereafter he died, in 1909.[75]

While they lasted, however, the bicycle crazes produced widespread consumption communities whose common interests revolved around the quality and meaning of life in the city. But equally important, it is unlikely that the crazes could have occurred without a combination of peculiarly urban situations, including population density, ready advertising media, superior road surfaces, and higher levels of discretionary income. Like the sporting club, then, the bicycle boom was a community form produced by the urban reality.

9/*Some Heroes & Their Fans*

SPORTS CLUBS HAD PROVIDED Bostonians with organized structures for sharing common activities and interests. Sporting crazes like the bicycle boom had encompassed a wider interest group than the club—the consumption community. A final form of group consciousness and cohesion also developed through the medium of sport during this period. This involved the fans, those enthusiastic spectators and rooters who were united in their devotion to a team or hero. Their community was much more spontaneous and fleeting than the club or the craze. Like the latter, however, sports fans existed, en masse, because collective identification with a team or hero served interests and needs acutely felt in the urban environment.

The importance of the sports hero lay in his ability to serve as a symbol by which his followers (or antagonists) could derive organization and meaning for their lives. As Anselm Strauss has pointed out, the city dweller is typically exposed to an "inevitably ambiguous mass of impressions and experiences . . . which he must collate and assess, not only for peace of mind but to carry on daily affairs."[1] Certain sports figures emerged periodically as particular symbols around whom the buzz of urban existence took form. He might represent a special life-style, for immigrants or for natives, for rich or for poor. He might boost morale for a small group or for the city as a whole. He might illustrate the achievements to be made through preparation and endurance, or the decline that followed indulgence and overconfidence.[2]

These were the same dramas that repeated daily on every street in the city. The sports figure, however, let the fan sit back and enjoy the play from a safe distance. Indeed, the special attraction

168

of this "symbolic" community was its ability to offer a sense of personal stake at little cost. It did not require the purchase of a commodity or the payment of membership dues (although of course the live event required an admission fee). It did not demand the time and effort of a political lobby, such as we saw at work in the park and playground issues. Yet at the same time the symbolic community provided a viable form of association, cemented by the common joy of victory and the shared anguish of defeat.

Conversely, as we shall see, some groups might be joined by a mutual antagonism to the symbolic leader of another group. The development of community was not always positive. But while the sports hero might generate group conflict, he might also nurture a fellow feeling among differing segments of the city, particularly when he upheld Boston's good name against Chicago or Baltimore even if he had himself been born (like "King" Kelly) in Troy, New York. Let us take a closer look at some of these heroes and their fans.

> His colors are the Stars and Stripes,
>   He also wears the green,
> And he's the grandest slugger that
>   the ring has ever seen;
> No fighter in the world can beat
>   Our true American,
> The Champion of all Champions
>   Is John L. Sullivan![3]

This popular vaudeville ballad captured some of the widespread affection for the "Boston Strong Boy" during the last two decades of the nineteenth century. Like the East India traders and the majestic clipper ships, he carried the name of Boston to distant points of America and the world. A braggart, a brawler, and a drunkard throughout most of his career, he squandered his earnings and ten years after his last fight was forced to file for bankruptcy. But he counted presidents and crown princes among his friends and admirers. His death and funeral in 1918 dashed the war effort from the headlines, and James Michael Curley paid homage to his legend by serving as a pallbearer.[4]

His life began humbly enough, on Roxbury's Harrison Avenue, in 1858. His father, a short but rugged hod carrier, came from Tralee, County Kerry; his mother, closer to his own size as a heavyweight, had emigrated from Athlone, County Roscommon. John Lawrence Sullivan attended local grammar schools. He completed his formal education at Boston College, then located in town, where he struggled vainly for a short while to fulfill his mother's wish that he enter the priesthood. While drifting through short stints at various trades, including semiprofessional baseball, he gained recognition as a boxer by competing in sparring exhibitions at local theaters.[5]

Boston did not tolerate pugilism, or bare-knuckle boxing; but the city aldermen granted entertainment licenses for "sparring," with gloves. This was a wee bit of casuistry, but as one alderman quipped in defense of the policy, "If you will go out some day and look at a football match between Harvard and Yale, you will never say anything about a sparring exhibition!"[6] At these affairs, Sullivan bulled his way to prominence with victories over local or itinerant fighters like Tom Scannel, Johnny "Cocky" Woods, Tom Dwyer (the Massachusetts champion), and "Professor" Mike Donovan, the middleweight champion of the world. In April of 1880 he scored a major exhibition victory by defeating the English heavyweight Joe Goss, who had lost the American crown to Paddy Ryan the year before. The *Pilot* concluded its report with profound understatement by noting: "Sullivan, who is about 22 years of age, is a remarkable man, and destined to rank among the leading heavyweights of the country."[7]

He certainly had the physical potential. In peak condition, Sullivan distributed 190 pounds solidly around his five-foot, ten-inch frame. In his early years he wore a close-cropped "butch" haircut that made his coarse black hair bristle. With powerful shoulders and arms, a deep, thick chest, a heavy but solid middle, and short, strong legs, he was a formidable fighting machine.[8] John Boyle O'Reilly, assessing the heavyweight's skill in *Athletics and Manly Sports,* asserted that Sullivan was the most remarkable and interesting boxer in history, largely because of his "extraordinary nervous force." Where other boxers began slowly, Sullivan started round one swinging at full tilt, and he never let up. He was "as fierce, relentless, tireless as a cataract . . . as distinct from other boxers as a bulldog is from a spaniel. He is a fighting man."[9] Frequently using more strength than science, Sullivan often rushed at his opponents with a ferocity seldom seen in boxing circles.

By 1880 he was ready for national recognition. He issued a

The Great John L.

public challenge to the American champion, Paddy Ryan; but Ryan wisely held off until Sullivan had built a bigger reputation, which would help swell the purse for a championship match. This the Bostonian did, in the first of his major barnstorming trips, on which he offered to pay fifty dollars to any man who could last four rounds under the Queensbury rules. With Billy Madden as manager, Sullivan traveled the East Coast and into Ohio and Michigan. Within a year, the *Pilot* was calling him "the champion of America."[10] Ryan could no longer avoid a match. The site and date were set: February 6, 1882, in New Orleans. The purse was five thousand dollars, with each man putting up a one-thousand-dollar side bet. The match would be fought, bare knuckles, under the London Prize Ring Rules.[11]

Publicity for the illegal prize fight built so quickly that the promoters, fearing police action, moved the site at the last minute to neighboring Mississippi City. Waving his personal handerchief—white silk, with a green border on which were sewn alternating flags of America and Ireland—Sullivan promised to surrender it to Ryan if he lost the match. Then he knocked the champion out to gain the throne. Ryan said later, "When Sullivan struck me, I thought a telegraph pole had been shoved against me sideways."[12]

Boston was elated over her new champion, even though the victory had come in an illegal and unsavory "prize fight." Every paper in the country had published a "detailed report of the contest," the *Pilot* noted, despite many editorials condemning the affair as "brutal and degrading." If it was, asked the *Pilot*, "why did respectable and intelligent people feel an interest in so unworthy a struggle?" The only answer could be that the pugilists displayed three most admirable manly traits: courage, skill, and endurance. The *Pilot* continued, "It is highly to the credit of the winning man, John Sullivan, that he wished to fight with gloves. . . . John Sullivan will earn another championship if he refuses henceforth to box with bare hands."[13] The *Globe* was more pragmatic, concluding in its editorial, "We abhor prizefighting as a species of sporting, but as long as the 'mill' came off at all, we are glad the Boston boy won."[14]

Gloves or no gloves, his friends and admirers grew in number, within Boston and without. According to Sullivan, a "Bostonian rhymer" popularized the following epinician verse:

Just fancy what mingled emotions
Would fill the Puritan heart
To learn what renown was won for his town
By means of the manly art!
Imagine a Winthrop or Adams
In front of a bulletin board
Each flinging his hat at the statement that
The first blood was by Sullivan scored.
Thy bards, henceforth, O Boston!
Of this triumph of triumphs will sing,
For a muscular stroke has added a spoke
To the Hub, which will strengthen the ring!
Now Lowell will speak of the "ruby,"
And Aldrich of "closing a match,"
And Longfellow'll rhyme of "coming to time,"
Of "bunches of fives" and "the scratch"![15]

The *New York Herald* ridiculed the euphoria. While the victory in the prize ring might be cause for "high hopes" in Boston, it said, the fact remained that New York still excelled the Hub as a shipping port and a literary center. It even disputed Boston's claim to the baked bean championship![16]

Disregarding such criticism, Sullivan's friends held a public reception upon his return, where he was presented a gold watch and chain. That summer he appeared as the principal attraction at the annual picnic of the Irish Athletic Club. The *Republic* billed him as the "Terror of Terrors" who was "bidding fair to outshine his valorous namesake, 'Yankee Sullivan,'" who had enjoyed success a quarter-century before.[17]

For the next ten years, John L. Sullivan's career consisted largely of tours throughout the country to places like Pottsville, Pennsylvania; Steubenville, Ohio; Keokuk, Iowa; Macon, Georgia; and Corsicana, Texas, as well as trips abroad to England, Ireland, France, and Australia. He defended his championship both in the ring and in the barroom. Before leaving on one early trek, he bade farewell to his cheering fans, described by the *Globe* as "delegations from almost every city in New England, including every class of society; politicians, actors, musicians, artists, merchants, writers, in short, people of all walks of life." In patriotic fashion, Sullivan exclaimed: "I will strive to return to the place of my birth with a reputation unsullied and undiminished."[18]

Many of the challengers who faced the great John L. had the financial support of Richard K. Fox, a New Yorker, publisher of the enormously popular *Police Gazette* and Sullivan's bitter enemy. By 1887, Fox had picked Jake Kilrain as the man to silence the braggart from Boston. Claiming that Sullivan was avoiding a title match with Kilrain, Fox presented his protégé with a "championship" belt.[19]

In direct reaction to this insolent challenge, the City of Boston officially recognized its own boxer as champion of the world. On August 8, 1887, four thousand people crammed the Boston Theatre as Councilman Will Whall presented Sullivan with a magnificent gold belt, studded with 397 diamonds, and valued at eight thousand dollars. Mayor Hugh O'Brien and seven other members of the City Council represented the city government, a fact that caused great consternation among conservatives. The *Evening Transcript* railed at the mayor's "amazing performance." Where was his sense of humor, since his sense of decency had obviously deserted him? Didn't the mayor and his fellows realize that by acting so seriously and formally they were reinforcing a standing joke among American journalists? Orators and poets were no longer Boston's first citizens. That honor now belonged, by official recognition, to "Mr. J. Lawrence Sullivan."[20] But the wry play on the boxer's name was a joke only on the Brahmin class. Following a similar criticism of Mayor O'Brien in the *New York Tribune*, the *Pilot* sharply responded that it was only New York's envy that prompted the attack.[21]

Two years later, the Boston Strong Boy defeated Jake Kilrain under the blazing sun in Richburg, Mississippi. The match lasted seventy-five rounds, and was the last bare-knuckles championship fought in America. Sullivan continued on top for three more years, before losing the crown to James Corbett in September of 1892. In that bout, age lost to youth and slugging to "scientific" boxing. Sullivan was corpulent from incessant drinking, his hips as wide and bulging as his shoulders. His training routine of long walks, swimming, sweat baths, sparring, and occasional doses of a "physic" composed of zinnia, salts, manna, and black stick licorice helped him lose some weight, but did not condition him for the quick Corbett. The *Republic* hoped that the loss would teach him "moderation and sense," but added that his "manly acknowledgement of defeat" had won him the "favor and respect of many who had come to regard him as a rude bully and an unfeeling brute."[22]

John L. Sullivan never regained the championship. Yet, as his chief biographer emphasized, "to the great majority of Bostonian Irishmen, John was still the unbeaten and unbeatable champion of the world and in particular the champion of the Irish race."[23] With good reason, for the Irish immigrants in Boston were still buried under the tremendous weight of Boston's older traditions and families. What is more, despite their growing control of city politics, they were still, in Stephan Thernstrom's words, "highly distinctive in their inability to find jobs that offered security, prestige and financial rewards."[24] So the Irish, perforce, sought their heroes elsewhere. Indeed, one contemporary social study concluded that the social solidarity found in sports helped the Irish overcome their "inferiority" as individuals.[25]

Sullivan's popularity extended beyond the boundaries of his native city and kinfolk. Reports of the Corbett fight competed favorably for front-page space with the news of John Greenleaf

Whittier's death.[26] At the same time, however, he was vilified in many quarters as a drunken, brawling pugilist. Ironically, some of the severest criticism came from Irish Bostonians, in this case the middle class "lace-curtain Irish." *Donahoe's Magazine,* the voice of this group, ran a number of editorials complaining about the interest in pugilism which their kinsmen were showing. John L. Sullivan was included among the sons of Erin who disgraced their heritage by pursuing such a "barbarous business." In a stinging review of O'Reilly's book, *Ethics of Boxing and Manly Sports,* the magazine argued that only the smart set "who have never done an honest day's work in their lives" would approve of boxing. The rest of the nation, it declared, "except the loafers and drunkards, the gamblers, sports, outlaws, thieves, and pimps of every description, has nothing but execrations for the brood of blackguards who live by and encourage the wretched boxers."[27]

Donahoe's Magazine notwithstanding, it is probable that John L. Sullivan's supporters far outnumbered his detractors, especially among Boston's Irish. Moreover, his personal appeal had helped usher a disreputable sport into a new era of broader acceptance. Always an advocate of the less brutal Queensbury rules, he had donned gloves for the Corbett match, possibly to his disadvantage. His efforts in the ring and out, despite his lapses in sobriety, had gained greater respectability for boxing in Boston and America. His successes had provided a sense of cohesion and united interest to many segments of Boston's varied population.

BLACK FIGHT FANS were doubtless unmoved by John L. Sullivan's exploits. To begin, they had heroes of their own race. More important, the great John L. had on several occasions backed out of scheduled fights against black boxers. Within twenty years, however, the unrivaled heavyweight champion of the world, Jack Johnson, was black. And when, in 1910, a white hope named Jim Jeffries came out of retirement to challenge him, the tension in Boston, as elsewhere, was extraordinary. While many blacks looked to Jack Johnson as a symbol of achievement, the community of white fans was virulent in its racial fear and hatred. Their attitudes serve as a telling reminder that, as one historian argues, "a community can sometimes be formed not for the 'positive' reasons of creating social bonds, but also as a negative reaction to other groups."[28]

Black Bostonians had adopted a number of boxers as favorite sons well before Jack Johnson made his dramatic ascent. George Godfrey, a native of Prince Edward Island, was quite popular in the 1880s, especially when he laid claim to being the first colored heavyweight champion. Unfortunately, Godfrey never had a chance to vie for the "world" championship, as Sullivan chose to dodge him. But Godfrey's fights with the local "Black Star," McHenry Johnson, attracted up to five hundred fans; his bouts with white fighters even more. One historian of Boston's black community notes that in some cases, "black attendance at boxing matches outdrew the Sunday sermon at the black church." And even during Jack Johnson's reign as world champion from 1908 to 1915, local fans had a more popular hero in Sam Langford, a Nova Scotia transplant called the "Boston Tar Baby."[29] As admired as they were, however, these boxers never raised the consciousness of blacks, or whites, to anything near the level achieved on July 4, 1910 when Jim Jeffries was pummeled into submission in Reno, Nevada, by the man many recognize as the top heavyweight of all time.

Born in Galveston, Texas, in 1878, Jack Johnson had taken to the road at an early age in pursuit of a career in pugilism. His odd jobs and sparring exhibitions had even taken him to Boston for a short time in the mid-nineties. In his autobiography, Johnson recalled that he had roused the contempt of "Irish gangs" in Boston because of his outspoken admiration for Jim Corbett, the man who had dethroned John L. Sullivan.[30]

Over six feet tall, Johnson was a well-muscled and skillful boxer, but the color line held him from a shot at the championship until 1908, when Tommy Burns took him on, in return for the promise of lucrative gate receipts. The match went off in Sydney, Australia. Johnson toyed with Burns before knocking him out in the four-teenth round, and the calls began for a "white hope." Within a year, five were quickly dispatched. White fans put pressure on Jim Jeffries to emerge from retirement in defense of his race. "But one thing remains," urged Jack London. "Jeffries must emerge from his alfalfa farm and remove that smile from Johnson's face. Jeff, it's up to you!"[31]

In December of 1909, Jim Jeffries finally agreed to fight the black champion on the following July Fourth in San Francisco. Because of the wider publicity for this fight, protests immediately erupted, both from opponents of prize-fighting and from black and white groups fearful of racial backlash. In June, California's governor James Gillette succumbed to the mounting campaign and announced that the match would not occur in his state. The fight's promoter, Tex Rickard, quickly made arrangements with the governor of Nevada, who thought that a bout in Reno made good business sense. His resolve was welcomed by the many Americans who viewed the boxers and the fight in symbolic terms.

The *Boston Globe* had no doubt that Jim Jeffries would prove again the supremacy of the white race. On July 2 the paper began a scornful and satirical comic strip which followed the hopeful pilgrimage to Reno of "Mr. Sambo Remo Rastus Brown." Sambo Brown was depicted as a bumbling fool, and the message in the strip was clear—like his hero, Jack Johnson, Sambo would be put in his rightful place by the jabs, hooks, and uppercuts of the redoubtable Jeffries. Boston's blacks were quieter than the *Globe*, although a local black trainer named Joe Hicks announced his $180 bet on Johnson, who was a slight underdog.[32]

Joe Hicks should have put up more money. Jeffries was no match for the champion. As the *Globe* reported, "Johnson worked with the precision and attention to detail that a cooper uses in putting hoops around a barrel. He landed lefts and rights almost at will on his bulky opponent." With blood flowing from his mouth and nose, Jeffries staggered through the last rounds before falling for good in the fifteenth.[33]

Boston's reaction was mild compared to that in other cities. Racial conflicts were reported in more than fifty; thousands of injuries and at least eight deaths were attributed to the fight and its aftermath. White mobs roamed southern and northern streets in search of "uppity niggers." The *Globe*, changing course, tried to minimize the fight's racial significance, but at the same time it printed an inflammatory cartoon of Johnson strutting, cigar in hand, bejeweled in regal robe, crown on head, and crowing "Har! Har! Harrr!! I golly ah copped de bun!!!" One of his smiling entourage, in top hat and spats (Sambo Brown?) was shown shoving a white man aside with the remark, "Off de sidewalk, w'ite trash!" A headline lamented, WHITE RACE IN BOSTON SORRY FOR FIGHTER; a story noted that "white men appeared wrapped in gloom." The paper also reported that in the South and West Ends particularly "the colored people were greatly elated everywhere, and their jollification was pretty general, even if it was rather tame." The restraint shown by blacks limited the danger of confrontation, but one occurred when two black youths allegedly taunted passersby about the fight's importance. Two sturdy sailors intervened, "and they demonstrated to the satisfaction of even the most skeptical that the white race still reigns," crowed the *Globe*.[34]

In a real sense, the *Globe* was right. Jack Johnson's victory was not transferable. The city's black newspaper, the *Guardian*, could reprint sermons which extolled the boxer as "the greatest hero the colored race has ever had." It could run advertisements for special medallions commemorating the victory. Indeed Jack Johnson, the symbol, might have been cause for hope. But the euphoria died quickly. On July 6 the United Society of Christian Endeavor, headquartered in Boston, announced plans for a national campaign to prevent the showing of the fight film. Mayor John F. Fitzgerald indicated his full support of the initiative. He did not wish to see local morals diminished by a repeat of the spectacle. The *Evening Transcript*, a Fitzgerald adversary, relished the chance to remind its readers that the mayor imposed no similar ban on live fights. The films, said the *Transcript*, "are not very wicked and probably will not cause any great drop in the morality in the city." Fitzgerald held fast, however, despite the public outrage of the *Guardian*'s editor, William Monroe Trotter, who demanded a similar campaign to ban pictures of southern lynch mobs. And there was little white protest of Thomas Dixon's racist play, *The Clansman*, then opening in theaters around the country.[35]

The champion himself faced a troubled future. Dogged by his enemies, who despised him especially for his open affairs and his two marriages to white women, Jack Johnson fled the country in 1913 to avoid imprisonment on a trumped-up charge of violating the Mann Act. In 1915, when he was knocked out by Jess Willard in Havana, Cuba, he maintained that he had thrown the fight. Willard, the ultimate white hope, took no chances. Refusing to fight any black boxers, he redrew the color line.

Jack Johnson divided many black communities around the nation. Many moderate and conservative leaders, like Booker T. Washington and his followers, saw Johnson and his fast, prodigal life-style as an improper and challenging model, in sharp contrast to their program, which emphasized humility, thrift, and honest work. Others saw him as a direct and important defender of black

The Globe *Views Jack Johnson, July 5, 1910*

Courtesy of the *Boston Globe*

rights, and as Al-Tony Gilmore has demonstrated, this is the image that pervades black folklore.[36]

Whites were far more united in their opposition to Jack Johnson. As the Jeffries fight had illustrated in Boston, the foundation for symbolic community sometimes had firmer mortar when it supported a feeling of common resentment. This could be especially true when the symbols in question fought out fundamental issues like racial equality.

BOXING WAS A BRUTAL SPORT, and its promoters recognized the need to soften its image in order to attract a wider audience. Golf and golfers suffered from a completely different problem, as a Boston alderman discovered in 1899 when he submitted to his colleagues a proposal that the Parks Department be ordered to "place the golf links in Franklin Park in proper condition." The proposal met with instant laughter and derision; the alderman sheepishly added that he had never played the game and knew nothing about it. He was, he said, simply conveying an appeal from a constituent group of "ladies and gentlemen."[37] This episode typified the jaundiced view many Americans took toward golf in its early days. Jerome Travers, one of the game's outstanding amateurs, recalled vividly this common antagonism. "All the fun that was poked at it, and the actual indignities that its supporters had to endure," he said, made him feel that golf was "the only sport that has grown and flourished in the face of ridicule." Travers could not explain why golf was ever so marked, but he added that as late as the twenties some Americans still considered it a game fit only for "old men, women and dudes."[38]

It is a commonly accepted bit of golf legend that a single young man created a watershed for the sport, by winning a major tournament in 1913; that after his victory the image of golf changed from "dude" sport to wholesome, challenging outdoor competition for all Americans; that his personal popularity helped swell the ranks of America's golfers in ten years from under a half million to over two million. The young man's name was Francis Ouimet; the tournament was the United States Open.

American golf's best annalist has summarized the spirit of this legend. "Had a pleasant young man from a good Fifth Avenue family or some stiff and staid professional defeated Vardon and Ray," writes Herbert Warren Wind, "it is really doubtful if his victory would have been the wholesale therapeutic for American golf that was Ouimet's."[39] Francis Ouimet was something else again; a hero whose glitter attracted a following much larger than the golfing set. He was the poor boy who made good through hard work, the ex-caddie who vanquished the world's top professionals, the young gentleman who retained his modesty despite his monumental achievement. Ouimet had fired the shots heard round the sporting world. He was embraced by Americans from all walks of life; and his personal acceptance meant acceptance of the sport as well.[40]

To be sure, Francis Ouimet did not introduce golf to Boston. The son of a French-Canadian father and Irish-American mother, he had been fortunate to grow up across the street from The Country Club in Brookline. The Country Club, a founding member of the United States Golf Association, had first contracted the golfing virus in 1892, and certainly had the region's most prominent links in Ouimet's youth. But it claimed neither the first nor the only.[41] As early as 1890, George Wright had secured the use of Franklin Park for Boston's earliest golfers. Wright had purchased English golf clubs to sell in his sporting goods store, and realized that his prospective customers needed assurance of pleasant and open spaces on which to practice this strange game. After six years of experimental play, some of which elicited near-combat between golfers and park patrons, the parks commissioners approved construction of a nine-hole course.[42] Many others followed those at Franklin Park and The Country Club. By 1899 no fewer than twenty-nine links could be found within a twelve-mile radius of City Hall.[43] It was against this backdrop of limited but growing popularity that Francis Ouimet grew up, and prepared to take the city and country in triumph.

After a brief flirtation with visions of professional baseball, Ouimet grew enchanted with the game he saw played across the street from his home. He gradually purchased a set of used clubs at Wright and Ditson's by trading in balls he had found along The Country Club's fairways. He practiced daily at a three-hole course laid out by his brother Wilfred on a nearby cow pasture, and he occasionally played a clandestine round at The Country Club, either in the early morning or in the rain, at least until driven off by the greenskeeper. Nonetheless, he remembered with fondness his caddie days at the club, where some members let him occasionally "hit along."[44] And in the wake of his great victory he advised young golfers that private clubs offered them the "opportunity to mingle with the finest classes of people, intellectually and socially." In the golf and country clubs, he said, they were sure to find "big" men, "men of influence, in the city, the state, or the country at large."[45]

Ouimet delighted equally in the competition on the course. He eagerly looked forward to enrolling at Brookline High School, so that he could compete on the golf team for the championship of the Greater Boston Interscholastic Golf Association. Later he would recall the ridicule endured by these school golfers, so biting that they tried to avoid it by checking their clubs through the janitor's back door, for use later in the day. His game steadily improved, and in 1909, at the age of sixteen, he won the Boston Interscholastic Championship. Sights set on National Amateur competition, he joined the Woodland Country Club, in Newton, the following year, but failed in the qualifying round for the Amateur.

The year 1913 was the eventful one, for Francis Ouimet and for American golf. He won the first of his six Massachusetts Amateur titles, closing out Frank Hoyt in the final, 10 and 9. After qualifying for the National Amateur, he traveled to Long Island, where he fought valiantly against defending champion Jerry Travers before bowing, 3 and 2. He returned to Brookline, bolstered by his strong showing, his mind set on doing even better at the National Open, scheduled to be held at The Country Club.[46]

Although Ouimet had developed a solid reputation among local golfing circles, his was not among the names of serious contenders as the field arrived in Boston. The clear favorites were Harry Vardon and Ted Ray, two British professionals who were recognized as the best in the world. After the qualifying rounds, the medal competition unfolded as expected, with Vardon and Ray beating back the early American challengers to surround a fellow English professional, W. E. Reid, in the top three spots after Thursday's thirty-six holes. Ouimet had stayed close to the pace, however, and settled in only four strokes from the lead. The *Boston Herald* noted prophetically that Ouimet and Alec Ross of nearby Brae Burn were the "only players that appear sufficiently capable to uphold the prestige of New England against Old England."[47]

Friday dawned gray and drizzling, and the day continued dismal for most of the golfers. Alec Ross faded with a 93 on his third round. Vardon and Ray fell off their early pace, and Reid blew up. But Ouimet played consistently, and found himself tied for the lead with the favorites, with only one round to play. This set the scene for the first of the young man's upsets. Vardon and Ray did not play particularly well on the day's second round, finishing with 79s, but their leads looked secure when the rest of the field faltered in the rain. Ouimet himself seemed finished when, after a poor first nine, he double-bogeyed the tenth hole, and continued to struggle. With only six holes to play he was faced with the task of making up at least two strokes to par in order to gain a tie. This he did, with a birdie, three pars, and another birdie at seventeen.

The two thousand fans who had braved the rain gathered round the eighteenth green as Ouimet chipped up on this third shot. He was left with a four-foot putt for par and a tie. Countless golfers had missed shorter putts when their goal was only to break 80 in

*Francis Ouimet
and Caddie, Eddie
Lowery—1913
National Open*

Courtesy of the Francis Ouimet Caddie
Scholarship Fund

a friendly match. Ouimet stroked the ball cleanly into the hole, and America had its first golfing hero.[48]

Boston's press had given fair coverage of the tournament to this point, but the magnificent tie was front-page news. Both the *Globe* and *Herald* carried pictures of the young golfer. The *Globe* described the new enthusiasm for the "dude" sport:

> We have seen, in other sports, the hero of the day cheered to the echo and hoisted upon the shoulders of his admirers, for a jerky ride of fame. We have seen it on the football field in recognition of the dropkick that saved the day or won the game; we have seen it on the diamond, for the man who has won the game with a homer or the pitcher who has struck out the opposing batter, with three on bases and two men out.
>
> But such enthusiasm has been generally foreign to the golf links until the modest Woodland boy, Francis Ouimet, carried the gallery completely off its feet at The Country Club yesterday afternoon.[49]

The *Herald* called the demonstration "unparalleled in the history of great golfing events," and its editorial on "Francis Ouimet's pluck" argued that "no true American, no matter how apathetic or how remote his interest in the game, can restrain a thrill of pride over the feat of our brilliant young golfer." The conservative *Evening Transcript* referred to the tie as "Ouimet's Great Victory."[50]

Boston made the most of this miraculous comeback in regulation, for in their hearts, few thought that Ouimet had a chance in the playoff the following day. But more than ten thousand people, sniffing greatness, disregarded another day of rain. They were not disappointed, as experience fell to youth, and Ouimet won by five strokes over Vardon, six over Ray. The *Evening Transcript* marveled that "ten thousand enthusiasts will follow a golf champion through a downpour but a heavy fog will keep them away from the polls on primary day." The crowd had followed him, said the *Globe*, "unmindful of the rain, the water-soaked course, the wet feet, the bedraggled skirts, the ruined feathers."[51]

In two days, a rags-to-riches legend had been made. Sports writers interpreted his early caddie days as an effort "to help out the slender revenues at home." Through the mob on the triumphant clubhouse lawn he had reached a gray-haired woman, squeezed her hand, and shouted above the din, "Thank you, Mother."[52] He did nothing to tarnish the image. Ever modest in victory, he elected to remain an amateur; and although he never again won the U.S. Open, he won both the French and U.S. Amateurs the following year, was a continuing power in future Amateurs, captained the country's Walker Cup team for twenty-seven years, and was initiated, in 1951, as an honorary "captain" by the Royal and Ancient Golf Club at St. Andrews.[53] But these honors only served to embellish the young man's name. As British golf writer Bernard Darwin described the impact of the Open victory, "In a way he could never be so great a man again if he rose to be President of the United States."[54] Ouimet had proven that even a golfer could capture the affection of a city and a country.

Of course in many ways Francis Ouimet was the dream hero. Unlike John L. Sullivan or Jack Johnson, his personal life and habits exuded modesty, frugality, and earnestness. Even those who scorned the game of golf had to admire the lad's pluck. Ouimet demonstrated that if he played the game properly, the underdog could win not only the laurels but also the ungrudging affection of allies and opponents alike. Of immigrant stock, Francis Ouimet was a hard-working American. He threatened no one; he charmed everyone. He was the stuff of legend.

AS SYMBOLIC LEADERS, John L. Sullivan, Jack Johnson, and Francis Ouimet had through their own prowess and personal appeal expanded the popularity of individual sports that, through social and legal prejudices, had been limited in favor. The source of expansion and enrichment, as all promoters knew, was the great middle class, of which so many Americans saw themselves as members. If there was a sport that tapped the interest of this vast constituency, it was baseball; and for this reason, baseball led the field in providing heroes for the city's masses. Moreover, the organization of the professional leagues nurtured the sense that the ball club was the representative of the city's fortunes.

The barons of baseball, like Albert G. Spalding, stressed that this was in name and essence the true national pastime.

> The professional Baseball player is no thug trained to brutality like the prize-fighter, no half-developed little creature like the jockey, no cruel coward like the bullfighter. He is the natural development of the American boy's inborn love of manly, skillful, outdoor sport— sport busying brain and body and not harming anyone or anything. The average boy who loves Baseball is not the sort of boy who loves to go off with a gun intent on killing some poor bird. Baseball has done a lot to keep the Yankee lad from being brutal.[55]

There was truth in Spalding's claim, certainly in the minds of his contemporaries. And so the citizens of cities like Boston—not just the "dudes" or the "pugs," but all sports-minded residents—eagerly embraced their baseball teams.

Ouimet and Sullivan could bolster many Bostonians' pride in their town with fleeting performances on the golf links or in the prize ring. On baseball fortunes a much wider collection of fans lived and died, from April to October, year after year. "Queer people, the fans," said one baseball reporter, "and, in their various kinds and species, well worth seeing, sharing and understanding."[56] Queer and curious indeed. But there was a more important fellow feeling among baseball fans which Rollin Hartt, in a light treatment of popular amusements, recognized as having the definite ability to draw the heterogeneous populace of the city together. "Mickey O'Houligan," said the author, "sees more of America at a baseball game, and hears more of it than anywhere else." Braced and elated by the democracy of the ball park, the Irish laborer would happily share the game's score and details with even the chance "plutocrat" he might encounter on the way home. Next day he would discuss the game with "Kranks" from any social group: Father Hogan, Morris Rosenberg, patrolman McNally, the settlement worker, the scab, and the walking delegate. In his discussions, concluded Hartt, the fan "finds always a glow of fellow feeling, so strong and so genuine as in some sort to be-speak a realization of that noble American ideal, the brotherhood of man."[57]

Recent historians have questioned the degree to which a city's various social classes actually "rubbed shoulders" at the ball park. For one thing, most workers had daytime leisure only on the Sabbath, and Sunday baseball broke through legal barriers only after protracted struggle during the first decades of the twentieth century. The color line was more solid in baseball than in boxing; in those days, black fans found their heroes in the ring, not on the diamond. Despite these real limitations, however, the belief in baseball's integrative powers was widespread. For this reason, baseball more than any other sport served as a continuing vehicle of civic pride and boosterism. With their many successful professional teams, Bostonians often shared this experience.[58]

The first professional baseball league, the National Association of Professional Baseball Players, began in 1871. The Boston Red Stockings, led by Harry Wright, his brother George, and Albert Spalding, dominated the league during its short existence, winning four out of five pennants.[59] Thereafter, Boston teams competed favorably in many of the leagues that rose and fell during professional baseball's first forty years. Indeed, during the early 1890s the Boston team was so successful in the National League that many rival cities wished to break them up, much as Boston fans wished to do with the Yankee dynasties, or recently with the Montreal Canadians.[60]

Nothing breeds popularity like success, and Boston was no different. During one pennant-winning year the *Globe* wrote:

> The hold that the game has in this city is well-shown by the fact that up to date almost 75,000 people have attended the games. . . . Unprecedentedly large throngs attend the games of all the associa-

tions, comprising youth of the tenderest ages, business and professional men, old men and ladies, in fact every class, every station, every color and every nationality will be found at a ball match.[61]

Doubtless the *Globe* exaggerated the crowd's democratic nature, but team championships would continue to fuel this enthusiasm. A closer look at two such Boston teams shows the "community" of baseball at work.

In 1897, the "Beaneaters" faced the task of regaining preeminence in the National League by overcoming the defending champion Baltimore Orioles. Few experts considered the Boston team a threat, but after a seventeen-game July win streak, Boston found itself with a chance to sew up the pennant in Baltimore.[62] The teams had split the first two games of the late September series, and whoever won the third and final game was virtually assured the pennant. It was a classic struggle between contenders; more than 70,000 persons turned out for the three games, with nearly 30,000 attending the final.[63]

Back in Boston, suspense ruled. The *Evening Transcript* captured the city's emotion on the day of the final game in Baltimore:

> Stocks may rise and fall, but the clerk, the broker, the student, the merchant, master and man, priest and people, have awaited with feverish interest the latest tidings from the diamond as the rounding-out of each recurring day's history. The first man or boy to bring the returns to a waiting crowd establishes a position for himself at once, especially if his news jumps with the hopes of those whom he enlightens.
>
> The attempt to analyze this universal enthusiasm would hardly be profitable. Enough of that exists. Enough to know that not only thousands, but possibly millions, are awaiting with interest more or less anxious the result of today's game. Music Hall will be thronged with an excited multitude. Washington Street in front of the newspaper offices will suggest a presidential election night. Until the final bulletin brings elation or despair, a stranger may know that some national event is agitating the breasts of the American people.[64]

When the results of Boston's 19–10 win appeared on the bulletin boards along Newspaper Row, "every man, woman and child in the city was imbued with a healthful spirit of local pride."[65]

The Bostons clinched the pennant several days later by defeating Brooklyn while Baltimore lost to Washington. The *Globe* headlines spoke for much of the country, which was tired of Baltimore's firm hold on the pennant: *National Sport Is Vindicated by Our City's Victory!* Its editorial basked only in civic pride, noting, "Everything seems to be coming Boston's way this year—the baseball championship, the Constitution, rapid transit, and now the whole North Atlantic squadron." As if the two were logically coupled, the *Globe* added that besides having the baseball championship, Boston was still the literary center of the country![66]

A loss to Baltimore in the meaningless Temple Cup series (between the top two teams, to provide extra money to the players) did not dampen the championship spirit, as the city hosted a testimonial banquet at Faneuil Hall. Congressman John F. Fitzgerald presided, and Mayor Quincy presented the players with diamond-studded watches. Unlike the earlier reaction to John L. Sullivan's testimonial, the mayor suffered no criticism for this politically wise gesture. It would have been unpatriotic.[67]

This season also brought the birth of Boston's first organized fan club, the Royal Rooters. At the head of this marvelous collection of baseball kranks was one Michael T. McGreevey, who had recently opened a saloon called "The Third Base" near the National League grounds. McGreevey's motto was "Nuf Ced"; and this became his nickname. Led by McGreevey, Fitzgerald, and Waltham's Michael J. Regan, the Royal Rooters had a decidedly Irish stamp to them. They frequently traveled by train to cheer their heroes on the road, and McGreevey himself later accompanied the Red Sox on their spring treks to Hot Springs. Their antics at the ball park suggested few social pretensions. Their fight song was "Tessie, You Make Me Feel So Badly," but they also belted out a doctored version of "The Good Old Summertime":

> In the good-old summer time,
> Our Boston Baseball Nine
> Beat the teams—East and West
> Now they're first in line,
> The Athletics they are after us,
> Oh, me! Oh, me! Oh, my!
> We'll do them as we did the rest
> In the good old summer time.

Begun to support the National League franchise, the Royal Rooters had no trouble adopting the later American League club.[68]

An Early View of the Boston "Nationals"
Courtesy of the Boston Public Library, Print Department

After 1897, the Boston team continued to enjoy occasional success in the National League, but its local popularity suffered considerably after 1901 when the Boston franchise in the rival American League opened its doors at the South End grounds. Quickly second best in attendance, the National League club had also to watch the Pilgrims' (after 1907, the Red Sox) success on the field.[69] But in 1914 the elder Braves performed a "miracle comeback" to win the World Series. For this season, at least, they were Boston's darlings.

Led by manager George Stallings, shortshop "Rabbit" Maranville, and the legendary Johnny Evers, the Braves surged from last place in mid-July to an October pennant, winning sixty of their last seventy-six games.[70] But the path to full glory for team and city was still quite formidable. The Boston tribe faced as a World Series opponent Connie Mack's Athletics, winners of the American League and World Series in three of the last four years. Worse, the first two games were in Philadelphia.

Most baseball fans were astounded when the Braves swept these openers. Boston gave them a rousing welcome at South Station, and keyed up for the Columbus Day clash. The *Globe* reported

189

*"Nuf Ced"
McGreevey—
A Peerless Fan*

Courtesy of the Boston Public Library, Print Department

every hotel "crowded to capacity," their lobbies jammed with avid fans from around the country; Boston was "surcharged with a suppressed excitement." Had a stranger arrived totally unaware of the clash, claimed the paper, "he could not have failed to realize that some momentous occasion was at hand."[71] Women, "and sensible women at that," stood all night in the long line waiting for the gates to open at 9:00 A.M. They proved to be quite durable and "an inspiration to those fortunate as to be near them."[72] Two-dollar seats sold at $30 a pair; four-dollar seats for $50. Young gamins hawked counterfeit tickets for $12. Twenty-five thousand people swarmed the Common opposite the *Herald* building to see the scores on the giant board.[73]

The Braves' victory in the third game pushed news of the Great War out of the headlines on the front page. The *Globe* described the 5–4 victory in twelve innings, the thirty-five thousand fans who

The Royal Rooters at Baltimore—September 1897

Courtesy of the Boston Public Library, Print Department

had filled the bleachers a full four hours before game time, the antics of ex-mayor Fitzgerald and the Royal Rooters, and the crowd-pleasing presentations of Fitzgerald's political opponent, incumbent mayor James Michael Curley. Notables from the "better classes" watched the game from box seats; Governor David Walsh and the Honorable Samuel McCall sat at Fenway, while thousands of less fortunate souls crowded downtown "Newspaper Row."[74]

Boston reveled when the Braves swept the fourth game, and the series, from the reigning champs. When the bedlam subsided, the City Council sponsored a testimonial banquet at the Copley Plaza. The local politicians affirmed their long-standing support of the team, each trying to outdo the other in this regard. Lieutenant Governor Edward Barry declared that winning the championship "means a wonderful asset to the city, its merchants and its hotels, which latter have been enriched by at least $500,000." Assistant Attorney General Thomas Riley spoke of "the proud distinction brought to Boston by the great baseball victory." But it was left to Daniel J. McDonald to sum up the meaning of a championship. "Boston is once again on the map," he claimed, "for the series just closed has put Boston much more prominently before the national public than anything that has happened there for many years."[75] Much of this was vote-getting rhetoric, but one must remember that successful politicians have always been adept at supporting causes that have universal appeal and few detractors. Boston, as a city, could unite its classes, its ethnic groups, and its neighborhoods in support of a baseball champion. A seat at Fenway Park, a spot on "Newspaper Row," a glance at the morning headlines could all thrust the individual into a sense of community feeling.[76]

THESE TEAM AND INDIVIDUAL HEROES were symbolic leaders in cities like Boston. They tell us something about the desires and needs of many Americans during these years of rapid change. Sports heroes boosted individual, group, and civic morale, provided role models for young and old, and helped frame the city's or group's image as winner or loser. While heroes existed in all walks of life, the sports figure had some distinct advantages. By the turn of the century, his exploits were given prominent coverage in daily newspapers and journals. As Greg Lee Carter has emphasized, the sports symbol was both salient and simple to understand. One need not analyze complex data to determine whether the player or team was a winner or loser.[77] We have grown so accustomed to the worship of sports figures that we tend to forget how strange and curious the cult was a hundred years ago. But we should not take the idea for granted.

Joseph Lee grappled with the question at the beginning of this century:

> Already there are discernible signs of suspicion on our part that there is something wrong, a sort of stirring in our sleep, a half consciousness of our exiled state. It is seen in our vicarious interest in sport, in the way which gray-haired men will pore [sic] over the last imaginary details about a coming prize fight, in our football hysteria, in our mania for professional baseball. We have a homesick sort of feeling that there or thereabouts lies something reminiscent of a happier life. We turn to a hired expression of that in ourselves that goes unexpressed with something of a child's pathetic desire to get back home.[78]

Lee, of course, advocated active play; to him, the increase of spectators was symptomatic of a "dislocation in civilized life." But others felt that these great outbursts or "sprees" of fan interest served important societal needs. One early sociologist claimed they acted as "outlets for emotional expression and satisfaction"; they helped break the "prosy humdrum of human existence," and, more important, supplied "joyous abandon" and "creative gladness" to workers divorced from the satisfaction of seeing a job through from start to finish.[79]

Further, athletic heroes appealed to urban residents because they were successful products of physical exercise. We have seen the continued promotion of exercise for all classes by such varied groups as school authorities, social reformers, park and playground advocates, bicycle manufacturers, and physical educators. The theme of exercise for health was ever present and compelling. Athletes were alluring because they could display expertise in these same heavily promoted skills. Victory was a simple measure of excellence and perfection. Deeds, not promises, made the man.[80]

In part, then, sporting heroes enjoyed popularity because they touched a chord of reaction to the sedentary life in the modern city. On the other hand, however, their following depended heavily upon the technological advances of the age. The newspaper and the telegraph lent an important sense of immediacy and presence to the fan who was separated from an event by income or distance. In describing the partisans who jammed the Music Hall for reports of the 1897 baseball series with Baltimore, the *Evening Transcript* captured the crucial dimension of instant communication:

> There may have been men there who have had their doubts of the value of the telegraph and the telephone, the trolley and the incandescent light, the phonograph and the vitascope, but there was evidently no one who questioned in his innermost consciousness its service in the dissemination of baseball intelligence.[81]

The detailed reports and instant wirephotos of the Johnson-Jeffries fight meant that the fan's impression would hardly have been more vivid had the two men slugged it out on the Common. Sporting heroes no longer depended upon the slow diffusion of oral tradition for their popularity; it was instantly conveyed to wide audiences.[82]

In the end, though, the great athletes and teams gained notoriety

193

because they served as images or symbols around which their community—be it neighborhood, social class, ethnic group, or entire city—could characterize and assess its own life or that of others. To many Irish Bostonians, John L. Sullivan symbolized the fighting spirit and gusto for life that were necessary for survival in the city. To Brahmins and lace-curtain Irish, however, he represented all the brutal traits that held the Irish back. We saw a similar division in the black community during Jack Johnson's reign. Regardless of these differences, Sullivan and Johnson lent meaning to the mass of impressions and experiences that accompanied the direct and indirect contacts between natives and immigrants, between blacks and whites. Similarly, Francis Ouimet's rags-to-riches story was rare in real life, and he was never wealthy; but his victory proved that all this *could* happen in America.

The symbolic leader was a complex force. He could at times split a city even while he was uniting a group within it. Ultimately, though, like the neighborhood lobby, the club, and the craze, his fan following indicated that Bostonians developed many forms of fellow feeling during these years of rapid change. As Jim Jeffries supporters might indicate, the motives were not always positive. But when the sport, the team, or the individual was right, a celebration of success could transcend class, ethnic, or neighborhood differences and make the city feel good about itself.

10/A Parting Glimpse

WHY THE GREAT EXPANSION of sport, exercise, and outdoor recreation in Boston during these years? Surely the causes were numerous and closely linked. Urban business opportunity provided more people than ever before with the income and free time necessary for enjoying many of these activities. Of course the booms and busts of unregulated capitalism resulted in periodic and severe hardships. The free time of many Bostonians was often enforced by economic depression; the poorest immigrants and laborers tasted few fruits of modern business. The private and public promoters of recreation and sport, however, benefited from the economic growth of the period, which slowly created the large-scale reserve of discretionary time and money upon which their enterprise depended.[1]

The appeal of active pursuits might vary. Workers could find in sports some vindication of the priority of physical skill, even in the machine age. Ironically, this worship of muscular ability could lead thousands to spend a sunny afternoon sitting in the stands! But even larger numbers became participants of one sport or another. Many doubtless found in active sports a nice balance to their stationary or sedentary routines in office or factory. Henry Ward Beecher had advocated this "rational" approach to amusements in an 1869 Boston lecture. "As the director in a dance cries out 'change partners,' so it is with amusements," he said; "the still people must stir; the bustling folks must be still; those who stand must sit; those who labor their hands should use their brains, and scholars should exercise their bodies." Bostonians found that many active amusements fit Beecher's call after the Civil War.

Thus the frequent rages for velocipedes, croquet, badminton, roller skating, tennis, and golf.[2]

There always seemed to be a novelty to try; one fad frequently gave way to another, as Thomas Wentworth Higginson noted in describing the gymnasium's lack of sustained popularity. "To be an American," he said, "is to hunger for novelty." Because of this, he claimed, all instruments and appliances required constant modification. "We are dissatisfied with last winter's skates, with the old boat, and with the family pony." No wonder the zealot found the gymnasium "insufficient long before he has learned half the moves."[3] To trace the rise and fall of the many amusement crazes and rages that have swept through Boston during her history would be a fascinating study. What were their sources?

In Boston, much of the sporting impulse stemmed from a tendency to mirror English social fashion. As one contemporary analyst noted, "Anglomaniacism" had much to do with the greater acceptance of outdoor sports by men and women alike. While the true patriot might cringe at the love of things English, there was some compensation, she concluded; for Anglomaniacism "has made it here in America, because in England, the fashion to ride, to cycle and to play games."[4]

However they germinated, the organized sports that we have examined were more than just passing fads. The larger undertakings like public parks and playgrounds—requiring millions of dollars of expenditures, much in times of financial distress—were not crazes to be picked up and discarded like a velocipede. Golf, baseball, football, school sports, athletic clubs, and bicycling all continued to grow in the urban environment. They are today incorporated into established industries, leagues, and powerful governing bodies.

More than any other reason, the activities we have examined thrived because they seemed to be virtuous and useful in the urban community. They satisfied the particular desires and interests of urban residents. During the nineteenth century, the continuing swell of immigration, both from rural America and from overseas, the expanding sprawl of housing and industry, the emergence of new political machinery, and the sharpening distinctions between social, economic, and ethnic groups, all combined to create a sense of disruption in community. The principal proponents, organizers, and consumers of sport and recreation adopted a product that appeared to offer order, identity, stability, and association in the face of this crisis.

Concerned residents examined the city and found it physically debilitating. Clusters of wretched housing, poor sewage systems, and polluted air made the city ripe for illness and disease. Even those who could avoid its noxious living environment could not escape its breakneck nervous pace. As Dr. Dudley A. Sargent reminded readers of the *Saturday Evening Post,* the speed of modern life was a double-edged sword: "The telegraph, the telephone and the swift flying mail train and ocean liner have quickened the pulses of life and revolutionized the methods of doing business." At the same time, he noted, "how to keep pace with this rapid method of doing things is getting to be a serious problem with a great many people . . . and a host of people are breaking down annually in their efforts to do so."[5] Urban citizens were "nervous, anaemic, with little appetite," added another observer; they had lost "the spring and vitality of life and the joy of mere existence."[6]

Worse than the destruction of individual lives was the shredding of the city's very social fabric. Urban historians have recognized the specialization of urban space and the residential sorting by race, ethnicity, income, and occupation that improved transit and communication had allowed. While modern technology might also tie this differentiated composite together, this fact was not appreciated by all contemporaries.[7] As the population increased and dispersed, many reformers feared the desiccation of neighborhood spirit. To Joseph Lee or Robert A. Woods, the burgeoning tenements and town houses were no insurance that the city dweller would have any neighbors or groups with whom he felt real membership or social bonds. The mass of humanity was no guarantee that people felt any measure of shared or mutual responsibility. Amid squalor and splendor, the artisan, the laborer, the banker, or the clerk might move accountable to no one.[8]

It was against this background of real concern over the city's physical environment, its social life, and its image that public and private sport and recreation promoters fashioned their arguments. In reality, of course, urban life was not as disordered as critics then and later made it out to be. Nonetheless, perceptions spurred actions. Residents in Boston and other cities continued to reshape and reestablish meaningful forms of community; often their efforts occurred within a sporting medium. Thus, as we have seen,

197

recreation and sport operated in two distinct patterns of what can be called a search for community. The first involved attempts to directly shape or control the city so as to create a consciously defined sense of community. The drives to erect public recreation spaces and fill them with adult-directed games fit here. At the same time, however, a growing number of residents were less interested in confronting the city than they were in nurturing the ties of association and identity that the urban reality had presented to them. This receptive establishment of community encompassed clubs, commodities, and charismatic heroes. But we should not be too rigid in creating categories. In fact, several common themes can be found within both the active and receptive patterns of community formation. These included the notions of escape, reform, and association.

To begin with, much of the promotional ethos focused on attempts to provide antidotes or escapes from the city, its expanding congestion, and its mental strain. This represented no outright denial of urban life and opportunity, but rather simply a means to gain temporary refuge and asylum from the struggle—*recreation* for another day's toil. Public parks were to act as the lungs of the city, purifying its air and the spirit of its people. In the open space of a park the urban resident would find fresh air, blue sky, green trees, meadows, and sparkling brooks—scenes in striking contrast to those found normally in the city. Those with the means and the temperament sought a similar tonic at the golf club or the country club. In the midtown playground, its advocates claimed, the child or adult found welcome relief from the clank and clatter of teamster wagon or trolley car. During the 1890s, thousands took to the "silent steed," the bicycle, for similar reasons.

There was an irony here, however, since every escape was supported by the same technology, rationality, and organization that were integral parts of the life to be left behind. Olmsted's parks were carefully planned and engineered; they grew not just from nature's bounty, but from modern sciences like surveying, botany, engineering, and hydraulics. Likewise, the bicycle that conveyed so many to the great outdoors was the product of modern technological genius.

In many respects this escapist thrust mirrored and even antedated the suburban movement that some contemporary social analysts had outlined. In describing the growth of the suburbs, Adna

Weber wrote in 1899: "Such a new distribution of population combines at once the open air and spaciousness of the country with the sanitary improvements, comforts and associated life of the city."[9] Much of organized sport and recreation made a similar promise—to offer urban residents a short respite from the city's problems, so that they might be better equipped to make the most of its benefits. At times, though, the illusion of escape could be rudely shattered. For instance, as early as 1887 the parks commissioners were calling for additional police patrols in Franklin Park, where a "noisy gang of roughs" was causing trouble.[10]

But sport was not just a vehicle of escape. It also claimed to be an important tool of urban reform. Luther Gulick, director of the New York Public School Athletic League, long argued along these lines:

> We must accept the city for what it is, necessary, artificial, congested, nervously organized; and we must discover how to make these very traits count in upward development. Not by opposing inevitable tendencies, but by discovering their possibilities for good and pushing these to their logical issues shall we aid in the solution of our greatest social problem.[11]

Thus the movement for supervised playgrounds; take the "gang" impulse of youth and transfer it to team loyalty, which could, in turn, be broadened to community loyalty. School sports served the same purposes, especially after they had fallen from the control of students into the open arms of school authorities.

The social reform tradition was closely linked to the notion that sport and recreation improved the individual's character. As Josiah Quincy put it in one inaugural speech, there was an inverse relation between physical exercise and crime. "An active interest in athletic exercise, and the practice of it," said the mayor, "tends to keep a person out of evil paths, while, on the other hand, an absence of any such interest makes many persons an easier prey to the temptations and influences which lead to crime." While athletic club leaders were not so concerned with crime rates as was Mayor Quincy, they too stressed the character improvements that usually followed dedication to individual exercise and group cooperation.[12]

Closely tied to the escapist position, the reform arguments also took aim at the city's physical environment. We saw this particularly in the movement for parks and playgrounds. But even the bicycle craze contained a strong element of environmental reform—the movement for good roads.

Escape and reform did not exhaust the attractive features of sport and recreation. The popularity of many games and exercise forms also rested on their ability to bind people together, to give them a sense of identity, to make them happier with themselves and their community. As one historian of Charlestown put it:

> Unavoidable change must of course attend the growth of a population from comparatively small numbers of similar descent, most of whom knew each other, and where some families were large, to several-fold greater numbers, coming from many sources and having less in common.[13]

Sporting clubs provided a common focus for many of the city's neighborhoods, ethnic groups, and social classes. Athletic heroes did the same. These associations could, of course, fragment the population in any number of ways. The ultimate promise of sport, though, lay in its ability to bind groups together in a spirit of city-wide boosterism.

The campaigns, products, and activities we have examined were not casually laid before the public. They were carefully packaged and promoted, in full rhythm with the methods of modern business. The advertising usually followed one or more of the themes we have just discussed. But the object was to sell the product—park, playground, ball club, or bicycle—to the target audience. With newspapers eager to print sporting news, and even suggest improvements, product marketing was made easy. This caused some consternation among moralists like the Reverend Henry Morgan. As one rural migrant complained in his sensational novel, *Boston Inside Out,* "Why, great hokey! Boston folks seems ter be half crazy on amusements. Why the pesky papers don't seem ter have any thin' else scarcely, 'cept sports an' theatricals." Neither the bumpkin nor his creator could understand why a pedestrian match drew greater coverage than a sermon. The answer was simple. Sports sold copy. Sermons didn't.[14]

The promotional themes so well covered in the popular press interacted in a number of ways. For instance, we have seen that students promoted sports as a means of fostering the spirit of community in the school. Administrators, however, later redirected these same games as a vehicle of urban social reform. In the same way, while public parks were designed as an antidote to unchecked urban growth, they also acted as a source of great civic pride. Likewise, although suburban golf or country clubs offered a temporary escape from the congestion and mental strain of the city, they also provided an important source of identity for a particular social group.

So it was in complex ways that sport and recreation appeared quite valuable to Boston's search for community order and stability. Because of this value, advocates and promoters conceived and built up organizations to ensure that the benefits of sport would be achieved. During these years we see a proliferation of clubs, associations, commissions, and leagues, both public and private. These were instrumental in nature; they had definite goals. And as a result of this growing organization, there arose a gradual stress on the *results* of participation, rather than on the joy of the actual doing.

One old-timer complained that all the hoopla and organization were killing the fun in games and sports. Writing to the *Evening Transcript* in 1891, he outlined some of the pastimes of his youth: "Beetle and Wedge," "Log," "I Spy the Bull," and "Snap the Whip." There were "many, many others," he lamented, "which our 'modern youth' seem to have no idea of, while the old-fashioned foot ball and base ball are now reduced to a science and utilized to gather wealth, whereas we simply played for fun."[15] Exaggerated criticism, to be sure; young and old alike continued to play countless games "for the fun of it"; in parks, on streets, and in clubs. There was, however, a kernel of truth to the old man's cry. The great progress in sports and recreation revolved around organized and goal-oriented activities. Producers and consumers usually had more than just fun in mind.[16]

I have argued throughout this book that the notions of community change and community formation are useful in helping us understand the growth of sport and recreation in Boston. Was Boston unique in this regard, or did her experience reflect that of other American cities? Although these questions cannot be answered with certainty until historians produce more case studies of individual cities, it seems likely that the growth of sport and recreation occurred along parallel lines throughout urban America. Residents and reformers in other cities felt the same sense of growing disorder, and they addressed their problems much as Bostonians did. The concern for vicious amusements was echoed in many of America's cities. Public parks and playgrounds developed elsewhere along similar lines, as an urban phenomenon. And city dwellers throughout America experienced the lure of the club, the freedom of the bicycle, and the civic pride induced by successful athletic teams and heroes. The visions were typically the same. Sporting activities would help resolve the pains that accompanied rapid growth and change; partially at least, they would close up many of the fissures in modern life.[17]

As we have seen, though, the process contained both contradictions and illusions. Park and playground issues might elicit intense parochial bickering; athletic clubs might aggravate distinctions of class, nationality, sex, or race; the ties that bound consumers and fans might be fleeting, artificial, or manipulated. But little of this mattered. The prevailing sentiment in Boston and elsewhere stressed the positive value of sport and recreation as mediums through which Americans could struggle to strengthen themselves and their communities in the face of larger economic and social forces. That popular view has changed but little in the past hundred years.

Notes

Notes to Chapter 1

1. James D'Wolf Lovett, *Old Boston Boys and the Games They Played* (Boston: privately printed, 1906; reprint edn., Boston: Little, Brown, 1908), p. 17.

2. Football ordinance in *Reports of the Records Commissioners of the City of Boston Containing Boston Town Records* (Boston: Rockwell and Churchill, 1881–85), 25 October 1657. For other sports, see Carl Bridenbaugh, *Cities in the Wilderness: The First Century of Urban Life in America, 1625–1742* (New York: Oxford University Press, 1971), pp. 120, 274, 487; idem, *Cities in Revolt: Urban Life in America, 1743–1776* (New York: Oxford University Press, 1971), p. 364; Jennie Holliman, *American Sports, 1785–1835* (Durham, NC: Seeman Press, 1931), pp. 109, 122, 140, 147; Foster Rhea Dulles, *A History of Recreation: America Learns to Play*, 2nd edn. (New York: Appleton-Century-Crofts, 1965), pp. 48–49; Nancy Struna, "The Cultural Significance of Sport in the Colonial Chesapeake and Massachusetts" (Ph.D. dissertation, University of Maryland, 1979); Frank G. Armitage, "A Reconsideration of Puritan Recreation in Massachusetts, 1620–1763" (Ph.D. dissertation, Clark University, 1927).

3. *Boston Herald*, 15 August 1886; *South Boston Inquirer*, 16 July 1881. See also Joseph E. Garland, *Boston's North Shore* (Boston: Little, Brown, 1978), pp. 118–24, 220–29; John Allen Krout, *Annals of American Sport*, Yale Pageant of America, vol. 15 (New Haven: Yale University Press, 1929), pp. 60, 67.

4. *Boston Post*, 29 July 1842, 17, 18, 29 August 1843.

5. The attendance was probably exaggerated. *Boston Herald*, 5 July 1854; *Boston Post*, 4, 5 July 1863; *Boston Globe*, 4 July 1910.

6. Charles W. Eliot, "Rowing in the Fifties," *The H Book of Harvard Athletics*, ed. John A. Blanchard (Cambridge: Harvard Varsity Club, 1923), p. 10; George S. Mumford, "Rowing at Harvard," ibid., pp. 16–30.

7. *Boston Herald*, 6 July 1858.

8. John Boyle O'Reilly, *Athletics and Manly Sports* (Boston: Pilot Publishing Co., 1890), p. 85. For samples of the expanding coverage of college sports, see: *Boston Daily Advertiser*, 15, 16 May 1874, 27 June 1877; *Boston Herald*, 31 May 1881, 31 May 1888, 9 October 1890, 23 May 1891, 3

October 1894, 15 November 1903. See also Blanchard, *H Book of Harvard Athletics*; Nathaniel J. Hasenfus, *Athletics at Boston College* (Worcester, MA: Heffernan Press, 1943); Guy M. Lewis, "The Beginning of Organized Collegiate Sport," *American Quarterly* 32 (Summer 1970): 222–29.

9. *Boston Herald*, 10, 13, 14 May 1896; *The Pilot*, 16 May 1896; *South Boston Bulletin*, 6 June 1896; Ellery H. Clark, *Reminiscences of an Athlete: Twenty Years on Track and Field* (Boston: Houghton Mifflin, 1911), pp. 124–41.

10. *Boston Herald*, 19 April 1897; "Clarence DeMar Scrapbook," Boston Tradition in Sports Collection, microfilm reproduction, Boston Public Library.

11. Thomas W. Lawson, *The Krank: His Language and What It Means* (Boston: Rand Avery Co., 1888), cited in Harold Seymour, *Baseball: The Early Years* (New York: Oxford University Press, 1960), p. 338; David Q. Voigt, *American Baseball: From Gentleman's Sport to Commissioner's System* (Norman, OK: Oklahoma University Press, 1966), p. 180.

12. *Boston Herald*, 18 August 1886, 4 October 1903.

13. William Phelon, "The Great American Fan," *Baseball Magazine* 7 (September 1911): 3.

14. David Q. Voigt, "The Boston Red Stockings: The Birth of Major League Baseball," *New England Quarterly* 43 (December 1970): 531–49.

15. *Boston Herald*, 15 February 1887, 9, 12 November 1894. George V. Touhey, *A History of the Boston Baseball Club* (Boston: M. V. Quinn, 1897); Ellery H. Clark, Jr., *Boston Red Sox: 75th Anniversary History, 1901–1975* (Hicksville, NY: Exposition Press, 1975).

16. *Boston Herald*, 4 September 1881; James Dwight, "Lawn Tennis in New England," *Outing* 18 (1891): 157–60.

17. Joanna Davenport, "Eleonora Randolph Sears," *Notable American Women: The Modern Period*, ed. Barbara Sicherman et al. (Cambridge: Belknap Press of Harvard University Press, 1980), pp. 638–39.

18. Boston, Parks Department, *13th Annual Report, City Document No. 14*, 1888, p. 59.

19. Boston, City Council, *Reports of Proceedings*, 29 March 1877, 18 October 1915 (published annually; hereafter cited as "City Council Proceedings").

20. Boston, Department of Baths, *1st Annual Report, City Document No. 3a*, 1899. For early gyms see "A Report by E. M. Hartwell, Director of Physical Training," Boston, *School Document No. 22*, 1891. For later statistics, see Department of Baths, *Annual Report, City Document No. 5*, 1910.

21. C. Frank Allen, "The School in the Civil War," *Forty Years On: The Old Roxbury Latin School on Kearsarge Avenue from the Civil War to the Twenties*, ed. Francis Russell (West Roxbury, MA: Roxbury Latin School, 1970), p. 22; Henry Adams, *The Education of Henry Adams* (Boston, 1906;

reprint edn., Boston: Houghton Mifflin, Sentry edn., 1961), p. 38; *The English High School Record* 11 (November 1895): 10–12.

22. Address by Mr. Frank Morison, 29 December 1888, in *Boston Athletic Association*, ed. Edward Rankin (n.p., n.d.).

23. Frederic L. Paxson, "The Rise of Sport," *Mississippi Valley Historical Review* 4 (September 1917): 143–68; Dulles, *A History of Recreation*, pp. 198–99; John Higham, "The Reorientation of American Culture in the 1890s," *The Origins of Modern Consciousness*, ed. Horace John Weiss (Detroit: Wayne State University Press, 1965), p. 27. This standard argument appeared in the widely cited urban histories of Arthur M. Schlesinger, *The Rise of the City, 1878–1898, A History of American Life* (New York: Macmillan, 1933), vol. 10, pp. 308–19; and Blake McKelvey, *The Urbanization of America, 1860–1915* (New Brunswick, NJ: Rutgers University Press, 1963), pp. 184–93. See also John Allen Krout, "Some Reflections on the Rise of American Sport," *Proceedings of the Association of History Teachers of the Middle States and Maryland* 26 (1928): 84–93; Ralph H. Gabriel, "Sport in American Life," in Krout, *Annals of American Sport*, pp. 1–8; John R. Betts, *America's Sporting Heritage* (Reading, MA: Addison-Wesley, 1974); Lewis Mumford, *Technics and Civilization* (New York: Harcourt, Brace, and World, 1963), pp. 303–7; John A. Lucas, "A Prelude to the Rise of Sport: Antebellum America, 1850–1860," *Quest* 11 (December 1968): 50–57; Fritz Redlich, "Leisure-Time Activities: A Historical, Sociological, and Economic Analysis," *Explorations in Entrepreneurial History*, 2nd Series, 3 (1965): 3–23; Dale Somers, "The Leisure Revolution: Recreation in the American City, 1820–1920," *Journal of Popular Culture* 5 (Summer 1971): 125–47.

24. John R. Betts, "The Technological Revolution and the Rise of Sport, 1850–1900," *Mississippi Valley Historical Review* 40 (September 1953): 231–56. See also Seymour, *Baseball: The Early Years*, pp. 14, 32–34; Dale Somers, *The Rise of Sports in New Orleans, 1850–1900* (Baton Rouge: Louisiana State University Press, 1972); John Lucas and Ronald Smith, *Saga of American Sport* (Philadelphia: Lea and Febiger, 1978), pp. 125–47.

25. Lucas and Smith, *Saga of American Sport*, p. 67; Benjamin Rader, "Modern Sports: In Search of Interpretations," *Journal of Social History* 13 (Winter 1979): 308. The instinct idea also appears in Dulles, *A History of Recreation*, p. ix; Somers, *The Rise of Sports in New Orleans*, p. viii.

26. Paxson, "The Rise of Sport," 154, claims that the wealth, leisure, and sedentary life-style found in cities "could not have failed" to develop sport.

27. Gunther Barth, *City People: The Rise of Modern City Culture in Nineteenth-Century America* (New York: Oxford University Press, 1980), pp. 148–91. In some respects, Barth's arguments follow those of Seymour, *Baseball: The Early Years*, pp. 350–51. The central role of records, regu-

lations, and performance standards is argued in Allen Guttmann, *From Ritual to Record: The Nature of Modern Sports* (New York: Columbia University Press, 1978); and Alan G. Ingham, "American Sport in Transition: The Maturation of Industrial Capitalism and Its Impact Upon Sport," (Ph.D. dissertation, University of Massachusetts, 1978).

28. Steven A. Riess, *Touching Base: Professional Baseball and American Culture in the Progressive Era* (Westport, CT: Greenwood Press, 1980).

29. For a fuller account of this literature see Stephen Hardy, "The City and the Rise of American Sport: 1820–1920," *Exercise and Sports Sciences Reviews* 9 (1981): 183–219.

30. Ralph Turner, "The Industrial City: Center of Cultural Change," *The Cultural Approach to History*, ed. Caroline Ware (New York: Columbia University Press, 1940), pp. 228–42. For "city-building" as a research model, see Roy Lubove, "The Urbanization Process: An Approach to Historical Research," *Journal of the American Institute of Planners* 33 (January 1967): 33–39; Eric Lampard, "Urbanization and Social Change; On Broadening the Scope and Relevance of Urban History," *The Historian and the City*, ed. Oscar Handlin and John Burchard (Cambridge: MIT Press, 1963), pp. 225–47.

31. Louis Wirth, "Urbanism as a Way of Life," *American Journal of Sociology* 44 (July 1938): 1–24. For a similar scheme, see Oscar Handlin, "The Modern City as a Field of Historical Study," in Handlin and Burchard, *The Historian and the City*, pp. 1–26. A solid review of Wirth's thought may be found in Michael P. Smith, *The City and Social Theory* (New York: St. Martin's Press, 1979): pp. 1–44.

32. Oscar Handlin, *Boston's Immigrants: A Study in Acculturation* (Cambridge: Harvard University Press, 1959; reprint edn. New York: Atheneum, 1974).

33. Brock Yates, "A Hot Time in the Bold Town," *Sports Illustrated* 39 (3 December 1973): 55.

34. Robert Lipsyte, "A Diamond in the Ashes," *Sports Illustrated* 44 (26 April 1976): 39.

35. Richard Coleman and Bernice Neugarten, *Social Status in the City* (San Francisco: Jossey-Bass, 1971), pp. 8, 41.

36. Steven A. Riess, "The Baseball Magnates and Urban Politics in the Progressive Era," *Journal of Sport History* 1 (May 1974): 64. See also idem, *Touching Base*, pp. 49–120.

Notes to Chapter 2

1. George A. Hillery, Jr., "Definitions of Community: Areas of Agreement," *Rural Sociology* 20 (1955): 111–23. See also Colin Bell and Howard Newby, *Community Studies: An Introduction to the Sociology of the Local Community* (New York: Praeger, 1972); Robert A. Nisbet, *The Sociological Tra-*

dition (New York: Basic Books, 1966), pp. 47–48; Roland Warren, *The Community in America* (Chicago: Rand McNally, 1963): pp. 9–14.

2. Thomas Bender, *Community and Social Change in America* (New Brunswick, NJ: Rutgers University Press, 1978), p. 7.

3. Ernest W. Burgess, "Can Neighborhood Work Have a Scientific Basis?" *The City*, ed. Robert E. Park, Ernest Burgess, Roderick McKenzie (Chicago: University of Chicago Press, 1925), p. 144.

4. Herbert Gans, *The Urban Villagers: Groups and Class in the Life of Italian-Americans* (New York: Free Press, 1962), p. 104; Max Weber, *The City*, ed. and trans. Don Martindale and Gertrud Neuwirth (Glencoe, IL: Free Press, 1958), pp. 80–81. David J. Russo, *Families and Communities: A New View of American History* (Nashville: American Association for State and Local History, 1974), calls for a new approach to American history that stresses the integrated nature of local, regional, and national communities. While Russo basically considers specific forms of community (e.g., family, small town, city, region, nation), he does realize the need to appreciate "community" beyond the boundaries of local space. See also James Borchert, "Urban Neighborhood and Community: Informal Group Life, 1850–1920," *Journal of Interdisciplinary History* 11 (Spring 1981): 607–31.

5. Gans, *Urban Villagers*, p. 104; David B. Clark, "The Concept of Community: A Re-examination," *Sociological Review* 21 (August 1973): 397–411; Park Dixon Goist, *From Main Street to State Street: Town, City and Community in America* (Port Washington, NY: Kennikat Press, 1977), pp. 3–9.

6. Burgess, "Neighborhood Work," p. 146; Robert M. French, ed., *The Community: A Comparative Perspective* (Itasca, IL: F. E. Peacock, 1969), especially the article by Roland Warren, "Toward a Reformation of Community Theory." See Daniel Boorstin's treatment of "everywhere communities" in *The Americans: The Democratic Experience* (New York: Vintage, 1973), pp. 1–244.

7. Don Martindale, "Prefatory Remarks: The Theory of the City," in Weber, *The City*, pp. 9–62.

8. Ferdinand Tönnies, *Community and Society*, trans. Charles P. Loomis (New York: Harper, 1963), pp. 33, 64–65. See also the discussions in Robert A. Nisbet, *The Quest for Community* (New York: Oxford University Press, 1969), pp. 75–97; Bender, *Community and Social Change*, pp. 17–21. For similar concerns among American intellectuals as far back as Jefferson see Harold Kaplan, "Beyond Society: The Idea of Community in Classic American Writing," *Social Research: An International Quarterly of the Social Sciences* 42 (Summer 1975), entire number devoted to "The Idea of Community." See also R. Jackson Wilson, *In Quest of Community: Social Philosophy in the United States, 1860–1920* (New York: John Wiley, 1968); Arthur M.

Schlesinger, Jr., *The Age of Jackson* (Boston: Little, Brown, 1945), pp. 3–29; 306–21.

9. *Classic Essays on the Culture of Cities*, ed. Richard Sennett (New York: Appleton-Century-Crofts, 1969), contains a fine introduction to excerpts from the works of Weber, Simmel, and Spengler. See also Carl E. Schorske, "The Idea of the City in European Thought: Voltaire to Spengler," in Handlin and Burchard, *The Historian and the City*, pp. 95–114; Michael P. Smith, *The City and Social Theory* (New York: St. Martin's Press, 1979), pp. 88–126.

10. Charles N. Glaab and A. Theodore Brown, *A History of Urban America*, 2nd edn. (New York: Macmillan, 1976), pp. 99–102; Harold U. Faulkner, *Politics, Reform and Expansion* (New York: Harper, 1959), pp. 1–22.

11. Josiah Strong, *Our Country: Its Possible Future and Present Crisis* (New York: Baker and Taylor, 1885), pp. 128–40. See also Morton and Lucia White, *The Intellectual Versus the City* (Cambridge: Harvard University Press, 1962). Paul Boyer has recently documented the continued concern for "moral order," in *Urban Masses and Moral Order in America, 1820–1920* (Cambridge: Harvard University Press, 1978).

12. Adna Weber, *The Growth of Cities in the Nineteenth Century: A Study in Statistics*, Columbia University Studies in History, Economics, and Public Law, vol. 11 (1899), p. 429. For changes in social relationships see Peter Goheen, "Industrialization and Growth of Cities in Nineteenth-Century America," *American Studies* 14 (Spring 1973): 49–65; Zane Miller, "Scarcity, Abundance, and American Urban History," *Journal of Urban History* 4 (February 1978): 141; Barth, *City People*, pp. 28–57. One should not lose sight of the fact that urban changes and urban problems were tightly linked to the expansion of mercantile and industrial capitalism. See Ira Katznelson, "Community, Capitalist Development and the Emergence of Class," *Politics and Society* 9 (1979): 203–38; Smith, *City and Social Theory*, pp. vii–ix, 171–229, 296–99. Most historical sources and modern scholars tend to equate class with occupation, e.g. blue-collar, white-collar. While I employ this basic formula, I am aware of its limitations. See Michael B. Katz, "Social Class in North American Urban History," *Journal of Interdisciplinary History* 11 (Spring 1981): 579–605.

13. Edward Bellamy, *Looking Backward* (New York, 1888; reprint edn., New York: New American Library, Signet edn., 1960), p. 50.

14. Robert H. Wiebe, *The Search for Order: 1877–1920* (New York: Hill and Wang, 1967), pp. 44–75.

15. Park, Burgess, and McKenzie, eds., *The City*, pp. 106–7. Park's attitude toward the city had hardened. In contrast to this passage see his earlier, more balanced view in "The City: Suggestions for the Investigation of Human Behavior in the City Environment," *American Journal of Sociology* 20 (March 1915): 577–612. Similar perceptions are examined in Goist,

From Main Street to State Street, pp. 110–20; David Price, "Community and Control: Critical Democratic Theory in the Progressive Period," *American Political Science Review* 68 (December 1974): 1663–78; Bender, *Community and Social Change,* pp. 19–21; Smith, *City and Social Theory,* pp. 1–44.

16. Bender, *Community and Social Change,* emphasizes this throughout his book. I have profited from his interesting analysis. For the persistence of community, see Tamara Hareven, "The Historical Study of the Family in Urban Society," *Journal of Urban History* 1 (May 1975), 262–63; Gans, *Urban Villagers;* Claude Fischer et al., *Networks and Places: Social Relations in the Urban Setting* (New York: Free Press, 1977), pp. 1–16, 189–205.

17. John T. Prince, "Boston in 1813: Reminiscences of an Old Schoolboy," *Bostonian Society Publications* 3 (1906): 76.

18. Quoted in Stanley K. Schultz, "Breaking the Chains of Poverty: Public Education in Boston, 1800–1860," *Cities in American History,* ed. Kenneth T. Jackson and Stanley K. Schultz (New York: Knopf, 1972), p. 307. See the similar sentiment in "Public and Private Charities in Boston," *North American Review* 61 (July 1845): 155–56.

19. *Society in America* (New York: Saunders & Otley, 1837), vol. 2, p. 290, quoted in Handlin, *Boston's Immigrants,* p. 19.

20. Ibid., p. 20; Edward Everett Hale, *A New England Boyhood* (Boston: Casell, 1893), ch. 4.

21. Robert A. McCaughey, "From Town to City: Boston in the 1820s," *Political Science Quarterly* 88 (June 1973): 191–213.

22. Ray Allen Billington, "The Burning of the Charlestown Convent," *The New England Quarterly* 10 (March 1937): 4–24; James P. Green and H. C. Donahue, *Boston's Workers: A Labor History* (Boston: Trustees of Boston Public Library, 1979), p. 22.

23. George Rogers Taylor, "The Beginnings of Mass Transportation in Urban America," *Smithsonian Journal of History* 1 (Summer 1966): 35. See also Handlin, *Boston's Immigrants,* table 2, p. 239. Population turnover in Peter Knights, *The Plain People of Boston, 1830–1860: A Study in City Growth* (New York: Oxford University Press, 1971), pp. 59, 119–26.

24. Knights, *Plain People,* p. 121; Handlin, *Boston's Immigrants,* pp. 51–53.

25. *The Massachusetts Teacher* 4 (October 1851): 289–91, quoted in Michael B. Katz, ed., *School Reform: Past and Present* (Boston: Little, Brown, 1971), p. 169.

26. Handlin, *Boston's Immigrants,* p. 206.

27. Quoted in Paul Hughes, "Edward Everett Hale and the American City" (Ph.D. dissertation, New York University, 1975), pp. 87, 89.

28. *Report of the Committee of Internal Health on the Asiatic Cholera* (Boston, 1849), p. 13; Schultz, "Breaking the Chains," 309.

29. Boston, *City Documents No. 11,* 1852, p. 3; quoted in Knights, *Plain People,* p. 114.

30. Handlin, *Boston's Immigrants*, pp. 151–77. On the Brahmins, see Ronald Story, *The Forging of an Aristocracy: Harvard and the Boston Upper Class, 1800–1870* (Middletown, CT: Wesleyan University Press, 1980).

31. Howard Mumford Jones, "The Wounds of War: A Tale of Two Cities," *Harvard Library Bulletin* (April 1972): 135–57; Handlin, *Boston's Immigrants*, pp. 207–11.

32. *The Census of Massachusetts for 1905* (Boston, 1909), vol. 1: xxxi; *Boston's Growth: A Bird's-Eye View of Boston's Increase in Territory and Population from Its Beginning to the Present* (Boston, printed for the State Street Trust Co., 1910).

33. Stephan Thernstrom, *The Other Bostonians: Poverty and Progress in the American Metropolis, 1880–1970* (Cambridge: Harvard University Press, 1973), p. 21.

34. Frederic Bushee, *Ethnic Factors in the Population of Boston*, Publications of the American Economic Association, Third Series, 4 (May 1903); Thernstrom, *Other Bostonians*, table 6.1, p. 113; Carroll D. Wright, *The Social, Commercial and Manufacturing Statistics of the City of Boston* (Boston, 1882).

35. Sam Bass Warner, *Streetcar Suburbs: The Process of Growth in Boston, 1870–1900* (Cambridge: Harvard University Press, 1962; reprint edn., New York: Atheneum, 1972), p. 2; Bellamy quotation in 1960 edition of New American Library, p. 29. On reclamation of land see Walter Muir Whitehill, *Boston: A Topographical History*, 2nd edn. (Cambridge: Belknap Press of Harvard University Press, 1968).

36. Massachusetts Bureau of Statistics of Labor, *Forty-first Annual Report*, 1910; Robert A. Woods, ed., *Americans in Process: North and West Ends of Boston* (Boston: Houghton Mifflin, 1902); idem, *The City Wilderness* (Boston: Houghton Mifflin, 1898); Paula Todiso, *Boston's First Neighborhood: The North End* (Boston: Trustees of Boston Public Library, 1975); William De Marco, "Ethnics and Enclaves: The Italian Settlement in the North End of Boston" (Ph.D. dissertation, Boston College, 1980); Sari Roboff, *The North End*, Boston 200 Neighborhood History Series (Boston: Boston 200 Corp., 1975); James R. Green, *The South End*, Boston 200 Neighborhood History Series (Boston: Boston 200 Corp., 1975).

37. Robert A. Woods and Albert Kennedy, eds., *The Zone of Emergence: Observations of the Lower Middle and Upper Working Class Communities of Boston, 1905–1914*, abridged and edited with a preface by Sam Bass Warner, Jr., 2nd edn. (Cambridge: MIT Press, 1969), p. 35; Sari Roboff, *East Boston*; Katie Kenneally, *Charlestown*; idem, *South Boston*, Boston 200 Neighborhood History Series (Boston: Boston 200 Corp., 1976).

38. Warner, *Streetcar Suburbs*, pp. 120, 157, notes that even here only one-quarter owned homes. See also Anne Millet, *Hyde Park*; Katie Kenneally, *Roslindale*; idem, *Brighton*; idem, *West Roxbury*; idem, *Dorchester*, all

in Boston 200 Neighborhood History Series (Boston: Boston 200 Corp., 1975–76).

39. B. O. Flower, *Civilization's Inferno, or, Studies in the Social Cellar* (Boston, 1893); E. M. Hartwell, *Report of the Director of Physical Training, School Document No. 8,* 1894, pp. 25–27.

40. Wakstein, "Boston's Search for a Metropolitan Solution," *Journal of the American Institute of Planners* 38 (September 1972): 288; Handlin, *Boston's Immigrants,* p. 215.

41. Geoffrey Blodgett, *The Gentle Reformers: Massachusetts Democrats in the Cleveland Era* (Cambridge: Harvard University Press, 1966); John T. Galvin, "The Dark Ages of Boston City Politics," Massachusetts Historical Society, *Proceedings* 89 (1977): 88–111.

42. Woods, *Americans in Process,* pp. 147–89; Blodgett, *Gentle Reformers,* pp. 166–71. Galvin, "Dark Ages of Boston Politics"; Robert A. Silverman, "Nathan Matthews: Politics of Reform in Boston, 1890–1910," *New England Quarterly* 50 (1977): 626–43.

43. Carroll D. Wright, *Strikes in Massachusetts, 1830–1880,* Massachusetts Bureau of Statistics of Labor, *Eleventh Annual Report,* 1880, reprinted 1889. See also the bureau's *Seventeenth Annual Report,* 1886, cited in Arthur Mann, *Yankee Reformers in the Urban Age* (Cambridge: Harvard University Press, 1954), p. 2. John Boyle O'Reilly, "The City Streets," *The Pilot* (Boston), 20 January 1883, reprinted in George E. McNeill, *The Labor Movement: The Problem of Today* (Boston: A. M. Bridgman and Co., 1887), pp. 457–59. See also Jama Lazerow, "'The Workingman's Hour': The 1886 Labor Uprising in Boston," *Labor History* 21 (Spring 1980): 200–20.

44. Hale, *New England Boyhood,* p. 240; "loneliness" quotation cited in Hughes, "Hale and the American City," 137.

45. Van Wyck Brooks, *New England: Indian Summer, 1865–1915* (New York: E. P. Dutton, 1940), p. 98.

46. Quoted in Geoffrey Blodgett, "Frederick Law Olmsted: Landscape Architecture as Conservative Reform," *Journal of American History* 62 (March 1976): 885. See also similar sentiments in John P. Bobock, "The Irish Conquest of Our Cities," *Forum* 16 (April 1894): 186–95.

47. Francis Parkman, "The Failure of Universal Suffrage," *North American Review* 127 (July 1878): 4.

48. Henry Cabot Lodge, *Boston* (London: Longmans, Green, 1892), pp. 198, 224.

49. Norton quotation in Barbara Miller Solomon, *Ancestors and Immigrants: A Changing New England Tradition* (Cambridge: Harvard University Press, 1956; reprint edn., New York: John Wiley, 1965), p. 15. On the Brahmin class and their reactions to industrialism see Frederic Cople Jaher, "The Boston Brahmins in the Age of Industrial Capitalism," in Jaher, ed., *The Age of Industrialism in America* (New York: Free Press, 1968),

pp. 188–262; idem, "Nineteenth-Century Elites in Boston and New York," *Journal of Social History* 6 (Fall 1972): 32–77. On their political adjustment, see Peter K. Eisinger, "Ethnic Political Transition in Boston, 1884–1933: Some Lessons for Contemporary Cities," *Political Science Quarterly* 93 (Summer 1978): 217–39.

50. Warner, *Streetcar Suburbs*, p. 162; James A. Merino, "Cooperative Schemes for Greater Boston," *New England Quarterly* (June 1972): 196–226.

51. Woods, *City Wilderness*, p. 3. On the larger role of the settlement house, see Allen F. Davis, *Spearheads for Reform: The Social Settlements and the Progressive Movement, 1890–1914* (New York: Oxford University Press, 1967).

52. Woods and Kennedy, eds., *Zone of Emergence*, p. 144.

53. Paul Boyer, *Urban Masses and Moral Order in America, 1820–1920*, p. 131. See also Mann, *Yankee Reformers in the Urban Age*.

54. McNeill, *The Labor Movement*, p. 455.

55. *Republic*, 10 May 1890, quoted in Blodgett, *Gentle Reformers*, pp. 151–52.

56. Isaac Goldberg, "A Boston Boyhood," *The American Mercury* 17 (July 1929): 356. See also Alvan Sanborn, *Moody's Lodging House and Other Tenement Sketches* (Boston: Copeland and Day, 1895), p. 110; Gans, *Urban Villagers*; Handlin, *Boston's Immigrants*, pp. 154–55, 176; Humbert Nelli, "Italians in Urban America: A Study in Ethnic Adjustment," *International Migration Review*, New Series, 1 (Summer 1967): 38–55.

57. Katznelson, "Community, Capitalist Development, and the Emergence of Class." I have profited greatly from Katznelson's analysis, especially his ideas about the importance of political linkages, consumption patterns, and ties of affect in restructuring community. On the segmentation of space, see also Barth, *City People*, ch. 2; David Ward, "The Industrial Revolution and the Emergence of Boston's Central Business District," *Economic Geography* 42 (1966): 152–71.

58. Nisbet, *Quest for Community*, p. 73. See Fischer et al., *Networks and Places*, pp. 7–12, for a critique of Nisbet's notions of community decline. Barth quotation in *City People*, p. 3.

59. Barth, *City People*, passim.

Notes to Chapter 3

1. Daniel T. Rodgers, *The Work Ethic in Industrial America, 1850–1920* (Chicago: University of Chicago Press, 1978), p. xiii.

2. Ibid., p. 7. For the type of ranking I am describing see Melvin Adelman, "The Development of Modern Athletics: Sport in New York City, 1820–1870" (Ph.D. dissertation, University of Illinois, 1980), pp. 651–705.

3. E. P. Thompson, "Time, Work-Discipline, and Industrial Capital-

ism," *Past and Present* 38 (1967): 98–125; Oscar Handlin, "The Modern City as a Field of Historical Study," p. 14; Alan Dawley, *Class and Community: The Industrial Revolution in Lynn* (Cambridge: Harvard University Press, 1976), passim. For the maintenance of traditional patterns of work and leisure, see Herbert Gutman, "Work, Culture, and Society in Industrializing America, 1815–1919," *American Historical Review* 78 (June 1973): 531–88; Bruce Laurie, "'Nothing on Compulsion': Life Styles of Philadelphia Artisans, 1820–1850," *Labor History* 15 (Summer 1974): 367–94. "Leisure" definition in Michael Marrus, *The Emergence of Leisure* (New York, 1974), p. 6. See also Sebastian de Grazia, *Of Time, Work and Leisure* (Garden City, NY: Anchor edition, 1964).

4. John Downame, *Guide to Godlynesse* (London, 1622), p. 164; quoted in Nancy Struna, "Puritans and Sport; The Irretrievable Tide of Change," *Journal of Sport History* 4 (Spring 1977): 3.

5. William Burkitt, *The Poor Man's Help, and the Young Man's Guide* (London, 1684), pp. 35–39; quoted in Peter Wagner, "Puritan Attitudes Towards Physical Recreation in 17th Century New England," *Journal of Sport History* 3 (Summer 1976): 143.

6. Mather quoted in Wagner, "Puritan Attitudes." See Wagner's companion article, "American Puritan Literature: A Neglected Field of Research in American Sport History," *Canadian Journal of History of Sport and Physical Education* (December 1977): 62–75. Besides the numerous sources cited in Wagner's and Struna's articles, see also Increase Mather, *Testimony Against Profane Customs* (1687, reprint edn. Univ. of Virginia Press, 1953); idem, *An Arrow Against Profane and Promiscuous Dancing Drawn from the Quiver of the Scriptures* (Boston, 1684).

7. See *Acts and Resolves, Public and Private, of the Province of Massachusetts Bay* (Boston, 1869), pp. 58, 681; *The Colonial Laws of Massachusetts* (Boston, 1887), pp. 58, 347; *The Charters and General Laws of the Colony and Province of Massachusetts Bay* (Boston, 1814), p. 780; *Reports of the Records Commissioners of the City of Boston Containing Boston Town Records* (Boston, 1881–85).

8. John Danforth, *The Vile Prophanations of Prosperity* (Boston: Samuel Phillips, 1704), p. 40, quoted in Wagner, "American Puritan Literature," 67. See also Bernard Bailyn, *The New England Merchants in the Seventeenth Century* (New York: Harper Torchbooks edn., 1964), pp. 139–42.

9. "The Harm of Innocent Amusement," *Massachusetts Missionary Magazine* 1 (1803): 465; see also *Monthly Magazine and American Review* 1 (1799): 188.

10. Jill Siegel Dodd, "The Working Classes and the Temperance Movement in Ante-bellum Boston," *Labor History* 19 (Fall 1978): 510–31.

11. Paul Boyer, *Urban Masses and Moral Order*, p. 5. Boyer examines the problem as it was discerned in a number of antebellum cities.

12. Adrienne Siegel, "When Cities Were Fun: The Image of the Amer-

ican City in Popular Books, 1840–1870," *Journal of Popular Culture* 9 (1975): 573–82. Robert Toll, *Blacking Up! The Minstrel Show in Nineteenth-Century America* (New York: Oxford University Press, 1974), ch. 1, makes an interesting argument about the importance of the stage as a source of identity to rural immigrants.

13. Foster's series on Philadelphia and New York appear in the *New York Tribune*, October 1848–February 1849. See George Rogers Taylor, "Philadelphia in Slices," *Pennsylvania Magazine of History and Biography* 93 (1969): 23–72.

14. Boston, City Missionary Society, *Seventh Annual Report*, pp. 31, 32; quoted in J. L. Dunstan, *A Light to the City: 150 Years of the City Missionary Society of Boston, 1816–1966* (Boston, 1966).

15. William Clapp, "The Drama in Boston," *The Memorial History of Boston*, ed. Justin Winsor, 4 vols. (Boston, Ticknor and Co., 1880), vol. 4, p. 380. See also Claudia D. Johnson, "That Guilty Third Tier: Prostitution in Nineteenth-Century American Theaters," in Daniel Walker Howe, ed., *Victorian Culture* (Philadelphia: University of Pennsylvania, 1976), pp. 111–20. On Ann Street, see Edward H. Savage, *Police Records and Recollections; or, Boston by Daylight and Gaslight for Two Hundred and Forty Years* (Boston: John P. Dale, 1873), pp. 254–62.

16. *Boston Post*, 18 August 1843, 6 May 1852; Clapp, "The Drama in Boston."

17. Savage, *Police Records and Recollections*, pp. 155–66.

18. *Massachusetts Teacher* 2 (May 1849): 139; *Massachusetts Senate Document*, no. 12 (1850): 21–22; both quoted in Michael B. Katz, *The Irony of Early School Reform: Educational Innovation in Mid-Nineteenth Century Massachusetts* (Cambridge: Harvard University Press, 1968; reprint edn., Boston: Beacon Press, 1970), pp. 121, 172.

19. Rev. Robert Hunter, *On Cruelty to Animals* (Troy: N. Tuttle, 1835), pp. 13–17, 215; A. Chalmers, "On Cruelty to Animals," *The Methodist Magazine* 9 (July 1826): 259–66, quoted in Jack W. Berryman, "Anglo-American Blood Sports: A Study in Changing Morals" (M.A. thesis, University of Massachusetts, 1974), p. 110.

20. Charles Dickens, *American Notes* (London, 1842, reprint edn. London: Macmillan, 1923), p. 49.

21. The split among Protestant sects over the amusement question clearly related to basic issues such as the role of the environment in individual morality. Unitarians led the liberalization of ideas in this regard. See Daniel Walker Howe, *The Unitarian Conscience: Harvard Moral Philosophy, 1805–1861* (Cambridge: Harvard University Press, 1970).

22. "Ministry for the Poor," *The Works of William E. Channing*, new edn. (Boston: American Unitarian Association, 1889), p. 77.

23. "Address on Temperance," "Self-Culture," ibid., pp. 34, 101, 110–12.

24. Frederick W. Sawyer, *A Plea for Amusements* (New York: D. Appleton, 1847), p. 291; see the reaction to Sawyer in "Amusements," *New Englander* 9 (August 1851): 345–59. Parker quotation in Henry Steele Commager, ed., *Theodore Parker: An Anthology* (Boston: Beacon Press, 1960), pp. 157–58.

25. E. E. Hale, "Public Amusements and Public Morality," *Christian Examiner* 62 (July 1857): 51, 52.

26. E. E. Hale, *Public Amusement for Poor and Rich* (Boston: Phillips, Sampson and Co., 1857), p. 8; idem, *Sybaris and Other Homes, to Which Is Added, "How They Live in Hampton"* (Boston, 1900), pp. 383–84.

27. Hale, *Public Amusement for Poor and Rich*, pp. 10, 11.

28. See Guy Lewis, "The Muscular Christianity Movement," *Journal of Health, Physical Education and Recreation* 37 (May 1966): 27–28; John A. Lucas, "A Prelude to the Rise of Sport: Ante-bellum America, 1850–1860," *Quest* 11 (December 1968): 50–58; John R. Betts, "Mind and Body in Early American Thought," *Journal of American History* 54 (March 1968): 787–805.

29. Edwin Bacon, ed., *Men of Progress* (Boston: New England Magazine Publishing Co., 1896), p. 970. See the fine article by John A. Lucas, "Thomas Wentworth Higginson: Early Apostle of Health and Fitness," *Journal of Health, Physical Education and Recreation* 42 (February 1971): 30–33.

30. Thomas Wentworth Higginson, "Saints and Their Bodies," *Atlantic Monthly* 1 (March 1858): 582–95 (reprinted in his *Outdoor Papers* [Boston, 1871]). See also his "Physical Courage," *Atlantic Monthly* 2 (November 1858): 727–37; "Letter to a Dyspeptic," ibid., 3 (April 1859): 465–74; and "The Health of Our Girls," ibid., 9 (June 1862): 722–31; all ably reviewed by Lucas.

31. "Gymnastics," *Atlantic Monthly* 7 (March 1861): 283–302. Boston had experienced an interesting and fleeting gymnastics craze in the 1820s. See Granville Putnam, "The Introduction of Gymnastics in New England," *New England Magazine* 3 (September 1890): 110–13.

32. For broader scope on these issues see John R. Betts, "Public Recreation, Public Parks, and Public Health Before the Civil War," *The History of Physical Education and Sport,* ed. Bruce Bennett (Chicago: Athletic Institute, 1972), pp. 33–52. John Lucas and Ronald Smith, *Saga of American Sport,* pp. 70–121, illustrate the lingering resistance to this newer philosophy. For an extensive examination of the popular press, see Adelman, "Development of Modern Athletics," pp. 651–705. Peter Levine, "The Promise of Sport in Antebellum America," *Journal of American Culture* 2 (Winter 1980): 623–34, claims that middle-class advocates of sport made "no attempt to control a group or class considered to be subordinate." The sources examined above were concerned about the behavior of several groups or classes, including subordinates.

33. John R. Betts, "Home Front, Battlefield, and Sport During the Civil War," *Research Quarterly* 42 (1971): 131.

34. Massachusetts Bureau of Statistics of Labor, *Annual Reports*, 1875, 1889, 1910; Joseph Zeisel, "The Workweek in American Industry, 1850–1956," *Monthly Labor Review* 81 (January 1958): 23–29; James R. Green and Hugh Carter Donahue, *Boston's Workers: A Labor History* (Boston: Trustees of the Boston Public Library, 1979); Philip S. Foner, *History of the Labor Movement in the United States*, 3 vols. (New York: International Publishers, 1947), vol. 1, pp. 202–18.

35. George E. McNeill, *The Labor Movement: The Problem of Today*, p. 474. See also Lazerow, "The Workingman's Hour."

36. Rev. O. B. Frothingham, *A Plea for Amusement: A Sermon* (New York, 1874), p. 13; Rodgers, *Work Ethic*, pp. 106, 156.

37. American Christian Committee, Document No. 1, 1867, pp. 20–22. BYMCA, *The Necessity of Moral and Christian Effort Among Young Men Made Evident by the Following Statements* (1867), cited in William B. Whiteside, *The Boston YMCA and Community Need* (New York: Association Press, 1951), p. 63.

38. *Boston Daily Advertiser*, 9 May 1870; *Boston Herald*, 7, 18 August 1886; *South Boston Inquirer*, 26 June 1880; *Charlestown News*, 27 August 1881.

39. Henry Morgan, *Boston Inside Out! Sins of a Great City! A Story of Real Life!* (Boston: Shawmut Publishing Co., 1880), pp. 43, 90, 99.

40. Jane McCrady, "South End Amusements," *New Boston* 1 (November 1910): 318–20; Robert A. Woods, ed., *The City Wilderness*, p. 181; idem, *Americans in Process*, pp. 190–223, 251–54; Alvan Sanborn, *Moody's Lodging House and Other Tenement Sketches* (Boston: Copeland & Day, 1895), p. 120; Robert A. Woods and Albert Kennedy, eds., *The Zone of Emergence*, p. 41.

41. Woods and Kennedy, *Zone of Emergence*, p. 129.

42. "Amusements," *New Englander* 26 (July 1867): 399–424; James Freeman Clarke, *Self-Culture* (Boston: James R. Osgood Co., 1880), p. 393. See also Rev. F. E. Clark, "The Positive Side of the Amusement Question," *Homiletic Review* 10 (1885): 356; Rogers, *Work Ethic in Industrial America*, pp. 102–24; Washington Gladden, "Christianity and Popular Amusements," in his *Applied Christianity* (Boston: Houghton Mifflin, 1886).

43. Rev. Charles A. Dickinson, "The Problem of the Modern City Church," *Andover Review* 12 (October 1889): 355–67. On the BYMCA see the association's magazine *Leisure Hours (Boston Young Man's Magazine)*, which began in 1887; *Boston Herald*, 3 June 1888; B. Deane Brink, *The Body Builder, Robert J. Roberts* (New York: Association Press, 1916); Whiteside, *The Boston YMCA*, pp. 74–80, 150. On the BYMCU see George Hutchinson, "Boston Young Men's Christian Union," *Lend a Hand* 15 (January 1895): 37–45. See also Richard A. Swanson, "The Acceptance and Influence of Play in American Protestantism," *Quest* 11 (December

1968): 58–70; idem, "American Protestantism and Play" (Ph.D. dissertation, Ohio State University, 1967).

44. Richard H. Edwards, *Popular Amusements,* "Studies in American Social Conditions" (New York: Association Press, 1915), p. 91. Jacob Riis, *The Battle with the Slum* (New York: Macmillan, 1902), p. 283; Robert A. Woods and Albert Kennedy, *The Settlement Horizon: A National Estimate* (New York, 1922), p. 296. See also Jacob Riis, "Fighting the Gang with Athletics," *Collier's* 46 (11 February 1911): 17.

45. For good overall treatments, see Jon M. Kingsdale, "The 'Poor Man's Club': Social Functions of the Urban Working-Class Saloon," *American Quarterly* 25 (October 1972): 472–89; Boyer, *Urban Masses and Moral Order,* pp. 121–205.

46. Quoted in John T. Galvin, "The Dark Ages of Boston City Politics," *Proceedings of the Massachusetts Historical Society* 89 (1977): 99.

47. *The Liquor Problem: A Summary of Investigations Conducted by the Committee of Fifty, 1893–1903* (Boston, 1893), pp. 147–48.

48. For the police headcount see B. O. Flower, "Practical Measures for Promoting Manhood and Preventing Crime," *Arena* 18 (November 1897): 678; Francis Peabody, "Substitutes for the Saloon," *Forum* 21 (July 1896): 595, 598. On the role of saloons in political and criminal machines see Woods, *City Wilderness,* pp. 137–47, 154–68; idem, *Americans in Process,* pp. 190–223; Woods and Kennedy, *Zone of Emergence,* pp. 129–30. See also E. C. Moore, "The Social Value of the Saloon," *American Journal of Sociology* 3 (July 1892): 1–12.

49. Raymond Calkins, *Substitutes for the Saloon* (Boston, 1901, revised edn. Boston: Houghton Mifflin, 1919), pp. 151, 159, 202, 205. See also John Barker, *The Saloon Problem and Social Reforms* (Boston, 1905).

50. James Freeman Clarke, "Rational Sunday Observance," *North American Review* 131 (1880): 504; C. D. Wright, *Sunday Labor, Sixteenth Annual Report of the Massachusetts Bureau of Statistics of Labor* (Boston, 1885).

51. Elmer O. Cappers, *Centennial History of The Country Club: 1882–1982* (Brookline: printed by the Club, 1981), p. 44. Waverly arrest in *Boston Globe,* 11 October 1897. For more evidence of Sunday sports see *Boston Herald,* 30 May 1881, 9 August 1886, 4, 18 June 1888, 6 October 1890.

52. Park Department, *Annual Report,* 1909–10, p. 8. The same complaint appeared in the next two annual reports.

53. Joseph Lee, "Sunday Play," *Survey* 25 (October 1910): 55–62; *Massachusetts Acts and Resolves,* 1920, ch. 240; 1928, ch. 406.

54. Boyer, *Urban Masses and Moral Order,* pp. 220–51. See also Alan Dawley, *Class and Community,* pp. 97–128, for a distinction between authoritarian and "manipulative" forms of control.

55. A recent book examining the struggle over space and time in the leisure arena is Cary Goodman, *Choosing Sides: Playgrounds and Streetlife on the Lower East Side* (New York: Schocken, 1978). Although I don't agree

with all of his conclusions, I have profited a great deal from Goodman's lucid discussion of the basic questions.

56. John Boyle O'Reilly, *Athletics and Manly Sports*, pp. 149–52. For Irish temperance groups see Dennis P. Ryan, "Beyond the Ballot Box: A Social History of the Boston Irish, 1845–1917" (Ph.D. dissertation, University of Massachusetts, 1979). Ryan also discusses the Sunday baseball issue, but Archbishop O'Connell's opposition may be found in the *Boston Globe*, 16 February 1911. The concern of black clergy may be found in Elizabeth Pleck, *Black Migration and Poverty: Boston, 1865–1900* (New York: Academic Press, 1979), p. 111.

Notes to Chapter 4

1. Boston, *City Document No. 1*, 1847.
2. See Mayor Nathan Matthews, *The City Government of Boston, Valedictory Address* (Boston, 1895), p. 112; John Koren, *Boston, 1822 to 1922: The Story of Its Government and Principal Activities during One Hundred Years, City Document No. 39*, 1922, p. 127.
3. Geoffrey Blodgett, "Frederick Law Olmsted: Landscape Architecture as Conservative Reform," *Journal of American History* 62 (March 1976): 869–89.
4. For the "progressive" interpretation see Blake McKelvey, "An Historical View of Rochester's Parks and Playgrounds," *Rochester History* 11 (January 1949): 1–24; Charles Doell and Gerald Fitzgerald, *A Brief History of Parks and Recreation in the United States* (Chicago: Athletic Institute, 1954); John R. Betts, *America's Sporting Heritage, 1850–1950*, pp. 174–76; K. Gerald Marsden, "Philanthropy and the Boston Playground Movement, 1885–1907," *Social Service Review* 35 (1961): 48–58. The "social control" interpretation may be seen in Michael P. McCarthy, "Politics and the Parks: Chicago Businessmen and the Recreation Movement," *Journal of the Illinois State Historical Society* 65 (1972): 158–72; Lawrence Finfer, "Leisure as Social Work in the Urban Community: The Progressive Recreation Movement, 1890–1920" (Ph.D. dissertation, Michigan State University, 1974); Cary Goodman, *Choosing Sides: Playgrounds and Street Life on the Lower East Side* (New York: Schocken, 1979). A more balanced analysis may be found in Paul S. Boyer, *Urban Masses and Moral Order in America, 1820–1920*, pp. 233–51.
5. Roy Rosenzweig, "Middle-Class Parks and Working-Class Play: The Struggle Over Recreational Space in Worcester, Massachusetts, 1870–1910," *Radical History Review* 21 (Fall 1979): 32. I have profited greatly from Rosenzweig's analysis, which concentrates on the activism of working-class interest groups.
6. City Council, *Proceedings*, 21 October 1869; *Boston Daily Advertiser*, 9 November 1870.

7. See, for instance, Ernest Bowditch, "Rural Parks for Boston," *Boston Daily Advertiser*, 24 June 1875; or the debate, resulting in postponement of the issue, in City Council *Proceedings*, 22 December 1873. For other important arguments see Boston, *Council Report on the Establishment of a Public Park, City Document No. 105*, 1874, City Council *Proceedings*, 18 February, 1 March, 1 April, 5 April 1875. The 1875 act fared better than its predecessor in part because its approval required only a simple majority of votes. The 1870 act had required a two-thirds majority.

8. Minutes of the Board of Commissioners of the Boston Parks Department, 1 January 1876, residing with the executive secretary of the Parks Department, City Hall, Boston (hereafter referred to as "Parks Minutes"). See also the *Second Annual Report of the Board of Commissioners of the Department of Parks for the City of Boston* (hereafter referred to as *"Parks Reports"*), 1876, in which the board cited their criteria as (1) *accessibility*: "for all classes"; (2) *economy*: lands that "would least disturb the natural growth of the city in its business and domestic life, and those which would become relatively nearer the centre of population in future years"; (3) *adaptability*; (4) *sanitary advantages*. On Olmsted's appointment, see Parks Minutes, 10 December 1878.

9. *Boston Post*, 17 June 1874.

10. *Boston Daily Advertiser*, 9 June 1875.

11. City Council, *Report on the Establishment of a Public Park, City Document No. 105*, 1874, pp. 11–12.

12. City Council *Proceedings*, 7 November 1881.

13. *Second Annual Parks Report, City Document No. 42*, 1876, p. 13; see also City Council, *Report of the Committee on Public Parks Recommending the Purchase of Land for West Roxbury and City Point Parks, City Document No. 61*, 1880.

14. *Parks for the People. Proceedings of a Public Meeting held at Faneuil Hall, June 7, 1876* (Boston: Franklin Press, 1876), p. 39. City Council *Proceedings*, 3 December 1874.

15. *City Document No. 105*, 1874, p. 8; *City Document No. 123*, 1869, pp. 58–59. See also two interesting "scientific" works, not specifically on Boston: John Rauch, M.D., *Public Parks: Their Effects upon the Moral, Physical, and Sanitary Condition of the Inhabitants of Large Cities: With Special Reference to Chicago* (Chicago: S. C. Briggs, 1869); John Toner, M.D., "Free Parks and Camping Grounds or Sanitariums for the Sick and Debilitated Children of the Poor in Crowded Cities During the Summer Months," *The Sanitarian* (May 1873).

16. City Council *Proceedings*, 28 May 1877.

17. *City Document No. 105*, 1876, p. 6.

18. *The Boston Common, or Rural Walks in Cities, by a Friend of Improvement* (Boston: G. W. Light, 1838), pp. 55–56.

19. *Parks for the People,* pp. 12, 29, 42. See also comments in *City Document No. 105,* 1876; *Report and Accompanying Statements and Communications Relating to a Public Park for the City of Boston, City Document No. 123,* 1869, p. 18.

20. City Council *Proceedings,* 7 May 1877.

21. See the comments of Dr. Holmes in *Parks for the People,* p. 25. See also City Council *Proceedings,* 28 May 1877; *Second Annual Parks Report, City Document No. 72,* 1876, p. 4; *City Document No. 61,* 1880, p. 3.

22. "*Boston's Uncommon Parks,*" Boston 200 Broadside Series (Boston, 1976). For a good contemporary description see Sylvester Baxter, "The Public Parks, Playgrounds, Baths and Gymnasiums," in *A Civic Reader for New Americans* (New York: American Book Company, 1908), pp. 42–49.

23. See the *Second Annual Parks Report, City Document No. 42,* 1876, which outlines the proposed system. The Common Council was the large body (elected by ward) which, along with the small Board of Aldermen (elected at large) comprised the bicameral City Council.

24. City Council *Proceedings,* 12 July 1877. The Back Bay loan was passed only when it was cloaked in the garb of sewage improvement. See City Council *Proceedings,* 19 July 1877.

25. *Seventh Annual Parks Report,* 1881, pp. 24–25.

26. City Council, *Report of the Committee on Public Parks, City Document No. 93,* 1881, p. 2.

27. See City Council *Proceedings,* 7 July, 3 October, 7 November, 8 December 1881.

28. Map C includes more than the Back Bay Park proper because the councilors clearly recognized its ultimate link to improvements in the connecting river and pond system. Although distance from proposed parks appears to have influenced voting patterns, one might also pursue the effect of ethnocultural tensions. While the Irish-Yankee division comes quickly to mind, however, the suggestion is complicated by the fact that the powerful Irish politician, Patrick Maguire, who became a parks commissioner, had real-estate interests that begged support of the suburban parks. See Blodgett, "Olmsted," 885. Also, by 1880, the Irish population had spread out into outer zones as well. It was no longer clustered in the inner city. See Warner, *Streetcar Suburbs,* pp. 79–80; Thernstrom, *Other Bostonians,* pp. 163–65.

29. *Boston Daily Advertiser,* 10 June 1875. For a recent critique of the central reform vs. local politics model see David Thelen, "Urban Politics: Beyond Bosses and Reformers," *Reviews in American History* (September 1979): 406–12.

30. See similar lobbies in Parks Minutes, 15 December 1879, 17 June, 11 December 1880, 15 September 1885, 21 April 1892, 8 May 1894. On the difference between private attachments and public alienation see

Claude S. Fischer, "The Public and Private Worlds of City Life," *American Sociological Review* 46 (June 1981): 306–16. While Gunther Barth sees this localism in *City People*, ch. 2, he doesn't clearly indicate its presence in public parks issues.

31. *South Boston Inquirer*, 17 September, 1, 15 October, 26 November, 17 December 1881.

32. Parks Minutes, 29 April, 13 May 1887, 19, 26 June 1891, 2 August 1897, 8 December 1902; *Annual Parks Report*, 1891, p. 35.

33. Charles Davenport, *The Embankment and Park on the Charles River Bay* (n.d., n.p.), pamphlet residing in the Boston Athenaeum; Uriel Crocker, *Plan for a Public Park* (Boston, 1869), p. 6.

34. *Boston Daily Advertiser*, 9 June 1875. Indeed, Wards 1 and 2 voted heavily against the Park Act.

35. City Council *Proceedings*, 1 April 1875.

36. Ibid., 28 May 1877, 25 May 1908.

37. See Parks Minutes, 14 February 1889, 27 January 1891, 6 March 1891, 10 April 1891, 22 May 1891 for Charlestown pressure; 20 June 1892, 7 December 1893, 26 February 1894, 1 July, 30 September 1895, 19 November 1896 for North End pressure. Fitzgerald's "monument" is discussed in Woods, *Americans in Process*, p. 182. See the speed with which $5000 was appropriated to open the Charlesbank in City Council *Proceedings*, 28 April 1892.

38. Blodgett, "Olmsted," 886–87, suggests that "Olmsted was able to respond to the growing public taste for active recreation." I would suggest that his response was a result of considerable pressure and was, in the end, unsatisfactory to the "new tastes." On Olmsted, see also Laura Wood Roper, *FLO: A Biography of Frederick Law Olmsted* (Baltimore: Johns Hopkins, 1973); F. L. Olmsted, Jr., and Theodora Kimball, eds., *Frederick Law Olmsted: Landscape Architect, 1822–1902*, 2 vols. (New York: Putnam, 1922).

39. See F. L. Olmsted, *Public Parks: Two Papers Read Before the American Social Science Association in 1870 and 1880*, entitled "Public Parks and the Enlargement of Towns" and "A Consideration of the Justifying Value of a Public Park" (Brookline, MA, 1902), p. 37.

40. "Notes on the Plan of Franklin Park and Related Matters," in *Eleventh Annual Parks Report*, 1885, p. 42.

41. *Thirteenth Annual Parks Report*, 1887, pp. 86–87.

42. Parks Minutes, 9 September 1884; "Report of the Landscape Architects on Provisions for the Playing of Games," *Fifteenth Annual Parks Report*, 1889, pp. 14–19.

43. Olmsted views in Frederick Law Olmsted, Jr., "Neighborhood Pleasure Grounds in Boston," *Harper's Weekly* 41 (25 December 1897): 1290–91; letter from Olmsted firm in City Council *Proceedings*, 25 June 1896. The development of active sports in the parks may be followed in the

Parks Minutes; 17 November, 5 December 1890, 7 November, 19 December 1892, 20 November 1893, 23 December 1895, 14, 21 December 1896, 11 July, 17 October 1898, 1 October 1900, 11 October 1902, 2 May 1905.

44. Parks Minutes, 1 June 1885, 5 August 1885, 12 June 1886, 3 June 1895. For an interesting interpretation of the role played by commercialized amusements in the modern city see John Kasson's analysis of Coney Island, *Amusing the Millions* (New York: Hill and Wang, 1979).

45. City Council *Proceedings*, 31 July 1893.

46. Parks Minutes, 24 April, 22 May 1893, 21, 28 May 1894, 7, 14 October 1895, 6 April 1896, 22 May 1914.

47. See the evaluation by the Olmsted firm in the *36th Annual Parks Report*, 1910–11, pp. 73–77. See also the comments on parks in *1915: The Official Catalogue of the Boston Exposition* (Boston, 1909), p. 31.

48. F. L. Olmsted, "Justifying Value of a Public Park," quoted in Roper, *FLO*, p. 318. For the Boston park system's lasting impact on local environment, see Department of Landscape Architecture, Harvard Graduate School of Design, *Olmsted's Park System as a Vehicle in Boston* (Cambridge, 1973); William Weismantel, "How the Landscape Affects Neighborhood Status: The Conserving and Renewing Influence of Boston's Charles River Basin and Park System," *Landscape Architecture* 56 (April 1966): 190–94.

Notes to Chapter 5

1. *Boston Daily Advertiser*, 13 December 1869. See also James D'Wolf Lovett, *Old Boston Boys and the Games They Played* (Boston: privately printed, 1906; reprint edn., Boston: Little, Brown, 1908), p. 198.

2. E. E. Hale, *A New England Boyhood and Other Bits of Autobiography* (Boston: Casell, 1893), ch. 4.

3. City Council *Proceedings*, 7 November 1881.

4. *Annual Report* of the Board of Parks Commissioners, 1914–15, p. 9. See also statistics in City Council *Proceedings*, 18 October 1915.

5. K. Gerald Marsden, "Philanthropy and the Boston Playground Movement, 1885–1907," *Social Service Review* 35 (March 1961): 48–58. See the similar arguments in Allen F. Davis, *Spearheads for Reform: The Social Settlements and the Progressive Movement, 1890–1914* (New York: Oxford University Press, 1967), ch. 4; Dominick Cavallo, "Social Reform and the Movement to Organize Children's Play During the Progressive Era," *History of Childhood Quarterly* 3 (Spring 1976): 509–22; idem, *Muscles and Morals: Organized Playgrounds and Urban Reform, 1880–1920* (Philadelphia: University of Pennsylvania Press, 1981); Benjamin McArthur, "The Chicago Playground Movement; A Neglected Feature of Social Justice," *Social Service Review* 49 (September 1975): 377–78; Finfer, "Leisure as Social Work"; Goodman, *Choosing Sides*; Boyer, *Urban Masses and Moral Order*. The works tend to fall into either the "progressive" or "social control" camps discussed in ch. 4.

6. Works almost universally cited include: Joseph Lee, *Play in Education* (New York: Macmillan, 1915); Everett B. Mero, *American Playgrounds* (Boston: Dale Association, 1908); Henry Curtis, *Education Through Play* (New York: Macmillan, 1915); idem, *The Play Movement and Its Significance* (New York; Macmillan, 1917); Clarence Rainwater, *The Play Movement in the United States* (Chicago: University of Chicago Press, 1922); Luther H. Gulick, *A Philosophy of Play* (New York: Scribner, 1920).

7. *Massachusetts Acts and Resolves*, 1898, ch. 412.

8. City Council *Proceedings*, 4 May 1873.

9. Ibid., 28 April 1873.

10. Ibid., 4 May 1873.

11. Ibid., 4, 12 May 1873.

12. See, for instance, *Report and Accompanying Statements and Communications Relating to a Public Park for the City of Boston, City Document No. 123*, 1869; editorial in the *Boston Post*, 17 July 1874; City Council *Proceedings*, 21 October 1869.

13. City Council *Proceedings*, 29 March 1877.

14. *Second Annual Parks Report, City Document No. 42*, 1876.

15. City Council *Proceedings*, 10 May 1877.

16. Cavallo, *Muscles and Morals*, pp. 49–72.

17. City Council *Proceedings*, 27 June 1878.

18. Ibid., 1, 26 May 1879; *Charlestown News*, 10 June 1882.

19. *Fourth Annual Parks Report, City Document No. 15*, 1879.

20. City Council *Proceedings*, 7 July, 3 October, 7 November, 8 December 1881.

21. Parks Minutes, 11 May 1883.

22. Ibid., 20 May 1884.

23. Ibid., 9 September 1884. See also the prohibition of baseball at Marine Park "on account of the danger to other visitors in the park"; ibid., 12 August 1885.

24. See the early petitions for playground space on the parks or nearby areas, in City Council *Proceedings*, 11 May 1885, 21 April 1887; Parks Minutes, 13 May 1887.

25. City Council *Proceedings*, 17 May 1886, 20 January 1887.

26. For a measure of the mounting local pressure for playgrounds see the many requests forwarded to the City Council. Ibid., 1 June 1886, 14, 18 April, 23, 26 May, 7, 23 June 1887, 10, 17 May 1888.

27. *Thirteenth Annual Parks Report, City Document No. 14*, 1888, p. 34.

28. "Report of the Landscape Architects on Provisions for the Playing of Games," *Fourteenth Annual Parks Report*, 1889.

29. Boston School Committee, *A Notice to Parents of Grammar School Children Regarding the Opening of Franklin Park Playstead*, 10 June 1889, pamphlet in Boston Public Library. See also *Fifteenth Annual Parks Report*, 1890, for a report on the gala opening.

30. *Boston Journal,* 27 July 1889.

31. City Council *Proceedings,* 28 April 1892. See a brief history and description in the *Sixteenth Annual Parks Report,* 1891; F. L. Olmsted, Jr., "Neighborhood Pleasure-Grounds in Boston," *Harper's Weekly* 41 (25 December 1897): 1290–91.

32. Robert A. Woods et al., *The City Wilderness,* p. 198; Alvan F. Sanborn, *Moody's Lodging House and Other Tenement Sketches* (Boston: Copeland and Day, 1895), pp. 125–32.

33. The Parks Minutes abound with requests in the early nineties. See, for instance, 19 June 1891; *Report of a Special Committee of the Common Council on a Playground in Ward 23, City Document No. 114,* 1893.

34. *Massachusetts Acts and Resolves,* 1898, ch. 412; City Council *Proceedings,* 29, 31 December 1898.

35. *Mayoral address of His Honorable Josiah Quincy, City Document No. 1,* 1897.

36. For instance, Marsden, "Philanthropy and the Boston Playground Movement," 51, states that "before 1896, Boston had done almost nothing to develop city playgrounds." For the relationship of playgrounds to Quincy's overall plans see Geoffrey Blodgett, *The Gentle Reformers: Massachusetts Democrats in the Cleveland Era* (Cambridge: Harvard University Press, 1966), pp. 249–55.

37. Some were the old "rental" variety; some were controlled by the Department of Public Grounds. See *Twenty-Third Parks Report,* 1897–98, pp. 23–24.

38. See the comments in Leonard Simutis, "Frederick Law Olmsted Sr.: A Reassessment," *Journal of the American Institute of Planners* 38 (September 1972): 279.

39. City Council *Proceedings,* 18 October 1915.

40. *Report of Special Committee of the Common Council on a Playground in Ward 13, City Document No. 187,* 1896, p. 2.

41. Warner, *Streetcar Suburbs,* p. 45. Typical outlying groups can be found in *City Document No. 114,* 1893; *City Document No. 69,* 1896.

42. *Report of Special Committee of Aldermen on the Investigation of the Park Department, City Document No. 115,* 1900, pp. 1138–39. The occupations included ten clerks, two lathers, two printers, two machinists, two bevelers, and one each of the following: real estate, assistant superintendent (janitor?), carriage painter, upholsterer, caterer, plumber, salesman, boilermaker, agent, janitor, gas fitter, porter, musician, carpet factory worker, shoemaker. Four of the clerks were clearly the sons of laborers, living at home.

43. Joseph Lee, "Playgrounds, Beaches and Baths," in ed. Elizabeth Herlihy, *Fifty Years of Boston* (Boston: Tercentenary Committee, 1932), p. 680; idem, "Boston's Playground System," *New England Magazine* 27

(January 1903): 521–36. A good discussion of Lee appears in Cavallo, *Muscles and Morals*, passim. See also Neva R. Deardorff, "Joseph Lee," *Dictionary of American Biography, Supplement Two*, ed. R. L. Schuyler (New York: Charles Scribner's Sons, 1958), pp. 374–75.

44. In 1866, a vacation school operated at the Old First Church on Chauncey St. In 1879, the Women's Education Association funded a vacation school, and in 1881, the Associated Charities sponsored a larger number. See Lee, "Boston's Playground System"; Rainwater, *Play Movement*, p. 22.

45. Massachusetts Emergency and Hygiene Association, *Annual Report*, 1889, p. 32; quoted in Marsden, "Philanthropy and the Boston Playground Movement," 50.

46. *Annual Parks Report*, 1907, appendix; *Annual Parks Report*, 1894, pp. 89–90; Parks Minutes, 8 May 1891.

47. Boston School Committee, *School Document No. 14*, 1902, p. 23.

48. Massachusetts Civic League (hereafter cited as "MCL"), *Annual Report*, 1900, pp. 17–18.

49. MCL, *Playground Committee Report*, 1900, p. 1.

50. Parks Minutes, 19, 26 February 1900, 19 February 1901.

51. MCL, *Playground Committee Report*, 1900, p. 8.

52. Letter from Lee to Robert Treat Paine II, September 1903, in Paine's letters, residing with the Massachusetts Historical Society; Lee, "Boston's Playground System," 531.

53. MCL, *Report on Supervised Play in the Commonwealth*, 1913.

54. Cavallo has outlined this well in *Muscles and Morals*. See also Bernard Mergen, "The Discovery of Children's Play," *American Quarterly* 27 (1975): 399–420; Mark Kadzielski, "'As a Flower Needs Sunshine,' The Origins of Organized Children's Recreation in Philadelphia, 1886–1911," *Journal of Sport History* 4 (Summer 1977): 169–88.

55. Joseph Lee, "Play for Home," *Playground* 6 (1912): 146; idem, "Play and Congestion," *Charities and the Commons* 20 (April 1908): 43–48.

56. Joseph Lee, *Play and Playgrounds*, American Civic Association, Department of Public Recreation, Leaflet No. 11 (January 1908), p. 26. See the same notions in Lee, *Play in Education*, p. 336; "Boston's Playground System," 534.

57. Joseph Lee, "Boston's Playground System," 535.

58. Barbara Miller Solomon, *Ancestors and Immigrants: A Changing New England Tradition* (Cambridge: Harvard University Press, 1956; reprint edn., New York: John Wiley, 1965).

59. Joseph Lee, "Assimilation and Nationality," *Charities* 19 (1908): 1453–55, quoted in Solomon, *Ancestors and Immigrants*, p. 131.

60. Joseph Lee, *Expensive Living—The Blight on America* (Boston, 1900), p. 19, quoted in Solomon, *Ancestors and Immigrants*, p. 139.

61. MCL, *Playground Committee Report on North End Playground,* 1900; MCL *Annual Report,* 1901, pp. 4, 23.

62. MCL *Annual Report,* 1909, p. 20; 1913, p. 30. My views on Royce and Cooley stem from David E. Price, "Community and Control: Critical Democratic Theory in the Progressive Era," *American Political Science Review* 68 (December 1974): 1670–73.

63. MCL, *Annual Report,* 1909, p. 20. For similar beliefs see Otto Mallery, "The Social Significance of Play," *Annals of the American Academy of Political and Social Science* 25 (March 1910): 156; Jacob Riis, "Fighting the Gang with Athletics," *Collier's* 45 (11 February 1911): 17; Luther Gulick, "Team Games and Civic Loyalty," *Social Review* 14 (1906): 677.

64. Boston 1915, *Yearbook and Official Catalogue "1915"* (Boston, 1909).

65. Cavallo, *Muscles and Morals,* properly recognizes this problem (p. 9).

66. William Foote Whyte, *Street Corner Society: The Social Structure of an Italian Slum* (Chicago: University of Chicago Press, 1943; enlarged edn., 1955, pp. 3–8); Joseph Lee, "What Are the Best Games for Boys in Crowded Cities?" *Playground* 6 (January 1913): 373. Gans found the West End's playground deserted but the streets full of playing children when he studied the area in the 1950s. See Herbert J. Gans, *Urban Villagers: Group and Class in the Life of Italian-Americans* (New York: Free Press, 1962; paperback, 1965), p. 18. Goodman, in *Choosing Sides,* claims that playgrounds helped wipe out street culture in New York's Jewish Lower East Side. This certainly did not happen in Boston's ethnic neighborhoods. On the "unbridled freedom," see Philip Davis, *Street-Land: Its Little People and Big Problems* (Boston: Small, Maynard & Company, 1915), pp. 13–19.

67. Belle Beard, *Juvenile Probation, An Analysis of Case Records of Five Hundred Children Studied at the Judge Baker Guidance Clinic and Placed on Probation in the Juvenile Court of Boston* (New York: American Book Company, 1934), pp. 109, 113, 158–59.

68. William Foote Whyte, "Race Conflicts in the North End of Boston," *New England Quarterly* 12 (December 1939): 623–42.

69. Raymond Calkins, *Substitutes for the Saloon* (Boston, 1901; revised edn., Boston: Houghton Mifflin, 1919), p. 189.

70. Parks Minutes, 31 December 1906; City Council *Proceedings,* 9 June 1898; Massachusetts Acts and Resolves 1907, ch. 295, sec. 2.

71. "Vacation Schools and Playground Report," *School Document No. 15* (1907), p. 18; Parks Minutes, 10 November 1908, 22 September 1910; *38th Annual Parks Report,* 1912–13; from 1907 to 1912 the parks commissioners consulted with a number of "experts" in areas of school hygiene, social work, public recreation. On the call for Sunday play see *35th Annual Parks Report,* 1909–10, p. 8.

72. Robert A. Woods et al., *The City Wilderness: A Settlement Study by Residents and Associates of the South End House* (Boston: Houghton Mifflin, 1898), p. 3.

Notes to Chapter 6

1. George Wright, *Record of the Boston Baseball Club Since Its Organization, with a Sketch of All Its Players for 1871, '72, '73, '74, and Other Items of Interest* (Boston: Rockwell & Churchill, 1874), p. 6.

2. Rule 10, Chapter 5, Rules and Regulations of the Primary School Committee, in *Report of the Director of Physical Training, School Document No. 22*, 1891, p. 26. See also *School Document No. 7*, 1929, which contains a useful history and chronology of Boston public schools.

3. Stanley Schultz, *The Culture Factory: Boston Public Schools, 1789–1860* (New York: Oxford University Press, 1973), pp. 68–69. See also, Michael Katz, *The Irony of Early School Reform: Educational Innovation in Mid-Nineteenth Century Massachusetts* (Cambridge: Harvard University Press, 1968; reprint edn., Boston: Beacon Press, 1970); David Nasaw, *Schooled to Order: A Social History of Public Schooling in the United States* (New York: Oxford University Press, 1979), pp. 7–84.

4. "Physical Exercise," *Common School Journal* 7 (16 June 1845): 177–78, quoted in Schultz, *Culture Factory*, p. 93.

5. Boutwell quotation cited in the historical report by Edward M. Hartwell, *Boston School Document No. 22*, 1891, p. 32. For the life and ideas of Dio Lewis see Dio Lewis, *The New Gymnastics for Men, Women and Children* (Boston: Ticknor and Fields, 1864); Mary F. Eastman, *The Biography of Dio Lewis* (New York: Fowler and Wells, 1891).

6. *Report of Special Committee on the Subject of Physical Training in the Public Schools, City Document No. 94*, 1860, p. 5.

7. Ibid., p. 12.

8. *Third Semi-annual Report of the Superintendent of Public Schools*, 1861, pp. 22–23.

9. See the *Minutes of the Boston School Committee*, 11 December 1860, 4 February, 12 March 1861, 3 November 1863. (The bound manuscript minutes of the committee, to 1869, are in the Rare Book Room of the Boston Public Library. After 1869, the minutes were published.)

10. *Annual Report of the School Committee*, 1864, p. 36.

11. *School Committee Minutes*, 8 December 1863, 27 December 1864; *Report of the Director of Physical Training, School Document No. 22*, 1891, pp. 48–50; *Boston Herald*, 28 May 1892.

12. Isabel Barrows, ed., *Physical Training: A Full Report of the Papers and Discussions of the Conference Held in Boston in November 1889* (Boston: George H. Ellis, 1889); *Report of the Director of Physical Training, School Document No. 22*, 1891, pp. 43–68.

13. *Boston Herald*, 27 November 1890; *School Committee Minutes*, 25 June 1889; *Report of the Director of Physical Training, School Document No. 8*, 1894, pp. 101–05.

14. Barrows, *Physical Training*, pp. 112–13; *Report of Board of Supervisors*

of Physical Training, School Document No. 10, 1889, p. 10; *School Document No. 15,* 1890, p. 15; *Report of Director of Physical Training, School Document No. 8,* 1894, p. 65.

15. *Latin School Register* (hereafter referred to as *Register*) 9 (June 1890): 153.

16. *English High School Record* (hereafter referred to as *Record*) 1 (October 1885).

17. Winthrop Saltonstall Scudder, "An Historical Sketch of the Oneida Football Club of Boston, 1862–1865," Manuscript at Massachusetts Historical Society, Boston; idem, "The First Organized Football Club in the United States," *Old-Time New England* 15 (July 1924). Scudder was a member of the Oneidas. His claim for the club's primary was corroborated by Walter Camp and Park Davis. For other school sports, see Lovett, *Old Boston Boys,* pp. 82–90; *Boston Daily Advertiser,* 27 May 1878.

18. Parks Minutes, 10 March 1889; *Register* 8 (September 1888): 9; (November 1888): 41; Roger Ernst, "The School in the Nineties," *Forty Years On: The Old Roxbury Latin School on Kearsarge Avenue from the Civil War to the Twenties,* ed. Francis Russell (West Roxbury: Roxbury Latin School, 1970), pp. 35–36.

19. *Wright and Ditson Football Guide* (Boston: Wright and Ditson, 1890), pp. 44–55, contains the league constitutions.

20. *Register* 8 (March 1889): 101, 102; *Record* 11 (November 1895), 11 (January 1896); *South Boston High Chandelier* (hereafter referred to as *Chandelier*) 4 (January 1905); *Spalding's Official Football Guides* (1909), pp. 85–87; (1910), pp. 97–99; (1911), pp. 207–11; *Boston Journal,* 4 April 1895; *Boston Herald,* 7 October 1890, 23 May 1891, 7 November 1891. By 1895, the Interscholastic Athletic Association had 30 member schools. See the association's *Constitution and By-Laws* (Boston, 1895).

21. *Register* 8 (April 1889): 117.

22. *Chandelier* 3 (February 1904). For the antebellum class football scraps, "that awful hour when Sophs met Fresh, power met opposing power," see Morton H. Prince, "Football at Harvard, 1800–1875," *The H Book of Harvard Athletics, 1852–1922,* ed. John A. Blanchard (Cambridge: Harvard University Club, 1923), pp. 311–42; Thomas Wentworth Higginson, *Cheerful Yesterdays* (Boston: Houghton Mifflin, 1898), p. 61. For the changes in American college football that occurred as a result of intercollegiate championships, see Guy Lewis, "The American Intercollegiate Football Spectacle, 1869–1917" (Ph.D. dissertation, University of Maryland, 1965).

23. *Chandelier* 4 (June 1905): 5.

24. *Chandelier* 3 (February 1904): 7. As was common for the day, even among advocates of women's athletics, schoolgirls were steered away from the "hazards" of interscholastic competition. Therefore, intramural teams were stressed. See also *Chandelier* 3 (April 1904): 5.

25. *Record* 1 (1886): 44, 54; 11 (November 1895): 8–10; *Register* 8 (April 1889): 119; *Chandelier* 1 (April 1902): 10; 2 (October 1902): 9.

26. *Record* 11 (November 1895): 10; *Register* 8 (December 1888): 53.

27. *Boston Journal,* 2 May 1897; 8–10 June 1902. All of the local papers that had any kind of sports page covered the schoolboys.

28. *Record* 8 (October 1902): 25. See also *Register* 8 (September 1888): 8; 10 (March 1891): 85.

29. *Chandelier* 3 (November 1903): 8.

30. *Chandelier* 2 (October 1902): 1–5; 3 (November 1903). For other complaints, see *Record* 1 (1886): 67. League rules appear in *Wright and Ditson Football Guide,* pp. 44, 46; Interscholastic Athletic Association, *Constitution and By-Laws* (Boston, 1895).

31. *Register* 9 (January 1890): 73.

32. *Report of U.S. Commissioner of Education* (1897–98): 558–59.

33. P. D. Boynton, "Athletics and Collateral Activities in Secondary Schools," *Proceedings of National Education Association,* 1904, pp. 213–14. For similar arguments, see "Athletics in Schools," *Popular Science Monthly* 16 (March 1880): 677–84; Nathaniel S. Shaler, "The Athletic Problem in Education," *Atlantic Monthly* 63 (January 1889): 79–88; W. J. S. Bryan, "School Athletics," *Proceedings of National Education Association,* 1902, pp. 485–88.

34. Dudley Sargent, "The Place for Physical Training in the School and College Curriculum," reprinted in *The American Physical Education Review* 5 (March 1900). For Sargent's life, see Bruce Bennett, "The Life of Dudley Allen Sargent, M.D., and His Contributions to Physical Education" (Ph.D. dissertation, University of Michigan, 1947). Both Boston University and Harvard University hold collections of Sargent's papers, articles, and addresses, which include biographical material.

35. "Athletics in Secondary Schools," *American Physical Education Review* 8 (June 1903): 69; idem, "Place for Physical Training," 9. See also "The Necessity for the Medical Supervision of Athletics" (typescript, n.d.), in Sargent Papers, Harvard University Archives. The arguments continued into the next decade and beyond; see Dudley Sargent, "Abolish Evils and Games," *Boston Sunday Herald,* 8 March 1914; John L. Morse, "Athletics in the Schools," *Harvard Graduates Magazine* 23 (March 1915): 371–74; A. E. Stearns, "Athletics and the School," *Atlantic Monthly* 113 (February 1914): 145–48; M. K. Gordon, "Reform of School Athletics," *Century,* new series, 57 (January 1910): 469–71.

36. *Report of the Director of Physical Training, School Document No. 3,* 1903, pp. 196, 203; *School Committee Minutes,* 24 February 1903.

37. This was an age of "slugging" football, when the brutality of the sport called its very survival into question, at the collegiate and scholastic levels. See Lewis, "American Intercollegiate Football Spectacle."

38. *Annual Reports of the Superintendent of Schools, School Document No. 3,*

1904, pp. 42–44; *School Document No. 7*, 1905, p. 29; *School Committee Minutes*, 23 May 1905.

39. Massachusetts *Acts and Resolves*, 1906, chapter 251; *Annual Report of School Committee, School Document No. 17*, 1906, p. 34; *School Committee Minutes*, 4 June 1906.

40. *School Committee Minutes*, 20 May, 10 June 1907, 22 November 1910, 20 March, 2 October 1911, 15 January 1912; Massachusetts *Acts and Resolves*, ch. 295, 1907; ch. 314, 1911; *Annual Reports of School Committee and Superintendent of Schools, School Documents No. 13, 16*, 1907.

41. Joel Spring, "Mass Culture and School Sports," *History of Education Quarterly* 14 (Winter 1974): 485, 497; Timothy P. O'Hanlon, "Interscholastic Athletics, 1900–1940: Shaping Citizens for Unequal Roles in the Modern Industrial State" (Ph.D. dissertation, University of Illinois, 1979). I disagree with Spring and O'Hanlon in terms of timing more than in the ultimate philosophy of school athletics.

42. Dudley Sargent, "Physical Training as a Compulsory Subject," *The School Review* 16 (1908): 53. See also notes 34, 35 above. Sargent stressed that, with proper regulation, these values would emerge. Lee had conducted an experimental league with four grammar schools. See Massachusetts Civic League, *Annual Report*, 1902, pp. 33–35.

43. Thus, a certain consensus existed between the "controllers" and the "controlled." For similar cautions on stark interpretations of social control, see Paul S. Boyer, *Urban Masses and Moral Order in America, 1820–1920* (Cambridge: Harvard University Press, 1978), p. 59; William Muraskin, "The Social-Control Theory in American History: A Critique," *Journal of Social History* 9 (June 1976): 559–70.

44. See Guy Lewis, "Adoption of the Sports Program: The Role of Accommodation in the Transformation of Physical Education," *Quest* 12 (May 1969): 34–46; Betty Spears, "Influences on Early Professional Physical Education Curriculums in the United States," *Proceedings of the Second Canadian Symposium on the History of Sport and Physical Education*, Windsor, Ontario (May 1–3, 1972), pp. 86–103.

45. Schultz, *Culture Factory*, pp. 141–42; see also Michael Katz, "The Emergence of Bureaucracy in Urban Education: The Boston Case, 1850–1884," *History of Education Quarterly* 8 (Summer–Fall 1968): 155–88, 319–57.

46. *School Document No. 12* (1909); *School Document No. 8* (1910). The purpose of the new curriculum was to expose all students to the benefits of athletics, rather than "to produce a limited number of exceptional performers."

47. Marvin Lazerson, *Origins of the Urban School: Public Education in Massachusetts, 1870–1915* (Cambridge: Harvard University Press, 1971), p. ix; Lawrence Cremin, *The Transformation of the School; Progressivism in American Education, 1876–1957* (New York: Knopf, 1968); Joel Spring,

Education and the Rise of the Corporate State (Boston: Beacon Press, 1972). These authors differ in their ideological orientations toward education. See Diane Ravitch, *The Revisionists Revised: A Critique of the Radical Attack on the Schools* (New York: Basic Books, 1978).

48. "Some Relations of Physical Training to the Present Problems of Moral Education in America," 1 June 1907, at Sanders Theater, reprinted in *Dudley Allen Sargent, Fiftieth Anniversary, 1869–1919* (n.p., n.d.), pp. 63, 76, in the Sargent Papers, Boston University, Mss. File, Box 3.

49. Luther Gulick, "Team Games and Civic Loyalty," *School Review* 14 (1906): 676; Jacob Riis, "Fighting the Gang with Athletics," *Collier's* (11 February 1911): 17. Riis was discussing playgrounds and schoolboy athletic leagues. For similar optimism, see James Naismith, "High School Athletics and Gymnastics as an Expression of the Corporate Life of the High School," in ed. Charles H. Johnston, *The Modern High School* (New York: Charles Scribner's Sons, 1914), pp. 229–63.

50. *School Document No. 8*, 1910, p. 7.

51. *Register* 8 (September 1888): 8; *Chandelier* 1 (April 1902): 10.

52. Royce, "Some Relations of Physical Training"; Gulick, "Team Games and Civic Loyalty"; *Report of the Committee on Interscholastic Trophy, City Document 209*, 1895. For some interesting comments on the overall school program's role in this regard, see Bender, *Community and Social Change in America* pp. 136–42.

53. Robert S. Lynd and Helen M. Lynd, *Middletown: A Study in Modern American Culture* (New York: Harcourt, Brace and World, 1929; paper reprint edn., Harvest Books, 1956), pp. 484–87.

Notes to Chapter 7

1. This was actually a trial heat. See George Horton, "The Recent Olympian Games," *The Bostonian Magazine* 4 (July 1896): 215–29; Horton was the United States consul in Athens. See also Ellery H. Clark, *Reminiscences of an Athlete: Twenty Years on Track and Field* (Boston: Houghton Mifflin, 1911), pp. 124–41.

2. Henry Hall, ed., *The Tribune Book of Open Air Sports* (New York: The Tribune Association, 1887), p. 332, quoted in John R. Betts, *America's Sporting Heritage, 1850–1950* (Reading, MA: Addison-Wesley, 1974), pp. 98–99. For New York clubs, see Melvin Adelman, "The Development of Modern Athletics: Sport in New York City, 1820–1870" (Ph.D. dissertation, University of Illinois, 1980), passim; Joe Willis and Richard G. Wettan, "Social Stratification in New York City Athletic Clubs, 1865–1915," *Journal of Sport History* 3 (1976): 45–63.

3. Jack C. Ross, *An Assembly of Good Fellows: Voluntary Associations in History* (Westport, CT: Greenwood, 1976), pp. 255–57.

4. Alexis de Tocqueville, *Democracy in America*, trans. George Lawrence, ed. J. P. Mayer (Garden City: Doubleday and Co., Anchor edn., 1969),

vol. 2, p. 513. Louis Wirth, "Urbanism as a Way of Life," *American Journal of Sociology* 44 (July 1938): 3–24; Walter Glazer, "Participation and Power: Voluntary Associations and the Functional Organization of Cincinnati in 1840," *Historical Methods Newsletter* 5 (1972): 151–68; Don H. Doyle, "The Social Functions of Voluntary Associations in a Nineteenth-Century Town," *Social Science History* 1 (1977): 344–55. For a good review of literature, see Constance Smith and Anne Freedman, *Voluntary Associations: Perspectives on the Literature* (Cambridge: Harvard University Press, 1972).

5. See the discussion of clubs in Adelman, "Development of Modern Athletics," p. 640.

6. Benjamin G. Rader, "The Quest for Sub-Communities and the Rise of American Sport," *American Quarterly* 29 (Fall 1977): 355–56. Rader stresses the role of ethnic and status clubs in this context. He also suggests neighborhoods, occupations, and religious preferences as sources of sports clubs and subcommunity. Although I emphasize these same club forms as responses to the search for local community in one city, my findings corroborate Rader's broader interpretation.

7. Stephen Freedman, "The Baseball Fad in Chicago, 1865–1870; An Exploration of the Role of Sport in the Nineteenth-Century City," *Journal of Sport History* 5 (Summer 1978): 42–64. For a fuller discussion of sports clubs during this period, see Stephen Hardy, "The City and the Rise of American Sport: 1820–1920," *Exercise and Sport Sciences Reviews* 9 (1981): 183–219.

8. Samuel Eliot Morison, *The Maritime History of Massachusetts, 1783–1860* (Boston: Houghton Mifflin, Sentry edn., 1961), pp. 241–49.

9. A. J. Kenealy, "Yacht Clubs of the East," *Outing* 18 (1891): 383–88, 475–80. See also Arthur Brayley, *A History of the Boston Yacht Club* (Boston, 1891); Charles Foster, *The Eastern Yacht Club Ditty Box, 1870–1900* (Norwood, MA: privately printed, 1932); Parks Minutes, 17 September 1894.

10. Howard Maynadier, *Sixty Years of the Union Boat Club* (Boston: printed by the club, 1913); James D'Wolf Lovett, *Old Boston Boys and the Games They Played*, pp. 55–62; Charles A. Peverelly, *The Book of American Pastimes, Containing a History of the Principal Baseball, Cricket, Rowing and Yachting Clubs of the United States* (New York: published by the author, 1866); Charles Hallock, *Hallock's American Club List* (New York, 1878).

11. Will Roffe, "Cricket in New England and the Longwood Club," *Outing* 18 (1891): 251–54; *Boston Herald*, 8, 15 August, 15 September 1886; Parks Minutes, 29 August 1893, 22 January 1894, 23 December 1895; Peverelly, *Book of American Pastimes*, 532–35; Lovett, *Old Boston Boys*, p. 76.

12. George V. Touhey, *A History of the Boston Baseball Club* (Boston: M. F. Quinn, 1897), pp. 17–27; Lovett, *Old Boston Boys*, pp. 78, 128–53;

Peverelly, *Book of American Pastimes*, pp. 337, 516. Descriptions of "Massachusetts" and "New York" games in Harold Seymour, *Baseball: The Early Years* (New York: Oxford University Press, 1960), pp. 26–30. The amateur clubs acted as feeders, on occasion, for the professional clubs. John Morrill, who captained the Bostons after George Wright, came up through the local amateur club circuit; see *Boston Journal*, 14 April 1895. A late "Massachusetts" game is cited in the *Charlestown News*, 22 July 1882.

13. Charles E. Pratt, "Our First Bicycle Club," *The Wheelman* 1 (March 1883): 402; *Bicycle World* 1 (27 December 1879): 50.

14. Ellery H. Clark, "Track Athletics," *The H Book of Harvard Athletics*, ed. John A. Blanchard (Cambridge: Harvard Varsity Club, 1923), pp. 463–68.

15. *Boston Herald*, 4 August 1881, 16 February 1887; *Boston Post*, 23 February 1861; *Boston Daily Advertiser*, 21 July 1875, 4, 8 September, 26 December 1879. I found an announcement for an athletic meet as far back as 1843! Promoted by the director of the Boston Gymnasium, the activities were called "gymnastic games," but included sprints, distance runs, leaping, and hammer throw. See *Boston Post*, 17 August 1843.

16. *Boston Daily Advertiser*, 31 July 1867, 12 June 1871; *Boston Herald*, 27 May 1881, 17 May 1896; John W. Linnehan and Edward D. Cogswell, eds., *The Driving Clubs of Greater Boston* (Boston: Atlantic Printing Co., 1914).

17. Alexander Williams, *A Social History of the Greater Boston Clubs* (Barre, MA: Barre Publishing Company, 1970); *The Boston Club Book for 1888* (Boston: Edward E. Clark, 1888); *The Clubs of Boston* (Boston: N. Wilson and Co., 1891).

18. Kenealy, "Yacht Clubs of the East," 384. Adelman, "The Development of Modern Athletics," pp. 234–35, refers to the perceptions of baseball as a child's game. For a more general treatment of subcultural development, see Claude Fischer, "Toward a Subcultural Theory of Urbanism," *American Journal of Sociology* 80 (1975): 1319–41.

19. *Boston Herald*, 31 May 1881, 3 June 1888; *Republic*, 7, 14 July 1883, 7 July 1890; *Charlestown News*, 30 April, 4 June, 2 July, 6 April, 3 September 1881, 15 July 1882; *South Boston Bulletin*, 10 August 1895. I traced as many club members listed in newspaper accounts as I could positively identify in city directories. This evidence is admittedly scanty, but I believe that my general point is valid.

20. Parks Minutes, 23 November 1903.

21. For Woods and other reformers' fears, see ch. 2. For Savin Hill Beach Association see *Boston Journal*, 12 May 1895. For the activities of other neighborhood clubs, see Parks Minutes, 5 August 1885, 25 September 1899, 5 February 1900, 3 April 1905; *The Pilot*, 18 March 1892; *Boston Journal*, 11 April 1895.

22. Oscar Handlin, *Boston's Immigrants*, p. 155.

23. Edward Mussey Hartwell, *Report of the Director of Physical Training, School Document No. 22*, 1891, p. 59. Description of picnic quoted in Augustus Prahl, "The Turner," in A. E. Zucker, ed., *The Forty-Eighters* (New York: Russell and Russell, 1950), p. 97. On Heizen, see Handlin, *Boston's Immigrants*, pp. 156, 172. See also Carl Wittke, *Refugees of Revolution* (Philadelphia: University of Pennsylvania Press, 1952), pp. 147–61; Albert B. Faust, *The German Element in the United States*, 2 vols. (Boston: Houghton Mifflin, 1909), vol. 2, ch. 8; Henry Metzner, *History of the American Turners*, 3rd rev. edn. (Rochester, NY: National Council of the American Turners, 1974).

24. *Boston Daily Globe*, 29 August 1879, quoted in Gerald Redmond, *The Caledonian Games in Nineteenth-Century America* (Rutherford, NJ: Fairleigh Dickinson University Press, 1971), p. 45. See also Rowland Tappan Berthoff, *British Immigrants in Industrial America, 1790–1950* (Cambridge: Harvard University Press, 1953), pp. 151–52, 167–68, 179.

25. Katie Kenneally, *West Roxbury*, Boston 200 Neighborhood History Series (Boston: Boston 200 Corp., 1976), p. 12; *Boston Herald*, 29 May 1881, 25, 26 August 1882.

26. *The Pilot*, 18 July 1854.

27. *The Pilot*, 4, 25 June 1881; *Republic*, 8, 22, 29 July, 19 August 1882; *Boston Herald*, 29 May, 18 June 1881, 12 August 1886; John R. Betts, "John Boyle O'Reilly and the American Paideia," *Eire-Ireland* 2 (Winter 1967): 36–52.

28. Dennis P. Ryan, "Beyond the Ballot Box: A Social History of the Boston Irish, 1845–1917" (Ph.D. dissertation, University of Massachusetts/Amherst, 1979), p. 125; *Boston Herald*, 31 May 1881; *Republic*, 4 June 1892, 8 July 1893, 6 June 1896.

29. O'Reilly, *Athletics and Manly Sports*, p. 235; *Boston Journal*, 6 May 1895.

30. John Daniels, *In Freedom's Birthplace: A Study of the Boston Negroes* (Boston: Houghton Mifflin, 1914; repinted edn., New York: Johnson Reprint Corp., 1968), p. 171; *The Guardian*, 3 July 1909, 2 July 1910; Parks Minutes, 19 February, 2 July 1894; Elizabeth Pleck, *Black Migration and Poverty: Boston, 1865–1900* (New York: Academic Press, 1979), pp. 73–74.

31. For other looks at the "push-pull" nature of ethnic sports see John Pooley, "Ethnic Soccer Clubs in Milwaukee: A Study in Assimilation," in M. Marie Hart, ed., *Sport in the Socio-Cultural Process* (Dubuque, IA: William C. Brown, 1972), pp. 328–45; Richard Sorrell, "Sports and Franco-Americans in Woonsocket, 1870–1930," *Rhode Island History* 31 (Fall 1972): 116–26; *The Armenians in Massachusetts*, American Guide Series (Federal Writer's Project of the WPA for the State of Massachusetts, 1937), pp. 44–45.

32. Richard Coleman and Bernice Neugarten, *Social Status in the City* (San Francisco: Jossey-Bass, 1971), p. 8. Rader also argues this point well in "The Quest for Sub-communities and the Rise of American Sport," 361–63. See also E. Digby Baltzell, *Philadelphia Gentlemen: The Making of a National Upper Class* (New York: Free Press, 1958), pp. 335–63. The best work on the relationship of sport to social class and status is Richard Gruneau, "Sport, Social Differentiation, and Social Inequality," *Sport and Social Order: Contributions to the Sociology of Sport*, Donald W. Ball and John W. Loy, eds. (Reading, MA: Addison-Wesley, 1975), pp. 121–84.

33. *The Clubs of Boston: Containing a Complete List of Members and Addresses of All Boston Clubs of Social and Business Prominence, Endorsed by All the Leading Clubs* (Boston: N. Wilson and Co., 1891), preface.

34. Henry L. Nelson, "The Clubs of Boston," *Harper's Weekly* 34 (25 January 1890): 58.

35. Williams, *Social History of the Greater Boston Clubs*, ch. 8, 9; Cleveland Amory, *The Proper Bostonians* (New York: E. P. Dutton, 1947), pp. 276, 357.

36. Edwin Bacon, ed., *Boston of Today. A Glance at Its History and Characteristics* (Boston: Boston Post Publishing Co., 1892), p. 106. The Country Club's forerunner was the Myopia Club, which began in 1876 under the leadership of the Prince family and was fused into The Country Club in 1882. Its successor, the Myopia Hunt Club, still thrives. See Allan Forbes, *Early Myopia* (Boston: published by the author, 1942); Edward Weeks, *Myopia: A Centennial Chronicle* (Lunenburg, VT: Stinehour Press, 1976); Elmer O. Cappers, *Centennial History of The Country Club: 1882–1982* (Brookline, MA: printed by the club, 1981), pp. 2–4.

37. Frederic H. Curtiss and John Heard, *The Country Club, 1882–1932* (Brookline, MA: privately printed, 1932); Elmer O. Cappers, "The Country Club, Brookline, Massachusetts," *Proceedings of the Brookline Historical Society*, 1968, pp. 58–64; idem, *Centennial History*. I am indebted to Mr. Cappers for providing me both information and a tour of The Country Club. A full description of the club and grounds can also be found in David Paine, "Prominent Country Clubs," *New England Magazine* (May 1905): 322–36.

38. Sarah Forbes Hughes, ed., *Letters and Recollections of John Murray Forbes* (Boston: Houghton Mifflin, 1899), pp. 43–46; *Reminiscences of John Murray Forbes*, 3 vols. (Boston: George H. Ellis, 1902), vol. 1, pp. 68–88; *Letters (Supplementary) of John Murray Forbes*, 3 vols. (Boston: George H. Ellis, 1905), vol. 1, pp. 18, 26, 176–77.

39. Ronald Story, *The Forging of an Aristocracy: Harvard and the Boston Upper Class* (Middletown, CT: Wesleyan University Press, 1980), pp. 160–82. Story tabulated the number of Harvard graduates, p. 177, p. 249 n. 30. I tabulated the linkage with the Union and Somerset clubs by comparing the original membership list in Curtiss and Heard, *The Country*

Club, pp. 169–74, with lists of Somerset and Union members in *Clubs of Boston*, 1891, 363–71, 405–15; *The Constitution, By-Laws and House Rules of the Union Club* (Boston: George H. Ellis, 1882); *A Brief History of the Somerset Club of Boston, with a List of Past and Present Members, 1852–1913* (Boston: published by the club, 1913), pp. 37–68. Some were members of both other clubs.

40. Curtiss and Heard, *The Country Club*, p. 4.

41. The Country Club, *Constitution, By-Laws and List of Members* (Boston: by the club, 1888); The Tennis and Racquet Club, *Constitution, By-Laws, Rules, Member-list* (Boston: by the club, 1908); Union Boat Club, *Constitution and By-Laws* (Boston: by the club, 1873); Foster, *The Eastern Yacht Club Ditty Box*, p. 20; Brayley, *History of the Boston Yacht Club*. These followed the same formats used by the in-town men's clubs. Ingham found that country-club memberships were of similar importance to the iron barons of Pennsylvania and Ohio. See John N. Ingham, *The Iron Barons: A Social Analysis of an American Urban Elite, 1874–1965* (Westport, CT: Greenwood Press, 1978), p. 97.

42. City Council *Proceedings*, 17 May 1886.

43. Quoted in Amory, *Proper Bostonians*, p. 357. Reactions to exclusion underscored the importance of club membership to social status, but more research is needed into the attitudes of excluded groups. For a good example see Robert Rockaway, "Anti-Semitism in an American City: Detroit, 1850–1914," *American Jewish Historical Quarterly* 64 (1974): 42–54.

44. Allen Chamberlain, "Boston's First Attempt at a Country Club," *Boston Evening Transcript*, 20 January 1926. The document now hangs proudly in the hallway of The Country Club. Freedman, "The Baseball Fad in Chicago," found that the same concerns motivated many Chicago clubs.

45. Edward Rankin, *Boston Athletic Association* (n.p., n.d.); *Boston Herald*, 16 February 1887; *South Boston Bulletin*, 9 May 1896; *Republic*, 7 June 1890. A check of random names from the BAA club list of 1888 indicated members whose occupations would likely have rendered them unacceptable at The Country Club.

46. *South Boston Bulletin*, 10 August 1895.

47. City Council *Proceedings*, 18 June 1896; *Leisure Hours* 1 (August 1888): 8; *Boston Daily Advertiser*, 14 May 1874.

48. Linnehan and Cogswell, *Driving Clubs of Greater Boston*, pp. 8–24.

49. *By-Laws and Rules of the Boston Bicycle Club* (Boston, 1882), p. 22. Amory, *Proper Bostonians*, p. 276. For complaints on this trend, see Duncan Edwards, "Life at the Athletic Clubs," *Scribner's* 18 (July 1895): 6. See also *Boston Journal*, 14 April 1895.

50. I am indebted to Professor Betty Spears, University of Massachusetts/Amherst, for sending me information from the Allen School Scrap-

books. Professor Spears's forthcoming study of Amy Morris Homans and the Boston Normal School should do much to illuminate the role of these gymnasiums. For more information, see Elizabeth Wilson, *Fifty Years of Association Work Among Young Women, 1866–1916* (New York: YWCA, 1916), p. 43; Hope Narey, "Physical Training for Women," *The Bostonian* 1 (1894–95): 98–106; Kate Gannett Wells, "An Open Air Gymnasium for Women," ibid., 4 (June 1896): 258–66; Mary Taylor Bissell, "Athletics for City Girls," *Popular Science Monthly* 46 (December 1894): 145–53; Elizabeth C. Barney, "The American Sportswoman," *Fornightly Review* 56 (1894): 263–77.

51. Barney, "American Sportswoman," 263.

52. W. G. Van Tassel Sutphen, "The Golfing Woman," *Outlook* 62 (June 1899): 254; *Boston Herald*, 25 August 1897. For similar sentiment linking sports with female vitality and family comradeship, see Anna de Koven, "The Athletic Woman," *Good Housekeeping* 55 (August 1912): 148–57, with coverage of the exploits of Eleonora Sears.

53. Lucille Hill, ed., *Athletics and Outdoor Sports for Women* (New York: Macmillan, 1903), p. 4.

54. Arthur Mann, *Yankee Reformers in the Urban Age* (Cambridge: Harvard University Press, 1954), ch. 9, notes that Kate Gannett Wells was an outspoken opponent of suffrage. Valuable treatment of women's sport history may be found in Stephanie L. Twin, "Jock and Jill: Aspects of Women's Sport History in America, 1870–1940" (Ph.D. dissertation: Rutgers University, 1978). Other good coverage is in Lucas and Smith, *Saga of American Sport*, pp. 250–66; Betty Spears and Richard A. Swanson, *History of Sport and Physical Activity in the United States* (Dubuque, IA: William C. Brown, 1978), passim; Ellen W. Gerber et al., *The American Woman in Sport* (Reading, MA: Addison-Wesley, 1974).

55. W. F. Dix, "The Influence of Sport in American Life," *The Independent* 55 (3 September 1903): 2094. Baltzell extends this argument to the level of a national aristocracy; see *Philadelphia Gentlemen*, pp. 335–63.

56. Robert Dunn, "The Country Club: A National Expression," *Outing* 47 (1905): 165.

57. Edward Martin, "Country Clubs and Hunt Clubs in America," *Scribner's Out of Door Library: Athletic Sports* (New York: Scribner, 1897), p. 275; Dunn, "Country Club," 165.

58. Chamberlain, "Boston's First Attempt at a Country Club."

59. Caspar W. Whitney, "Evolution of the Country Club," *Harper's* 90 (1894): 30.

60. Henry Howland, "Golf," *Scribner's* 17 (May 1895): 533–35; Arthur Tarbell, "Golf and Golf Clubs," *The (Boston) National Magazine* 4 (August 1896): 481–93. Occasionally, the caddies brought the golfers back to reality by striking for higher wages. See *Boston Herald*, 17 May 1896.

61. Nathan C. Shiverick, "The Social Reorganization of Boston," in Williams, *Social History of Greater Boston Clubs*, p. 143. See also *Boston Journal*, 21 April 1895.

62. Quoted in Lewis Mumford, *The City in History* (New York: Harcourt, Brace and World, 1961), p. 495. Handlin offers a similar analysis in *Boston's Immigrants*, p. 221.

63. Robert Anderson, "Voluntary Associations in History," *American Anthropologist* 73 (February 1971): 217–18. For a similar analysis of one Boston association, see Ronald Story, "Class and Culture in Boston: The Athenaeum, 1807–1860," *American Quarterly* 27 (May 1975): 178–99.

64. "The Fascination of Bicycling," *The Bicycling World* (Boston) 2 (4 February 1881): 195.

65. Betts, *America's Sporting Heritage*, p. 98.

Notes to Chapter 8

1. Sylvester Baxter, *Boston Park Guide, Including the Municipal and Metropolitan Systems of Greater Boston* (Boston: published by the author, 1895), p. 68.

2. City Council *Proceedings*, 11 April 1895; Parks Minutes, 29 April 1895.

3. Richard Harmond, "Progress and Flight: An Interpretation of the American Cycle Craze of the 1890's," *Journal of Social History* 5 (Winter 1971–72): 241. I have profited a great deal from Harmond's article. Where he stresses the bicycle as an escape from technology, I would emphasize its role as a release from urban living. The two were, of course, closely entwined, and my work does much to corroborate Harmond's broader interpretation. For the "machine in the garden," see Leo Marx, *The Machine in the Garden: Technology and the Pastoral Ideal in America* (New York: Oxford University Press, 1964). Parks Department response in City Council *Proceedings*, 25 June 1896; *Annual Parks Report*, 1896, p. 59.

4. I am indebted to Daniel Boorstin for his discussion of consumption communities in *The Americans: The Democratic Experience* (New York: Random House, 1973; Vintage Books edn., 1974), pp. 89–164.

5. The richest description of the bicycle's history in America is found in Norman L. Dunham, "The Bicycle Era in American History" (Ph.D. dissertation, Harvard University, 1956). Unfortunately Dunham became so engrossed in the three earlier forms that he had to "trim sail" upon reaching the safety bicycle. Besides Harmond's article, two other useful recent works are Gary Allan Tobin, "The Bicycle Boom of the 1890's: The Development of Private Transportation and the Birth of the Modern Tourist," *Journal of Popular Culture* 7 (Spring 1974): 838–49; Robert A. Smith, *A Social History of the Bicycle* (New York: American Heritage Press, 1972).

6. *Boston Intelligencer and Evening Gazette,* 24 April 1819, quoted in Dunham, "The Bicycle Era," p. 35. Descriptions may also be found in Smith, *Social History of the Bicycle,* ch. 1; John A. Krout, *Annals of American Sport,* p. 172; Axel Josephsson, "Bicycles and Tricycles," *Twelfth Census of the United States, 1900* (Washington, DC, 1902), vol. 10, p. 329.

7. Charles Pratt, *The American Bicycler* (Boston: Houghton Mifflin, 1879), p. 9. Pratt later embroidered the study and added that one of the students was Charles Sumner, but Dunham cautiously points out that Sumner was only eight years old in 1819! See Charles Pratt, "A Sketch of American Bicycling and Its Founder," *Outing* 18 (July 1891): 342–49; Dunham, "Bicycle Era," p. 36.

8. Dunham, "Bicycle Era," pp. 25, 26, 41.

9. Pratt, *American Bicycler,* pp. 15–18; Josephsson, "Bicycles and Tricycles," 330; Dunham, "Bicycle Era," pp. 47–49.

10. *Boston Daily Advertiser,* 18 August 1868, cited in Dunham, "The Bicycle Era," pp. 49–51.

11. "The Velocipede in Boston," *Boston Daily Advertiser,* 4 February 1869.

12. "The Velocipede," *Boston Daily Advertiser,* 9 March 1869.

13. See Dunham's analysis of the velocipede's demise, "The Bicycle Era," pp. 56f, 110–48.

14. Pratt, *American Bicycler,* p. 29; Josephsson, "Bicycles and Tricycles," 330–34.

15. Charles Pratt, "A Sketch of American Bicycling and Its Founder," *Bicycling World* 3 (22 July 1881): 129; Pratt, *American Bicycler,* pp. 23, 29; Albert A. Pope, "The Bicycle Industry," *One Hundred Years of American Commerce, 1795–1895,* ed. Chauncey M. Depew (New York: D. O. Haynes & Co., 1895), pp. 549–53; Dunham, "Bicycle Era," pp. 175–77.

16. *American Bicycling Journal,* 25 January 1879; *The Wheelman: An Illustrated Magazine of Cycling Literature and News* 1 (October 1882). Pope had founded *The Wheelman* with S. S. McClure as editor. The following year it merged with *Outing.*

17. Albert S. Parsons, "The Massachusetts Bicycle Club," *The Wheelman* 2 (June 1883): 165; *Boston Journal,* 28, 29 May 1886.

18. *Bicycling World* 2 (4 February 1881): 195.

19. *Bicycling World* 1 (27 December 1879): 50; *By-Laws and Rules of the Boston Bicycle Club* (Boston, 1882); Parsons, "Massachusetts Bicycle Club," 171.

20. "The Hum of the Hub," *League of American Wheelmen Bulletin* 3 (24 September 1886): 339. I found an ad for expensive ($100–$130) bicycles in the *Boston Advocate* (the black newspaper) of 27 June 1885.

21. Charles Pratt, "Our First Bicycle Club," *The Wheelman* 1 (March 1883): 402.

22. Charles Pratt, "Sketch of American Bicycling and Its Founder," 344.

23. *Boston Herald,* 30 May 1881.

24. *Bicycling World* 1 (27 December 1879): 50; *LAW Bulletin* 3 (1, 8 October 1886).

25. Parks Minutes, 31 May 1889; *Boston Journal,* 5 July 1889.

26. Parks Minutes, 25 June, 4 September 1891, 26 June 1893, 29 August 1896; *Boston Journal,* 5 July 1890.

27. *Bicycling World* 2 (11 March 1881): 278.

28. *Bicycling World* 2 (4 February 1881): 195; 25 (September 1892– March 1893): 214.

29. Pratt, "Our First Bicycle Club," 411.

30. Charles Pratt, *What and Why; Some Common Questions Answered* (Boston: Rockwell and Churchill, 1884), p. 44; idem, "Sketch of American Bicycling," 345.

31. Philip Mason, "The League of American Wheelmen and the Good Roads Movement, 1880–1905" (Ph.D. dissertation, University of Michigan, 1957).

32. Josephsson, "Bicycles and Tricycles," 325; Pratt, "Sketch of American Bicycling," 344–48, claimed there were more than 50 manufacturers, but this was probably promotional hyperbole.

33. Josephsson, "Bicycles and Tricycles," 331; Harmond, "Progress and Flight," 237; Dunham, "The Bicycle Era," p. 407.

34. *Boston Globe,* 19 August 1888.

35. Josephsson, "Bicycles and Tricycles," 331–33; Pope, "The Bicycle Industry," 551; Tobin, "The Bicycle Boom," 839; Harmond, "Progress and Flight," 238–40.

36. Joseph Bishop, "Social and Economic Influence of the Bicycle," *Forum* 21 (August 1896): 680.

37. *The Pilot,* 7 May 1892; "The Reign of the Bicycle," *Century* 49 (December 1895): 306–7.

38. *Boston Journal,* 22 April 1895.

39. *Boston Journal,* 28 April 1895.

40. *Boston Herald,* 21 June 1896.

41. Samuel Eliot Morison, *One Boy's Boston: 1887–1901* (Boston: Houghton Mifflin, 1962), p. 29. For bicycle schools, see also *Boston Herald,* 22 May 1892.

42. Charles Wingate, "Cycling in Boston," *Critic* 27 (12 October 1895): 235; James Fullerton Muirhead, *The Land of Contrasts* (London: John Lane, 1898; reprint edn., 1911), p. 127.

43. *Boston Globe,* 1 July 1894; *Boston Journal,* 26 May 1895; *Boston Evening Transcript,* 5 July 1892.

44. *Boston Journal,* 1, 7 April, 25 May, 18 August 1895; *Boston Herald,* 15 May 1892, 10 May 1896; *Boston Globe,* 1 July 1895.

45. *LAW Bulletin* 5 (August 1887): 125, 287; Isaac Potter, "The Bicycle's Relation to Good Roads," *Harper's Weekly* 40 (11 April 1896): 362; "Bicycle Problems and Benefits," *Century* 50 (May 1895): 474–75; Philip Mason, "The League of American Wheelmen and the Good Roads Movement."

46. *Boston Journal*, 26 May 1895.

47. *LAW Bulletin*, 27 (7 January 1898): 16; Sylvester Baxter, "Articles on the Civic Improvement of Boston," Scrapbook from 1904; in Rare Book Room, Boston Public Library, p. 21.

48. Parks Minutes, 10 July 1893; 29 June 1894.

49. *LAW Bulletin* 26 (2 July 1897): 5; 25 (14 May 1897): 543; Arthur K. Peck, "League of American Wheelmen," in William Van Rensselaer Miller, ed., *Select Organizations in the United States* (New York: Knickerbocker Publishing Co., 1896), p. 228.

50. *Century* 49 (December 1895): 306–07.

51. "Bicycle Boom," 840–41. Tobin's research shows that Pennsylvania, New York, New Jersey, Massachusetts, Ohio, and Illinois accounted for 75 percent of the total LAW membership in 1897. Further, bicycle repair shops were located mostly in the urban regions. His arguments are corroborated in Josephsson, "Bicycles and Tricycles," 325–28.

52. *Forum* 21 (August 1896): 683; *Bicycling World* 32 (15 May 1896): 11.

53. *LAW Bulletin and Good Roads* 23 (27 May 1896): 453; *Boston Herald*, 1 May 1892.

54. *Boston Herald*, 17 May 1896, 7 October 1894 (races). Smith, *Social History of the Bicycle*, chs. 4, 5, 13, provides good coverage of women and cycling.

55. *Boston Herald*, 3, 17 May 1896; *South Boston Bulletin*, 2 May 1896; *Pilot*, 7 May 1892.

56. "Why Bicycling Is the Best Form of Exercise," *Bicycling World* 2 (11 March 1881): 275.

57. "The Economic and Social Influences of the Bicycle," *Arena* 6 (October 1892): 581–83. See also *Scribner's* 27 (1895): 708–12; Luther Porter, *Cycling for Health and Pleasure* (New York, 1895), p. 182, cited in Harmond, "Progress and Flight," 243.

58. J. G. Dalton, *Lyra Bicyclica: Forty Poets on the Wheel* (Boston: the author, 1880), p. 31.

59. *Boston Herald*, 29 May 1892. See also the many examples cited in Harmond, "Progress and Flight," 246–48.

60. "The Selfish Side of Bicycling," *Bicycling World* 2 (25 February 1881): 243.

61. *Boston Journal* 1, 22 April, 2, 7, 23 July 1895; *Boston Herald*, 5 July 1896; Tobin, "The Bicycle Boom," 842.

62. *LAW Bulletin* 24 (16 October 1896): 513–14.

63. Tobin argues this subtle but important point in "Bicycle Boom," 242–45.

64. *Bicycling World* 2 (14 January 1881): 147.

65. *Boston Journal*, 28 April, 18 August 1895; *Century* 49 (December 1895): 306–7; *Mind and Body* 8 (July 1901): 116–17; *Harper's Weekly* 40 (11 April 1896): 354; *Forum* 21 (August 1896): 680; *LAW Bulletin* 24 (16 October 1896): 514.

66. Parks Minutes, 12 February, 5 March 1895.

67. *Century* 50 (May 1895): 474; *Arena* 6 (October 1892): 581.

68. *LAW Bulletin and Good Roads* 26 (30 July 1897): 150. See also, in the same magazine, 24 (18 December 1896): 803; 25 (21 May 1897): 576. Poem in Dalton, *Lyra Bicyclica*, p. 38.

69. Abbott Bassett, "Outdoor Season—Revival of Cycling," *Harper's Weekly* 47 (11 June 1904): 906–7. Mason, "League of American Wheelmen," pp. 44–48.

70. Bassett, "Outdoor Season," 907.

71. Charles W. Cheape, *Moving the Masses: Urban Public Transit in New York, Boston, and Philadelphia, 1880–1912* (Cambridge: Harvard University Press, 1980), pp. 103–53, 208–19.

72. Pope, "Bicycle Industry," p. 551.

73. Daniel Boorstin, *The Americans*, p. 147. Although they are miles apart ideologically, Boorstin and Karl Marx are curiously close in their descriptions of the ties of consumption and production. See Karl Marx, *The Grundrisse*, ed. and trans. David McLellan (New York: Harper Torchbooks, 1971), pp. 25–26, 66–68.

74. This possibility limited the usefulness of consumption as a measure of status. For an extended, if not abstruse, treatment of consumption and status, see Thorstein Veblen, *The Theory of the Leisure Class* (New York, 1899; reprint edn., New York: New American Library, Mentor Books, 1953).

75. Harold U. Faulkner, "Albert Augustus Pope," *Dictionary of American Biography*, ed. Dumas Malone (New York: Scribner, 1935), vol. 15, pp. 74–75.

Notes to Chapter 9

1. Anselm Strauss, *Images of the American City* (New York: Free Press, 1961), p. 17. See also Kevin Lynch, *The Image of the City* (Cambridge: MIT Press, 1960).

2. See Orrin Klapp, *Symbolic Leaders: Public Dramas and Public Men* (Chicago: Aldine Publishing Co., 1964), pp. 44, 259; idem, *Heroes, Villains, and Fools: The Changing American Character* (New York: Spectrum Books, 1962). See also David Q. Voigt's interesting use of Klapp's ideas in his discussion of umpires, in *American Baseball: From Gentleman's Sport to Commissioner's System* (Norman, OK: University of Oklahoma Press, 1966), pp. 183–84.

3. Quoted in Nat Fleischer, *The Boston Strong Boy: The Story of John L. Sullivan* (New York: C. J. O'Brien, Inc., 1941), p. 1.

4. *Boston Globe*, 2, 6 February 1918. The standard works on Sullivan's life are Roy Dibble, *John L. Sullivan: An Intimate Narrative* (Boston: Little, Brown, 1925); Donald B. Chidsey, *John the Great: The Times and Life of a Remarkable American, John L. Sullivan* (Garden City, NY: Doubleday, Doran, 1942); Fleischer, *Boston Strong Boy*; idem, *John L. Sullivan, Champion of Champions* (New York: Putnam, 1951). Sullivan himself wrote (or more likely coauthored with a ghost-writer) an autobiography, *Life and Reminiscences of a 19th-Century Gladiator* (Boston: J. A. Hearn, 1892).

5. Chidsey, *John the Great*, p. 27; Fleischer, *Boston Strong Boy*, pp. 5–19; Rex Lardner, *The Legendary Champions* (New York: American Heritage Press, 1972), p. 45.

6. City Council *Proceedings*, 2 July 1894. See also *City Document No. 167*, 1884; City Council *Proceedings*, 5 March 1888.

7. *The Pilot*, 17 April 1880.

8. Dibble, *John L. Sullivan*, p. 31. Our picture is taken from Sullivan's autobiography.

9. John Boyle O'Reilly, *Athletics and Manly Sports* (Boston: Pilot Publishing Co., 1890), pp. 75, 79. This book was originally published in 1888 as *Ethics of Boxing and Manly Sports*.

10. *The Pilot*, 25 June 1881. Accounts of the western swing may be found in Sullivan, *Life and Reminiscences*; Dibble, *John L. Sullivan*.

11. Basically, the London rules provided no limit to the number of rounds. A round ended when either man was knocked down. At that point, his seconds would assist him to his corner, and after a thirty-second rest, the boxers would come out for the next round. The fight ended only when either man could not begin the next round. The Queensbury rules called for gloves, rounds of three minutes' duration, and a rest of one minute between rounds. If a fighter was knocked down he had to get up, unassisted, within ten seconds, or be counted out. See Frank Menke, *The Encyclopedia of Sports* (New York: A. S. Barnes, 1953), pp. 231–36.

12. Chidsey, *John the Great*, p. 56.

13. *The Pilot*, 18 February 1882. *The Pilot* continued this appeal throughout Sullivan's career. See the issue of 13 August 1887.

14. *Boston Globe*, 8 February 1882. See also *Boston Post*, 8 February 1882.

15. "Ruby," "scratch," etc. were all common boxing terms. Quoted in Sullivan, *Life and Reminiscences*, p. 92.

16. Quoted in *Boston Globe*, 9 February 1882.

17. *Republic*, 29 July 1882. Sullivan's earlier reception is reported in the *Boston Globe*, 10 March 1882, and in his *Life and Reminiscences*, p. 95. For an account of Yankee Sullivan see Melvin Adelman, "The Development of Modern Athletics: Sport in New York City, 1820–1870," pp. 563–64.

18. *Boston Globe,* 9 August 1882.

19. Lardner, *Legendary Champions,* p. 50.

20. *Evening Transcript,* 9 August 1887. The *Transcript,* nonetheless, gave the story front-page coverage. One senses the strain such an action placed on the delicate relationship between the Brahmins and the Irish political machine. See Geoffrey Blodgett, *The Gentle Reformers,* p. 148.

21. *The Pilot,* 20 August 1887. See also *Boston Post,* 10 August 1887.

22. *Republic,* 10 September 1892. For his deteriorating condition, see Sullivan, *Life and Reminiscences,* pp. 254, 283–94, which includes a detailed physical report by Dudley Sargent. See also the interesting "A Day with Sullivan," *Boston Herald,* 10 July 1892.

23. Dibble, *John L. Sullivan,* p. 101.

24. Stephan Thernstrom, *The Other Bostonians; Poverty and Progress in the American Metropolis, 1880–1970* (Cambridge: Harvard University Press, 1973), p. 132. Handlin makes the same point in *Boston's Immigrants,* p. 223.

25. Frederick A. Bushee, *Ethnic Factors in the Population of Boston* (1903), p. 152. William V. Shannon makes a similar point in *The American Irish* (New York: Macmillan, 1963), ch. 7.

26. *Boston Globe,* 8 September 1892; *Boston Herald,* 8 September 1892; *The Pilot,* 17 September 1892. Visiting Briton James Fullarton Muirhead claimed that the fight news obscured Whittier's death; *The Land of Contrasts* (Boston, 1898), p. 158. I found that in Boston the coverage was roughly equal, with editorials focusing on Whittier rather than Sullivan-Corbett.

27. *Donahoe's Magazine* 20 (July 1888): 24–31; 20 (August 1888): 148–57; 9 (May 1883): 466–67; 14 (November 1885): 444–46. I am indebted to Dennis Ryan for citing and discussing these articles in "Beyond the Ballot Box: A Social History of the Boston Irish, 1845–1917," (Ph.D. dissertation, University of Massachusetts, 1979), p. 128. Chidsey makes a similar claim in *John the Great,* p. 3.

28. Kenneth L. Kusmer, "The Concept of 'Community' in American History," *Reviews in American History* 7 (September 1979): 385. This piece contains a good review of Thomas Bender, *Community and Social Change in America.*

29. Elizabeth Pleck, "Black Migration to Boston in the Late Nineteenth-Century" (Ph.D. dissertation, Brandeis University, 1974), p. 188. Pleck's excellent book, *Black Migration and Poverty,* contains less material on boxing. For more on these black fighters, the best source is Nathaniel S. Fleischer, *Black Dynamite: The Story of the Negro in the Prize Ring from 1782–1938* (New York: C. J. O'Brien, 1938). See also Edwin B. Henderson, *The Negro in Sports,* rev. edn. (Washington, DC: Associated Publishers, 1939); Lucas and Smith, *Saga of American Sport,* pp. 267–84. On the color line erected by John L. Sullivan and other white fighters, see Jack Orr, *The*

Black Athlete: His Story in American History (New York: Lion Books, 1969), p. 28; John R. Betts, "Organized Sport in Industrial America" (Ph.D. dissertation, Columbia University, 1951), p. 602.

30. Jack Johnson, *Jack Johnson is a Dandy: An Autobiography* (New York: Chelsea House Publishers, 1969), p. 42. Besides his autobiography, the best works on Johnson are Finis Farr, *Black Champion* (Greenwich, CT: Fawcett Publications, 1964); Al-Tony Gilmore, *Bad Nigger! The National Impact of Jack Johnson* (New York: Kennikat Press, 1975).

31. Quoted in Gilmore, *Bad Nigger!*, p. 32. I have relied throughout on Gilmore's thorough and scholarly account of Johnson and his impact in Boston and other cities.

32. *Boston Globe*, 2 July 1910.

33. Ibid., 5 July 1910.

34. Ibid. For a national account see Gilmore, *Bad Nigger!*, pp. 59–72.

35. *Boston Guardian*, 6 August 1910; *Boston Globe*, 6, 8 July 1910; *Boston Evening Transcript*, 6, 9 July 1910.

36. Gilmore, *Bad Nigger!*, pp. 19–21, passim.

37. City Council *Proceedings*, 12 April 1899.

38. Jerome Travers and James Crowell, *The Fifth Estate: Thirty Years of Golf* (New York: Alfred A. Knopf, 1926), p. 11.

39. Herbert Warren Wind, *The Story of American Golf*, 3rd edn., rev. (New York: Knopf, 1975), p. 85.

40. Travers called it "the most stimulating single incident the game has ever known," *Fifth Estate*, p. 187. See also John R. Betts, *America's Sporting Heritage*, p. 160; Tom Flaherty, *The U.S. Open: 1895–1965* (New York: E. P. Dutton, 1966), p. 34; Harry B. Martin, *Fifty Years of American Golf* (New York: Dodd, Mead, 1936); Jack Mahoney, *The Golf History of New England* (Wellesley, MA: New England Golf, 1973), p. 58. Mahoney is a bit more cautious, noting that while Ouimet's victory was undoubtedly the turning point, this transition "did not occur overnight."

41. Frederic H. Curtiss and John Heard, *The Country Club, 1882–1932* (Brookline, MA, 1932), pp. 62–67; Elmer Cappers, "The Country Club, Brookline, Massachusetts," *Proceedings of the Brookline Historical Society* (1968), pp. 61–62; idem, *Centennial History of The Country Club, 1882–1982* (Brookline, MA, 1981), pp. 22–31.

42. Parks Minutes, 5 December 1890, 7 November 1892, 23 October 1893, 18 April, 14 December 1896. Today's serious golfers would be happy to note that "learners' permits" were required of all neophytes! See also Mahoney, *Golf History of New England*, pp. 24–27.

43. G. H. Sargent, "Golfing round the Hub," *Outing* 34 (May 1899): 129–35; Allan Forbes, *Sport in Norfolk County* (Boston: Houghton Mifflin, 1938), ch. 7; James P. Lee, *Golf in America: A Practical Manual* (New York: Dodd, Mead, 1895), p. 46.

44. Francis Ouimet, *A Game of Golf: A Book of Reminiscence* (Boston: Houghton Mifflin, 1932).

45. Francis Ouimet, "The Game I Love," *St. Nicholas* 41 (March–August 1914): 592.

46. Ibid., 484; Ouimet, *Game of Golf*, pp. 10–55; Mahoney, *Golf History of New England*, p. 54.

47. *Boston Herald*, 19 September 1913. Both the *Herald* and the *Globe* offered thorough accounts of the tournament, although the young college football season still dominated the sports page. The *Globe* was less optimistic about American prospects, lamenting that "little is left save a hope that the open championship title of the United States will remain at home this year."

48. *Boston Globe*, 20 September 1913. Mahoney has a good summary of the final rounds in *Golf History of New England*, pp. 56–58. See also Cappers, *Centennial History*, pp. 50–56.

49. *Boston Globe*, 20 September 1913.

50. *Boston Evening Transcript*, 20 September 1913; *Boston Herald*, 20 September 1913.

51. *Sunday Globe*, 21 September 1913; *Boston Evening Transcript*, 22 September 1913.

52. *Boston Herald*, 20 September 1913; *Globe*, 20 September 1913; "Open Golf Championship," *Outlook* 105 (4 October 1913): 243–45.

53. See Flaherty, *The U.S. Open: 1895–1965*; Mahoney, *Golf History of New England*, pp. 59–62.

54. Bernard Darwin, "My First Visit to the States," *The Realm of Sport*, ed. Herbert Warren Wind (New York: Simon and Schuster, 1966), p. 375.

55. Albert G. Spalding, *America's National Game* (New York: American Sports Publishing Co., 1911), p. 534.

56. William Phelon, "The Great American Fan," *Baseball Magazine* 7 (September 1911): 6.

57. Rollin L. Hartt, *The People at Play* (Boston: Houghton Mifflin, 1909), pp. 316–17.

58. Steven A. Riess has done much to sort fact from fancy in baseball's history. See his *Touching Base: Professional Baseball and American Culture in the Progressive Era* (Westport, CT: Greenwood Press, 1980). For examples of baseball and boosterism see Harold Seymour, *Baseball: The Early Years* (New York: Oxford University Press, 1960), pp. 350–51; Greg Lee Carter, "Baseball in Saint Louis, 1867–1875: An Historical Case Study in Civic Pride," *Missouri Historical Society Bulletin* 21 (July 1975): 253–63.

59. See David Q. Voigt, "The Boston Red Stockings: The Birth of Major League Baseball," *New England Quarterly* 43 (December 1970): 531–49; George Wright, *Record of the Boston Baseball Club Since Its Organization* (Boston: Rockwell & Churchill, 1874).

60. See George Touhey, *A History of the Boston Baseball Club* (Boston: M. V. Quinn, 1897); Seymour, *Baseball,* vol. 1, p. 285; Voigt, *American Baseball,* vol. 1, p. 249. Boston won National League Pennants in 1877, 1878, 1883, 1891, 1892, 1893, 1897, 1898.

61. *Boston Globe,* 19 August 1883.

62. *Boston Herald,* 25, 26 September 1897; Voigt, *American Baseball,* vol. 1, p. 262.

63. Touhey, *Boston Baseball Club,* pp. 9–10.

64. *Boston Evening Transcript,* 27 September 1897.

65. Touhey, *Boston Baseball Club,* p. 10.

66. *Boston Globe,* 1, 2 October 1897.

67. *Boston Evening Transcript,* 7 October 1897; *Boston Globe,* 5 October 1897.

68. "Nuf Ced McGreevey Scrapbook," Boston Tradition in Sports Collection, microfilm reproduction, Boston Public Library.

69. See Fred Lieb, *Boston Red Sox* (New York: G. P. Putnam's Sons, 1947).

70. Seymour, *Baseball,* vol. 2, pp. 152–53; Voigt, *American Baseball,* vol. 2, pp. 42–43.

71. *Boston Daily Globe,* 12 October 1914.

72. *Boston Evening Globe,* 12 October 1914.

73. *Boston Herald,* 12, 13 October 1914.

74. *Boston Daily Globe,* 13 October 1914.

75. Ibid., 15 October 1914.

76. Mayor Kevin White recently stated, "There's a community spirit which prevails when the Red Sox are on top. It's as if the public itself was in the pennant race." *Boston Herald American,* 11 June 1978, B-7. For more on fan community and Boston fans see Seymour, *Baseball,* vol. 1, pp. 325–30; vol. 2, pp. 3–6, 76–80; *Everybody's Magazine* 29 (October 1913): 528; *Baseball Magazine* 7 (September 1911): 1–6; 6 (April 1911): 21–26; *Literary Digest* 77 (28 April 1923): 74; Hartt, *People at Play,* p. 284.

77. Carter, "Baseball in Saint Louis," 257.

78. Joseph Lee, *Play in Education* (New York: Macmillan, 1915), p. 443.

79. J. L. Gillin, "The Sociology of Recreation," *American Journal of Sociology* 19 (1914): 830–32.

80. One philosopher has argued the pursuit of excellence as the core of sport's appeal. See Paul Weiss, *Sport: A Philosophic Inquiry* (Carbondale, IL: Southern Illinois University Press, 1969).

81. *Boston Evening Transcript,* 28 September 1897.

82. In this regard, these athletes fell somewhere between the older hero and the "instant celebrity," as distinguished by Daniel Boorstin in his interesting book *The Image: A Guide to Pseudo-Events in America* (New York: Harper, 1964). Like the older hero, the athlete won fame and

following only on the basis of achievement; like the "celebrity," his name was inflated and conveyed by what Boorstin calls the "Graphics Revolution." For instance, when Sullivan fought Kilrain, the Western Union reportedly needed fifty operators to handle the instant "specials" of journalists from all over the country. See Betts, "Organized Sport in Industrial America," p. 153. The best argument for sport as a product of improved technology is Betts's article "The Technological Revolution and the Rise of Sport," *Mississippi Valley Historical Review* 40 (September 1953): 231–56.

Notes to Chapter 10

1. While cities may not have produced *proportionately* larger amounts of discretionary time and money, the concentration of these necessities meant that cities were the crucial markets for recreation and sport, as they were for most commodities. For suggestive remarks on this urban link, see Alan G. Ingham, "American Sport in Transition: The Maturation of Industrial Capitalism and Its Impact Upon Sport" (Ph.D. dissertation, University of Massachusetts, 1978), pp. 105–19.

2. "Rational Amusements," *Boston Daily Advertiser*, 16 January 1869.

3. Thomas Wentworth Higginson, "Gymnastics," in his *Outdoor Papers* (Boston, 1871), p. 158.

4. Hope Narey, "Physical Training for Women," *The Bostonian* 1 (1894–95): 103.

5. Dudley A. Sargent, "Home Gymnastics for the Business Man," *Saturday Evening Post*, 10 February 1900. See also Sargent's article, "Physical Training," *The Sanitarium* (March 1884): 189–206.

6. Dorothy Ellingwood, "Gymnastics and City Life," *The Educational Bi-Monthly* 3 (February 1909): 222–25.

7. Samuel Hays, "The Changing Political Structure of the City in America," *Journal of Urban History* 1 (November 1974): 7; Zane Miller, "Scarcity, Abundance, and American Urban History," *Journal of Urban History* 4 (February 1978): 141.

8. Joseph Lee, "Play as a School of the Citizen," *Charities and the Commons* 18 (August 1907): 486–91.

9. Adna Weber, *The Growth of Cities in the Nineteenth Century: A Study in Statistics* (New York, 1899), pp. 458–59.

10. Parks Minutes, 16 June 1887. On the bicycle, see Richard Harmond, "Progress and Flight: An Interpretation of the American Cycle Craze of the 1890s," *Journal of Social History* 5 (Winter 1971–72): 252–57. On the sciences of landscape architecture, see Donald E. Simon, "The Public Park Movement in Brooklyn, 1824–1873" (Ph.D. dissertation, New York University, 1972), p. 172.

11. Luther Gulick, *A Philosophy of Play* (New York: Scribner, 1920), p. 213.

12. Boston, *City Document No. 1,* 1899, p. 55.

13. James F. Hunnewell, *A Century of Town Life: A History of Charlestown, Massachusetts, 1775–1887* (Boston: Little, Brown, 1888), p. 108.

14. Rev. Henry Morgan, *Boston Inside Out! Sins of a Great City! A Story of Real Life!* (Boston, 1880), p. 129. For an editorial suggestion on improving the July Fourth sports offerings, see *Boston Herald,* 29 May 1881. For appreciative accolades to the sporting press, see *The Official Catalogue of the New England Cycle Show* (Boston, 1897), pp. 31–33.

15. *Boston Evening Transcript,* 28 March 1891.

16. For suggestive reading on the nature of modern sport, see Alan Ingham, "American Sport in Transition," esp. pp. 187–342; Allen Guttmann, *From Ritual to Record: The Nature of Modern Sports* (New York: Columbia University Press, 1978).

17. Most of the literature on other cities has already been cited in prior chapters. For an attempt at synthesizing these books and articles see Stephen Hardy, "The City and the Rise of American Sport: 1820–1920," *Exercise and Sports Sciences Reviews* 9 (1981): 183–219.

Selected Bibliography

I. PRIMARY SOURCES

A. Manuscripts, Minutes, and Scrapbooks

BOSTON, MA. Boston Public Library, Rare Book Room. Sylvester Baxter Scrapbook of "Articles on the Civic Improvement of Boston"; Charles Folsom Scrapbook of "Newsclippings on Park Proposals"; Boston School Committee Manuscript Minutes, 1860–69.

———. Boston Public Library, Microform Room. Clarence DeMar Scrapbook; "Nuf Ced" McGreevey Scrapbook.

———. Boston University. Dudley A. Sargent Papers.

———. City Hall, Department of Parks and Recreation. Minutes of the Board of Commissioners, 1875–1915.

———. Massachusetts Historical Society. Typescript by Winthrop Saltonstall Scudder, entitled "An Historical Sketch of the Oneida Football Club of Boston, 1862–1865."

CAMBRIDGE, MA. Harvard University. Dudley A. Sargent Papers.

B. Public Documents

BOSTON, MA. *City Documents*. Published annually, 1865–1915. Volumes included the mayor's annual inaugural address, and annual reports of the Auditor, Parks Department, and Department of Baths.

———. *Reports of Proceedings of the City Council*. Published annually, 1860–1915.

———. *School Documents*. Published annually, 1870–1915. Volumes included School Committee Minutes and Reports, and the annual reports of the superintendent of schools and the director of physical training.

———. Massachusetts Bureau of the Statistics of Labor. *Annual Report*. Published annually, 1870–1915.

C. Newspapers and Newsletters

The Advocate
Boston Daily Advertiser
Boston Evening Transcript

Charlestown News
The Pilot
The Record (English High School)

Boston Globe
Boston *Guardian*
Boston Herald
Boston Journal
Boston Post
The Chandelier (South Boston High School)

The Register (Boston Latin School)
The Republic
South Boston Bulletin
South Boston Inquirer
The Unicorn (Boston Athletic Association)

D. Sporting Journals

American Bicycling Journal
The Bicycling World
League of American Wheelmen Bulletin
Leisure Hours (Boston Young Men's Christian Association)
Outing (incorporated *The Wheelman*)

E. Articles

"AMUSEMENTS." *New Boston* 1 (November 1910): 315–25.

"AMUSEMENTS." *New Englander* 9 (August 1851); 345–59.

"AMUSEMENTS." *New Englander* 26 (July 1867): 399–424.

BARNEY, ELIZABETH C. "The American Sportswoman." *Fortnightly Review* 56 (1894): 263–77.

BARROWS, ESTHER. "Boston's Amusement Resources." *New Boston* 1 (November 1910): 315–17.

BASSETT, ABBOTT. "Outdoor Season—Revival of Cycling." *Harper's Weekly* 47 (11 June 1904): 906–7.

BAXTER, SYLVESTER. "The Economic and Social Influences of the Bicycle." *Arena* 6 (October 1892): 578–83.

———. "The Public Parks, Playgrounds, Baths and Gymnasiums." *A Civic Reader for New Americans.* New York: American Book Company, 1908, pp. 42–49.

———. "Seaside Pleasure Grounds for Cities." *Scribner's Magazine* 23 (June 1898): 676–87.

BINGHAM, K. S. "Boston's Outdoor Winter Sports." *New England Magazine* 43 (February 1911): 600–6.

BISHOP, JOSEPH. "Social and Economic Influences of the Bicycle." *Forum* 21 (August 1896): 680–89.

CALKINS, RAYMOND. "A Summary of Investigations Concerning Substitutes for the Saloon." *The Liquor Problem: A Summary of Investigations Conducted by the Committee of Fifty, 1893–1903,* Boston, 1905.

CLARKE, JAMES FREEMAN. "Rational Sunday Observance." *North American Review* 131 (1880): 504.

DICKINSON, REV. CHARLES A. "Problem of the Modern City Church." *Andover Review* 12 (October 1889): 355–67.

DUNN, ROBERT. "The Country Club: A National Expression." *Outing* 47 (1905): 160–74.

DWIGHT, JAMES. "Lawn Tennis in New England." *Outing* 18 (May 1891): 157–60.

EDWARDS, DUNCAN. "Life at the Athletic Clubs." *Scribner's Magazine* 18 (July 1895): 4–23.

GARRIGUES, HENRY. "Woman and the Bicycle." *Forum* 20 (January 1896): 578–87.

GILLIN, J. L. "The Sociology of Recreation." *American Journal of Sociology* 19 (1914): 830–32.

GOLDBERG, ISAAC. "A Boston Boyhood." *The American Mercury* 17 (July 1929): 354–61.

GORDON, M. K. "Reform of School Athletics." *Century,* New Series 57 (January 1910): 469–71.

GULICK, LUTHER. "Team Games and Civic Loyalty." *School Review* 14 (1906): 676–78.

HALE, EDWARD E. "Public Amusements and Public Morality." *Christian Examiner* 62 (July 1857): 47–65.

HIGGINSON, THOMAS WENTWORTH. "Gymnastics." *Atlantic Monthly* 7 (March 1861): 283–302.

———. "Saints and Their Bodies." *Atlantic Monthly* 1 (March 1858): 582–95.

HOWLAND, HENRY. "Golf." *Scribner's Magazine* 17 (May 1895): 531–47.

HUTCHINSON, GEORGE. "Boston Young Men's Christian Union." *Lend a Hand* 15 (January 1896): 37–39.

JOSEPHSSON, AXEL. "Bicycles and Tricycles." U.S. Bureau of the Census. *Twelfth Census of the United States,* 1900, Washington, 1902, vol. 10, pp. 325–39.

KENEALY, CAPT. A. J. "Yacht Clubs of the East." *Outing* 18 (1891): 383–88, 475–580.

DE KOVEN, ANNA. "The Athletic Woman." *Good Housekeeping* 55 (August 1912): 148–57.

LEE, JOSEPH. "Boston's Playground System." *New England Magazine* 27 (January 1903): 521–36.

———. "Play and Congestion." *Charities and the Commons* 20 (April 1908): 43–48.

———. "Play as an Antidote to Civilization." *Playground* (1911): 110–26.

———. "Play for Home." *Playground* 6 (1912): 146.

———. "Playgrounds, Beaches and Baths." Elizabeth Herlihy, ed., *Fifty Years of Boston: A Memorial Volume.* Boston: Tercentenary Committee, 1932.

———. "Sunday Play." *Survey* 25 (October 1910): 55–62.

McCRADY, JANE. "South End Amusements." *New Boston* 1 (November 1910): 318–20.

NAREY, HOPE. "Physical Training for Women." *The Bostonian* 1 (1894–95): 98–106.

NELSON, HENRY L. "The Clubs of Boston." *Harper's Weekly* 34 (25 January 1890): 57–60.

O'HAGAG, ANNE. "The Athletic Girl." *Munsey's Magazine* 25 (August 1901): 730–37.

OLMSTED, FREDERICK LAW, JR. "Neighborhood Pleasure-Grounds in Boston." *Harper's Weekly* 41 (25 December 1897): 1290–91.

OUIMET, FRANCIS. "The Game I Love." *St. Nicholas* 41 (March–August 1914): 590–93.

PAINE, DAVID. "Prominent Country Clubs." *New England Magazine* (May 1905): 322–36.

PARKMAN, FRANCIS. "The Failure of Universal Suffrage." *North American Review* 127 (July 1878): 1–20.

PARSONS, ALBERT S. "The Massachusetts Bicycle Club." *The Wheelman* 2 (June 1883): 161–72.

PEABODY, FRANCIS. "Substitutes for the Saloon." *The Forum* 21 (July 1896): 595–606.

PHELON, WILLIAM A. "The Great American Fan." *Baseball Magazine* 7 (September 1911): 5–9.

POPE, ALBERT. "The Bicycle Industry." Chauncey M. Depew, ed., *One Hundred Years of American Commerce, 1795–1895,* 2 vols. New York: D. O. Hayes & Co., 1895, vol. 2, pp. 549–53.

PRATT, CHARLES. "Our First Bicycle Club." *The Wheelman* 1 (March 1883): 402.

————. "A Sketch of American Bicycling and Its Founder." *Outing* 18 (July 1891): 342–49.

PUTNAM, GRANVILLE. "The Introduction of Gymnastics in New England." *New England Magazine* 3 (September 1890): 110–13.

RIIS, JACOB. "Fighting the Gang with Athletics." *Collier's* 46 (February 1911): 17.

ROFFE, WILL. "Cricket in New England and the Longwood Club." *Outing* 18 (1891): 251–54.

SARGENT, DUDLEY A. "Athletics in Secondary Schools." *American Physical Education Review* 8 (June 1903): 57–69.

————. "The Place for Physical Training in the School and College Curriculum." *American Physical Education Review* 5 (March 1900).

SARGENT, G. H. "Golfing round the Hub." *Outing* 34 (May 1899): 129–35.

SCUDDER, WINTHROP SALTONSTALL. "The First Organized Football Club in the United States." *Old Time New England* 15 (July 1924).

TARBELL, ARTHUR. "Golf and Golf Clubs." *The [Boston] National Magazine* 4 (August 1896): 481–93.

VAN TASSEL SUTPHEN, W. G. "The Golfing Woman." *Outlook* 62 (June 1899): 249–57.

WHITNEY, CASPAR. "Evolution of the Country Club." *Harper's* 90 (1894): 17–32.

———. "Recreation on Sunday." *Outing* 53 (December 1908): 383–86.

WINGATE, CHARLES. "Bicycling in Boston." *Critic* 27 (12 October 1895): 235–36.

F. Books, Constitutions, Pamphlets

ADAMS, HENRY. *The Education of Henry Adams.* Boston, 1906; reprint edn., Boston: Houghton Mifflin, Sentry edn., 1961.

ALLSTON GOLF CLUB. *Constitution and Rules,* 1903.

BARKER, JOHN. *The Saloon Problem and Social Reforms.* Boston, 1905.

BARROWS, ISABEL, ED. *Physical Training: A Full Report of the Papers and Discussions of the Conference Held in Boston in November 1889.* Boston: George H. Ellis, 1889.

BAXTER, SYLVESTER. *Boston Park Guide, Including the Municipal and Metropolitan Systems of Greater Boston.* Boston: the author, 1895; reprint edn., Boston: Laurens Maynard, 1896.

BELLAMY, EDWARD. *Looking Backward.* New York, 1888; reprint edn., New York: New American Library, 1960.

BOSTON BICYCLE CLUB. *Bylaws and Rules.* Boston, 1882.

The Boston Club Book for 1888; Containing a Full List of Members and Addresses of All Boston Clubs of Any Social or Political Prominence. Boston: Edward E. Clark, 1888.

The Boston Common, or Rural Walks in Cities, by a Friend of Improvement. Boston: G. W. Light, 1838.

BRAYLEY, ARTHUR. *A History of the Boston Yacht Club.* Boston, 1891.

BUSHEE, FREDERICK A. *Ethnic Factors in the Population of Boston.* American Economics Association Publications. Series 3, 4: 2 (1903).

CALKINS, RAYMOND. *Substitutes for the Saloon: An Investigation Made for the Committee of Fifty.* Boston, 1901; 2nd edn. revised, Boston: Houghton Mifflin, 1919.

CHANNING, WILLIAM ELLERY. *The Works of William E. Channing.* New edn. Boston: American Unitarian Association, 1889.

CLARK, ELLERY H. *Reminiscences of an Athlete: Twenty Years on Track and Field.* Boston: Houghton Mifflin, 1911.

CLARKE, JAMES FREEMAN. *Self-Culture: Physical, Intellectual, Moral, and Spiritual.* Boston: James R. Osgood & Co., 1880.

The Clubs of Boston: Containing a Complete List of Members and Addresses of All Boston Clubs of Social and Business Prominence, Endorsed by All the Leading Clubs. Boston: N. Wilson & Co., 1891.

The Country Club. Constitution, By-Laws and List of Members. Boston: published by the club, 1888.

CROCKER, URIEL. *Plan for a Public Park.* Boston, 1869.

DALTON, J. G. *Lyra Bicyclica: Forty Poets on the Wheel.* Boston, 1880.

DANIELS, JOHN. *In Freedom's Birthplace: A Study of the Boston Negroes.* Boston: Houghton Mifflin, 1914; reprint edn., New York: Johnson Reprint Corp., 1968.

DAVENPORT, CHARLES. *The Embankment and Park on the Charles River Bay.* Pamphlet in the Boston Athenaeum, n.p., n.d.

EDWARDS, RICHARD. *Popular Amusements.* New York: Associated Press, 1915.

FLOWER, B. O. *Civilization's Inferno, or, Studies in the Social Cellar.* Boston: Arena Publishing Company, 1893.

HALE, EDWARD EVERETT. *A New England Boyhood and Other Bits of Autobiography.* Boston: Casell Publishing Company, 1893.

———. *Public Amusement for Poor and Rich: A Discourse.* Boston: Phillips, Sampson and Co., 1857.

———. *Sybaris and Other Homes, to Which Is Added, "How They Live in Hampton."* Boston, 1900.

HARTT, ROLLIN LYNDE. *The People at Play: Excursions into the Humor and Philosophy of Popular Amusements.* Boston: Houghton Mifflin, 1909.

HIGGINSON, THOMAS WENTWORTH. *Cheerful Yesterdays.* Boston: Houghton Mifflin, 1898.

———. *Out-door Papers.* Boston, 1871.

INTERSCHOLASTIC ATHLETIC ASSOCIATION. *Constitution and By-Laws.* Boston, 1895.

JOHNSON, JACK. *Jack Johnson is a Dandy: An Autobiography.* Reprint edn., New York: Chelsea House, 1969.

LAWSON, THOMAS. *The Krank: His Language and What It Means.* Boston: Rand Avery Co., 1888.

LEE, JOSEPH. *Constructive and Preventive Philanthropy.* New York: Macmillan, 1902.

———. *Play and Playgrounds.* American Civic Association, Department of Public Recreation. Leaflet no. 11, January 1908.

———. *Play in Education.* New York: Macmillan, 1915.

LINNEHAN, JOHN W., AND EDWARD D. COGSWELL, EDS. *The Driving Clubs of Greater Boston.* Boston: Atlantic Printing Co., 1914.

LODGE, HENRY CABOT. *Boston.* London: Longmans, Green, 1892.

LOVETT, JAMES D'WOLF. *Old Boston Boys and the Games They Played.* Boston: privately printed, 1906; reprint edn., Boston: Little, Brown, 1908.

MCNEILL, GEORGE E., ED. *The Labor Movement: The Problem of Today.* Boston: A. M. Bridgman & Co., 1887.

MASSACHUSETTS CIVIC LEAGUE. *Annual Reports.* 1900–10.

MAYNADIER, HOWARD. *Sixty Years of the Union Boat Club.* Boston: printed by the club, 1913.

MORGAN, HENRY. *Boston Inside Out! Sins of a Greaty City! A Story of Real Life!* 2nd edn. Boston: Shawmut Publishing Company, 1880.

MUIRHEAD, JAMES FULLARTON. *The Land of Contrasts*. London: John Lane, 1898.

OLMSTED, FREDERICK LAW. *Civilizing American Cities: A Selection of F. L. Olmsted's Writings On City Landscapes*. Ed. S. B. Sutton. Cambridge, MA: MIT Press, 1971.

———. *Notes on the Plan of Franklin Park and Related Matters*. Pamphlet published by Boston Parks Department. Boston, 1886.

———. *Public Parks: Two Papers Read Before the American Social Science Association*. Brookline, MA, 1902.

O'REILLY, JOHN BOYLE. *Ethics of Boxing and Manly Sports*. Boston: Pilot Publishing Company, 1888; reprinted as *Athletics and Manly Sports*, Boston: Pilot Publishing Company, 1890.

OUIMET, FRANCIS. *A Game of Golf: A Book of Reminiscence*. Introduction by Bernard Darwin. Boston: Houghton Mifflin, 1932.

Parks for the People: Proceedings of a Public Meeting Held at Faneuil Hall, June 7, 1876. Boston: Franklin Press, 1876.

PEVERELLY, CHARLES A. *The Book of American Pastimes, Containing a History of the Principal Baseball, Cricket, Rowing and Yachting Clubs in the United States*. New York: published by the author, 1866.

PRATT, CHARLES E. *The American Bicycler: A Manual for the Observer, the Learner, and the Expert*. Boston: Houghton Mifflin, 1879.

———. *What and Why: Some Common Questions Answered*. Boston: Rockwell & Churchill, 1884.

SAVAGE, EDWARD H. *Police Records and Recollections; or, Boston by Daylight and Gaslight for Two Hundred and Forty Years*. Boston: John Dale, 1873.

STRONG, JOSIAH. *Our Country; Its Possible Future and Its Present Crisis*. New York, 1885; reprint edn., Cambridge: Harvard University Press, 1963.

SULLIVAN, JOHN L. *Life and Reminiscences of a 19th Century Gladiator*. Boston: Hearn & Co., 1892.

THE TENNIS AND RACQUET CLUB. *Constitution By-Laws, Rules, Membership List*. Boston, 1908.

TÖNNIES, FERDINAND. *Community and Society*. Trans. Charles P. Loomis. New York: Harper, 1963.

TOUHEY, GEORGE V. *A History of the Boston Baseball Club . . . Being a Public Testimonial to the Players of the 1897 Team in Recognition of the Magnificent Work of the Past Season*. Boston: M. F. Quinn, 1897.

TRAVERS, JEROME, and JAMES CROWELL. *The Fifth Estate: Thirty Years of Golf*. New York: Alfred A. Knopf, 1926.

UNION BOAT CLUB. *Constitution and By-Laws*. Boston, 1873.

———. *Constitution, By-Laws and House Rules*. Boston: George H. Ellis, 1882.

WEBER, ADNA F. *The Growth of Cities in the Nineteenth Century: A Study in Statistics*. Columbia University Studies in History, Economics and Public Law, vol. 11 (1899); reprint edn., Ithaca: Cornell University Press, 1963.

WINSOR, JUSTIN, ED. *The Memorial History of Boston*, 4 vols. Boston: Ticknor & Co., 1880.

WOODS, ROBERT A., ED. *Americans in Process: North and West Ends of Boston.* Boston: Houghton Mifflin, 1902.

WOODS, ROBERT A., ET AL. *The City Wilderness: A Settlement Study by Residents and Associates of the South End House.* Boston: Houghton Mifflin, 1898.

WOODS, ROBERT A., AND ALBERT KENNEDY, EDS. *The Zone of Emergence: Observations of the Lower Middle and Upper Working Class Communities of Boston, 1905–1914.* Unpublished report, 1914; abridged and edited with a preface by Sam Bass Warner. Cambridge: MIT Press, 1969.

WRIGHT, GEORGE. *Record of the Boston Baseball Club Since Its Organization, with a Sketch of All Its Players for 1871, '72, '73, '74, and Other Items of Interest.* Boston: Rockwell & Churchill, 1874.

II. SECONDARY SOURCES

A. Articles

ANDERSON, ROBERT. "Voluntary Associations in History." *American Anthropologist* 73 (February 1971): 209–22.

BETTS, JOHN R. "John Boyle O'Reilly and the American Paideia." *Eire-Ireland* 2 (Winter 1967): 36–52.

———. "Public Recreation, Public Parks, and Public Health Before the Civil War." *The History of Physical Education and Sport.* Ed. Bruce Bennett. Chicago: Athletic Institute, 1972, pp. 33–52.

———. "The Technological Revolution and the Rise of Sport, 1850–1900." *Mississippi Valley Historical Review* 40 (September 1953): 231–56.

BLODGETT, GEOFFREY. "Frederick Law Olmsted: Landscape Architecture as Conservative Reform." *Journal of American History* 62 (March 1976): 869–89.

CAPPERS, ELMER O. "The Country Club. Brookline, Massachusetts." *Proceedings of the Brookline Historical Society* (1968): 58–64.

DAVENPORT, JOANNA. "Eleonora Randolph Sears." *Notable American Women: The Modern Period.* Ed. Barbara Sicherman et al. Cambridge: Belknap Press of Harvard University Press, 1980, 638–39.

DODD, JILL SIEGEL. "The Working Classes and the Temperance Movement in Ante-Bellum Boston." *Labor History* 19 (Fall 1978): 510–31.

FAULKNER, HAROLD U. "Albert Augustus Pope." *Dictionary of American Biography.* Ed. Dumas Malone. New York: Charles Scribner's Sons, 1935. Vol. 15, pp. 74–75.

FISCHER, CLAUDE. "The Public and Private Worlds of City Life." *American Sociological Review* 46 (June 1981): 306–16.

———. "Toward a Subcultural Theory of Urbanism." *American Journal of Sociology* 80 (1975): 1319–41.

GALVIN, JOHN T. "The Dark Ages of Boston City Politics." Massachusetts Historical Society, *Proceedings* 89 (1977): 88–111.

HARDY, STEPHEN. "The City and the Rise of American Sport: 1820–1920." *Exercise and Sports Sciences Reviews* 9 (1981): 183–219.

HARMOND, RICHARD. "Progress and Flight: An Interpretation of the American Cycle Craze of the 1890s." *Journal of Social History* 5 (Winter 1971–72): 235–57.

HAYS, SAMUEL. "The Changing Political Structure of the City in America." *Journal of Urban History* 1 (November 1974): 6–38.

HIGHAM, JOHN. "The Reorientation of American Culture in the 1890s." *The Origins of Modern Consciousness.* Ed. Horace John Weiss. Detroit: Wayne State University Press, 1965, 25–48.

JAHER, FREDERIC COPLE. "The Boston Brahmins in the Age of Industrial Capitalism." *The Age of Industrialism in America.* Ed. Frederic Cople Jaher. New York: Free Press, 1968, 188–262.

———. "Nineteenth-Century Elites in Boston and New York." *Journal of Social History* 6 (Fall 1972): 32–77.

JONES, HOWARD M. "The Wounds of War: A Tale of Two Cities." *Harvard Library Bulletin* 20 (April 1972): 135–57.

JOSEPHSSON, AXEL. "Bicycles and Tricycles." *Twelfth Census of the United States, 1900.* Washington, DC, 1902. Vol. 10, pp. 325–39.

KATZNELSON, IRA. "Community, Capitalist Development and the Emergence of Class." *Politics and Society* 9 (1979): 203–38.

KUSMER, KENNETH L. "The Concepts of Community in American History." *Reviews in American History* 7 (September 1979): 380–87.

LAZEROW, JAMA. "'The Workingman's Hour': The 1886 Labor Uprising in Boston," *Labor History* 21 (Spring 1980): 200–20.

LEWIS, GUY. "Adoption of the Sports Program: The Role of Accommodation in the Transformation of Physical Education." *Quest* 12 (May 1969): 34–46.

———. "The Beginning of Organized Collegiate Sport." *American Quarterly* 32 (Summer 1970): 222–29.

———. "The Muscular Christianity Movement." *Journal of Health, Physical Education and Recreation* 37 (May 1966): 27–28.

LUBOVE, ROY. "The Urbanization Process: An Approach to Historical Research." *Journal of the American Institute of Planners* 33 (January 1967): 33–39.

LUCAS, JOHN A. "A Prelude to the Rise of Sport: Antebellum America, 1850–1860." *Quest* 11 (December 1968): 50–57.

———. "Thomas Wentworth Higginson: Early Apostle of Health and Fitness." *Journal of Health, Physical Education and Recreation* 42 (February 1971): 30–33.

McCAUGHEY, ROBERT A. "From Town to City: Boston in the 1820's." *Political Science Quarterly* 88 (June 1973): 191–213.

MARSDEN, K. GERALD. "Philanthropy and the Boston Playground Movement, 1885–1907." *Social Service Review* 35 (March 1961): 48–58.

MILLER, ZANE. "Scarcity, Abundance, and American Urban History." *Journal of Urban History* 4 (February 1978): 131–55.

PAXSON, FREDERIC L. "The Rise of Sport." *Mississippi Valley Historical Review* 4 (September 1917): 143–68.

RADER, BENJAMIN. "Modern Sports: In Search of Interpretations." *Journal of Social History* 13 (Winter 1979): 307–21.

———. "The Quest for Subcommunities and the Rise of American Sport." *American Quarterly* 29 (Fall 1977): 355–69.

REDLICH, FRITZ. "Leisure-Time Activities: A Historical, Sociological, and Economic Analysis." *Explorations in Entrepreneurial History*, 2nd series, 3 (1965): 3–23.

RIESS, STEVEN A. "The Baseball Magnates and Urban Politics in the Progressive Era." *Journal of Sport History* 1 (May 1974): 41–62.

ROSENZWEIG, ROY. "Middle-Class Parks and Working-Class Play: The Struggle Over Recreational Space in Worcester, Massachusetts, 1870–1910." *Radical History Review* 21 (Fall 1979): 31–46.

SILVERMAN, ROBERT A. "Nathan Matthews: Politics of Reform in Boston, 1890–1910. *New England Quarterly* 50 (1977): 626–43.

SIMUTIS, LEONARD. "Frederick Law Olmsted, Sr.: A Reassessment." *Journal of the American Institute of Planners* 38 (September 1972): 276–83.

SOMERS, DALE. "The Leisure Revolution: Recreation in the American City, 1820–1920." *Journal of Popular Culture* 5 (Summer 1971): 125–47.

SWANSON, RICHARD A. "The Acceptance and Influence of Play in American Protestantism." *Quest* 11 (December 1968): 58–70.

THOMPSON, E. P. "Time, Work-Discipline, and Industrial Capitalism." *Past and Present* 38 (1967): 98–125.

TOBIN, GARY A. "The Bicycle Boom of the 1890s: The Development of Private Transportation and the Birth of the Modern Tourist." *Journal of Popular Culture* 7 (Spring 1974): 838–49.

TURNER, RALPH. "The Industrial City: Center of Cultural Change." *The Cultural Approach to History.* Ed. Caroline Ware. New York: Columbia University Press, 1940, 228–42.

VOIGT, DAVID Q. "The Boston Red Stockings: The Birth of Major League Baseball." *New England Quarterly* 43 (December 1970): 531–49.

WHYTE, WILLIAM FOOTE. "Race Conflicts in the North End of Boston." *New England Quarterly* 12 (December 1939): 623–42.

WIRTH, LOUIS. "Urbanism as a Way of Life." *American Journal of Sociology* 44 (July 1938): 3–24.

B. Books

AMORY, CLEVELAND. *The Proper Bostonians.* New York: E. P. Dutton, 1947.

BARTH, GUNTHER. *City People: The Rise of Modern City Culture in Nineteenth-*

Century America. New York: Oxford University Press, 1980.

BELL, COLIN, AND HOWARD NEWBY. *Community Studies: An Introduction to the Sociology of the Local Community*. New York: Praeger, 1972.

BENDER, THOMAS. *Community and Social Change in America*. New Brunswick, NJ: Rutgers University Press, 1978.

BETTS, JOHN R. *America's Sporting Heritage, 1850–1950*. Reading, MA: Addison-Wesley, 1974.

BLANCHARD, JOHN A., ED. *The H Book of Harvard Athletics*. Cambridge: Harvard Varsity Club, 1923.

BLODGETT, GEOFFREY. *The Gentle Reformers: Massachusetts Democrats in the Cleveland Era*. Cambridge: Harvard University Press, 1966.

BOORSTIN, DANIEL. *The Americans: The Democratic Experience*. New York: Vintage, 1973.

BOSTON 200. *Neighborhood History Series*. Boston: Boston 200 Corp., 1975–76.

BOYER, PAUL S. *Urban Masses and Moral Order in America, 1820–1920*. Cambridge: Harvard University Press, 1978.

BROOKS, VAN WYCK. *New England: Indian Summer, 1865–1915*. New York: E. P. Dutton, 1940.

CAPPERS, ELMER O. *Centennial History of the Country Club: 1882–1982*. Brookline, MA: printed by the club, 1982.

CAVALLO, DOMINICK. *Muscles and Morals: Organized Playgrounds and Urban Reform, 1880–1920*. Philadelphia: University of Pennsylvania Press, 1981.

CHIDSEY, DONALD BARR. *John the Great: The Times and Life of a Remarkable American, John L. Sullivan*. Introduction by J. P. Marquand. Garden City, NY: Doubleday, Doran, 1942.

CLARK, ELLERY, H., JR. *Boston Red Sox: 75th Anniversary History, 1901–1975*. Hicksville, NY: Exposition Press, 1975.

COLEMAN, RICHARD, AND BERNICE NEUGARTEN. *Social Status in the City*. San Francisco: Jossey-Bass, 1971.

CURTIS, H. S. *The Play Movement and Its Significance*. New York: Macmillan, 1917.

CURTISS, FREDERIC H., AND JOHN HEARD. *The Country Club, 1882–1932*. Brookline, MA: privately printed, 1932.

DAVIS, ALLEN F. *Spearheads for Reform: The Social Settlements and the Progressive Movement, 1890–1914*. New York: Oxford University Press, 1967.

DeGRAZIA, SEBASTIAN. *Of Time, Work, and Leisure*. Garden City, NY: Anchor, 1964.

DIBBLE, ROY F. *John L. Sullivan: An Intimate Narrative*. Boston: Little, Brown, 1925.

DULLES, FOSTER RHEA. *A History of Recreation: America Learns to Play*, 2nd edn. New York: Appleton-Century-Crofts, 1965.

FISCHER, CLAUDE S., et al. *Networks and Places: Social Relations in the Urban Setting.* New York: Free Press, 1979.

FLAHERTY, TOM. *The U.S. Open: 1895–1965.* New York: E. P. Dutton, 1966.

FLEISCHER, NAT. *The Boston Strong Boy: The Story of John L. Sullivan.* New York: C. J. O'Brien, 1941.

FOSTER, CHARLES. *The Eastern Yacht Club Ditty Box, 1870–1900.* Norwood, MA: privately printed, 1932.

FRENCH, ROBERT. *The Community: A Comparative Perspective.* Itasca, IL: F. E. Peacock, 1969.

GANS, HERBERT. *The Urban Villagers: Groups and Class in the Life of Italian-Americans.* New York: Free Press, 1962.

GARLAND, JOSEPH. *Boston's North Shore: Being an Account of Life Among the Noteworthy, Fashionable, Wealthy, Eccentric and Ordinary, 1823–1890.* Boston: Little, Brown, 1978.

GILMORE, AL-TONY. *Bad Nigger! The National Impact of Jack Johnson.* Port Washington, NY: Kennikat Press, 1975.

GOIST, PARK DIXON. *From Main Street to State Street: Town, City and Community in America.* Port Washington, NY: Kennikat Press, 1977.

GOODMAN, CARY. *Choosing Sides: Playgrounds and Street Life on the Lower East Side.* New York: Schocken, 1978.

GREEN, JAMES R., AND H. C. DONAHUE. *Boston's Workers: A Labor History.* Boston: Trustees of Boston Public Library, 1979.

GREEN, MARTIN. *The Problems of Boston: Some Readings in Cultural History.* New York: W. W. Norton, 1966.

GUTTMANN, ALLEN. *From Ritual to Record: The Nature of Modern Sports.* New York: Columbia University Press, 1978.

HANDLIN, OSCAR. *Boston's Immigrants: A Study in Acculturation,* rev. edn. Cambridge, MA: Belknap Press of Harvard University Press, 1959; reprint edn., New York: Atheneum, 1974.

———, AND JOHN BURCHARD, EDS. *The Historian and the City.* Cambridge: MIT Press, 1966.

HASENFUS, NATHANIEL. *Athletics at Boston College.* Worcester, MA: Heffernan Press, 1943.

KATZ, MICHAEL. *The Irony of Early School Reform: Educational Innovation in Mid-Nineteenth-Century Massachusetts.* Cambridge: Harvard University Press, 1968; reprint edn., Boston: Beacon Press, 1970.

KLAPP, ORRIN. *Symbolic Leaders: Public Dramas and Public Men.* Chicago: Aldine Publishing Co., 1964.

KROUT, JOHN A. *Annals of American Sport.* Yale Pageant of America Series, vol. 15. New Haven: Yale University Press, 1929.

LAZERSON, MARVIN. *Origins of the Urban School: Public Education in Massa-*

chusetts, 1870–1915. Cambridge: Harvard University Press, 1971.

LUCAS, JOHN, AND RONALD SMITH. *Saga of American Sport*. Philadelphia: Lea and Febiger, 1978.

MCKELVEY, BLAKE. *The Urbanization of America, 1860–1915*. New Brunswick, NJ: Rutgers University Press, 1963.

MAHONEY, JACK. *The Golf History of New England*. Wellesley, MA: New England Golf, 1973.

MANN, ARTHUR. *Yankee Reformers in the Urban Age*. Cambridge: Harvard University Press, 1954.

MARTINDALE, DON. "Prefatory Remarks: The Theory of the City," in Max Weber. *The City*. Ed. and trans. Don Martindale and Gertrud Neuwirth. Glencoe, IL: Free Press, 1958, pp. 9–62.

MORISON, SAMUEL ELIOT. *The Maritime History of Massachusetts, 1783–1860*. Boston: Houghton Mifflin, Sentry edn., 1961; reprint edn., Boston: Northeastern University Press, 1980.

————. *One Boy's Boston: 1887–1901*. Boston: Houghton Mifflin, 1962.

NASAW, DAVID. *Schooled to Order: A Social History of Public Schooling in the United States*. New York: Oxford University Press, 1979.

NISBET, ROBERT A. *The Quest for Community*. New York: Oxford University Press, 1969.

OLMSTED, FREDERICK LAW, JR., AND THEODORA KIMBALL. *Frederick Law Olmsted: Landscape Architect, 1822–1903*. New York: G. P. Putnam, 1922.

PLECK, ELIZABETH H. *Black Migration and Poverty: Boston, 1865–1900*. New York: Academic Press, 1979.

RAINWATER, CLARENCE. *The Play Movement in the United States*. Chicago: University of Chicago Press, 1922.

REDMOND, GERALD. *The Caledonian Games in Nineteenth-Century America*. Rutherford, NJ: Fairleigh Dickinson University Press, 1971.

RIESS, STEVEN A. *Touching Base: Professional Baseball and American Culture in the Progressive Era*. Westport, CT: Greenwood Press, 1980.

RODGERS, DANIEL. *The Work Ethic in Industrial America, 1850–1920*. Chicago: University of Chicago Press, 1978.

ROPER, LAURA WOOD. *FLO: A Biography of Frederick Law Olmsted*. Baltimore: Johns Hopkins University Press, 1973.

ROSS, JACK. *An Assembly of Good Fellows: Voluntary Associations in History*. Westport, CT: Greenwood Press, 1975.

RUSSELL, FRANCIS, ED. *Forty Years On, The Old Roxbury Latin School on Kearsarge Avenue from the Civil War to the Twenties*. West Roxbury, MA: Roxbury Latin School, 1970.

RUSSO, DAVID J. *Families and Communities: A New View of American History*. Nashville: American Association for State and Local History, 1974.

SCHLESINGER, ARTHUR M. *The Rise of the City: 1878–1898*. History of American Life Series, vol. 10. New York: Macmillan, 1933.

SCHULTZ, STANLEY. *The Culture Factory: Boston Public Schools, 1789–1860.* New York: Oxford University Press, 1973.

SENNETT, RICHARD, ED. *Classic Essays on the Culture of Cities.* New York: Appleton-Century-Crofts, 1969.

SEYMOUR, HAROLD. *Baseball: The Early Years.* New York: Oxford University Press, 1960.

SHANNON, WILLIAM V. *The American Irish.* New York: Macmillan, 1963.

SMITH, CONSTANCE, AND ANNE FREEDMAN. *Voluntary Associations: Perspectives on the Literature.* Cambridge: Harvard University Press, 1972.

SMITH, MICHAEL P. *The City and Social Theory.* New York: St. Martin's Press, 1979.

SMITH, ROBERT A. *A Social History of the Bicycle.* New York: American Heritage Press, 1972.

SOLOMON, BARBARA MILLER. *Ancestors and Immigrants: A Changing New England Tradition.* Cambridge: Harvard University Press, 1956; reprint edn., New York: John Wiley, 1965.

SOMERS, DALE. *The Rise of Sports in New Orleans, 1850–1900.* Baton Rouge: Louisiana State University Press, 1972.

SPEARS, BETTY, AND RICHARD A. SWANSON. *History of Sport and Physical Activity in the United States.* Dubuque, IA: William C. Brown, 1978.

STORY, RONALD. *The Forging of an Aristocracy: Harvard and the Boston Upper Class, 1800–1870.* Middletown, CT: Wesleyan University Press, 1980.

STRAUSS, ANSELM. *Images of the American City.* New York: Free Press, 1961.

THERNSTROM, STEPHAN. *The Other Bostonians: Poverty and Progress in the American Metropolis, 1880–1970.* Cambridge: Harvard University Press, 1973.

TODISCO, PAULA. *Boston's First Neighborhood: The North End.* Boston: Trustees of Boston Public Library, 1975.

VOIGT, DAVID Q. *American Baseball: From Gentleman's Sport to Commissioner's System.* Norman, OK: Oklahoma University Press, 1966.

WARNER, SAM BASS. *Streetcar Suburbs: The Process of Growth in Boston, 1870–1900.* Cambridge: Harvard University Press, 1962; reprint edn. New York: Atheneum, 1972.

WARREN, ROLAND. *The Community in America.* Chicago: Rand McNally, 1963.

WHITEHILL, WALTER MUIR. *Boston: A Topographical History,* 2nd edn. Cambridge: Belknap Press of Harvard University Press, 1968.

WHITESIDE, WILLIAM B. *The Boston YMCA and Community Need.* New York: Association Press, 1951.

WHYTE, WILLIAM FOOTE. *Street Corner Society: The Social Structure of an Italian Slum.* Chicago: University of Chicago Press, 1943; enlarged edn., 1955.

WILLIAMS, ALEXANDER. *A Social History of the Greater Boston Clubs.* Barre,

MA: Barre Publishing Company, 1970.

WIND, HERBERT WARREN. *The Story of American Golf*, 3rd edn. rev. New York: Alfred A. Knopf, 1975.

C. Unpublished Ph.D. Dissertations

ADELMAN, MELVIN. "The Development of Modern Athletics: Sport in New York City, 1820–1870." University of Illinois, 1980.

BENNETT, BRUCE. "The Life of Dudley Allen Sargent, M.D., and His Contributions to Physical Education." University of Michigan, 1947.

BETTS, JOHN R. "Organized Sport in Industrial America." Columbia University, 1951.

DEMARCO, WILLIAM M. "Ethnics and Enclaves: The Italian Settlement in the North End of Boston." Boston College, 1980.

DUNHAM, NORMAN. "The Bicycle Era in American History." Harvard University, 1956.

HUGHES, PAUL. "Edward Everett Hale and the American City." New York University, 1975.

INGHAM, ALAN G. "American Sport in Transition: The Maturation of Industrial Capitalism and Its Impact Upon Sport." University of Massachusetts, 1978.

LEWIS, GUY M. "The American Intercollegiate Football Spectacle, 1869–1917." University of Maryland, 1965.

MASON, PHILIP. "The League of American Wheelmen and the Good Roads Movement, 1880–1905." University of Michigan, 1957.

RYAN, DENNIS P. "Beyond the Ballot Box: A Social History of the Boston Irish, 1845–1917." University of Massachusetts, 1979.

SAPORA, ALLEN. "The Contributions of Joseph Lee to the Modern Recreation Movement and Related Social Movements in the United States." University of Michigan, 1952.

STRUNA, NANCY. "The Cultural Significance of Sport in the Colonial Chesapeake and Massachusetts." University of Maryland, 1979.

SWANSON, RICHARD A. "American Protestantism and Play." Ohio State University, 1967.

TWIN, STEPHANIE. "Jock and Jill: Aspects of Women's Sports History in America, 1870–1940." Rutgers University, 1978.

Index